GREAT DECISIONS 2023

D1711976

About the cover

A worker stands in front of pipes stacked at the NordStream 2 facility on October 19, 2017, in Sassnitz, Germany. The German-Russian project, to construct a dual-line pipeline to transport natural gas from Russia to Germany and Western Europe has been a casualty of the war between Russia and Ukraine. Although completed in September 2022, the controversial pipeline has not been used and has been subject to suspected sabotage. (Photo by Carsten Koall/ Getty Images)

GREAT DECISIONS IS A TRADEMARK OF THE FOREIGN POLICY ASSOCIATION.

© COPYRIGHT 2023 BY FOREIGN POLICY ASSOCIATION, INC., 551 FIFTH AVENUE, NEW YORK, NEW YORK 10176.

LIBRARY OF CONGRESS CONTROL NUMBER: 2022948788

ISBN: 978-0-87124-284-6

Researched as of November 10, 2022.

The authors are responsible for factual accuracy and for the views expressed.

FPA itself takes no position on issues of U.S. foreign policy.

WAR IN UKRAINE

Several of our articles this year touch upon the ongoing war in Ukraine. For this reason, we are providing a map of Ukraine with its surrounding geography in order to give the reader a sense of some of the major developments since the war began in February 2022.

Russian forces invaded Ukraine on February 24, 2022, after Russian President Vladimir Putin announced a "special military operation" with the goal to "demilitarize" and "denazify" Ukraine and to protect Russians in Ukrainian territory. The invasion has been widely condemned internationally and has resulted in charges that Russians have committed war crimes. The war has affected energy shipments to Europe, which was a major customer for Russian oil and gas, and has led Europeans to attempt to cut back on the use of Russian energy, and led to the abandonment of the NordStream 2 gas pipeline. Another effect of the war is that shipments of grain from Ukraine and Russia have been slowed or halted, which in turn will increase food insecurity in many parts of the world. The United States and many other countries have imposed sanctions on Russia in an attempt to discourage the continued war in Ukraine. There is concern that China might be emboldened by Russia's attempt to annex Ukraine and move on Taiwan. The repercussions from the war in Ukraine are being felt all over the world.

⊗ Moscow

RUSSIA

RUSSIAN ADVANCE

Pripyat

BELARUS

Chernihiv

Sumy

Nizhyn

Romny

POLAND

Lutsk

Rivne

Bucha ⊗ **Kyiv**

Pryluky

Kharkiv

Lviv

Zhytomyr

UKRAINE

Dnieper

Poltava

Izyum ▫ **LUHANSK**

Ternopil

Cherkasy

Luhansk

Ivano-Frankivsk

Khmelnytski

Vinnytsya

Dnipro

DONETSK *DONBAS*

SLOVAKIA

Uzhhorod

Dniester

Kirovohrad

Donetsk

Chernivtsi

MOLDOVA

Kryvyi Rih

Zaporizhzhia

ZAPORIZHZHIA

Rostov-On-Don

HUNGARY

ROMANIA

Chisinau ⊗

Mykolayiv

KHERSON

Mariupol

Odessa

Kherson

Sea of Azov

Kerch

CRIMEA
(ANNEXED IN 2014)

Krasnodar

Danube Delta

Simferopol

Sevastopol

LEGEND

✳ **MAJOR RUSSIAN BOMBARDMENT**

☢ **NUCLEAR FACILITY**

◉ **PROVINCIAL CAPITAL**

▫ **CONFIRMED SITE OF ATROCITIES**

⋯⋯ **ANNEXED BY RUSSIA**

▨ **DONBAS REGION UNDER PRO-RUSSIAN CONTROL SINCE 2014**

▧ **RUSSIAN OCCUPIED**

▨ **RETAKEN BY UKRAINE**

In March of 2014 Russian troops seized the Ukrainian region of Crimea. Russia then annexed the region after Crimeans voted to join Russia in a disputed referendum. The other annexed lands: Donetsk, Luhansk, Kherson, and Zaporizhzhia came after the February 2022 invasion and staged referendums in those regions.

Danube

BULGARIA

Black Sea

0 ——— 100 Miles

0 ——— 100 Kilometers

TURKEY

Istanbul

SOURCE: BLOOMBERG NEWS; NEW YORK TIMES.
LUCIDITY INFORMATION DESIGN, LLC

NOTE: GENERAL OVERVIEW OF COMBAT OPERATIONS RESEARCHED THROUGH NOV. 10, 2022.

GREAT DECISIONS

FPA: The Value of Informed Discourse

Former Yale University President Kingman Brewster, Jr., observed, "A nation, like a person, needs to believe that it has a mission larger than itself." Brewster, who went on to serve as United States Ambassador to the Court of St. James, advocated for a Declaration of International Interdependence. Such a declaration would provide for "at least the beginning of global arrangements and institutions to safeguard the common defense and the general welfare of humanity everywhere." Brewster elaborated in *Foreign Affairs*, "Then we would rediscover the sense of purpose, and once more know the satisfaction, of those who saved the peoples of the colonies by making them into a nation. We, in our turn, might save the peoples of nations by making them into a world community capable of survival."

There are generations that stand out for exerting a decisive influence on history. Speaking on the cusp of the Second World War, President Franklin Delano Roosevelt famously said: "This generation has a rendezvous with destiny." I believe that Brewster's vision has never been more compelling and that America today has a rendezvous with destiny. However, we must first address frontally the growing domestic polarization that undermines our democracy and contributes to a corrosive lack of mutual respect.

I think it is noteworthy that we rarely, if ever, hear disrespectful discourse at Foreign Policy Association meetings. Yet far too much of the debate about the future of diverse democracies consists of attempts to ridicule or vilify rather than to engage or persuade. Instead of denouncing others we need to enter into a real debate about the kind of future we seek to shape. I am pleased that this is one of the aims of the Foreign Policy Association's Great Decisions Discussion Program. When I spoke with the librarian at the Kanawa County Public Libray in Charleston, West Virginia, which sponsors a Great Decisions discussion group, she told me that participants, while seriously engaged in their discussions, do so constructively and with an eagerness to hear the opinions of others. Great Decisions participants live up to Mary Catherine Bateson's observation that "we are not what we know but what we are willing to learn."

To succeed in an increasingly competitive world, we must replace the valor of ignorance with the valor of learning. Michael Mazarr, political scientist at the Rand Corporation, writes: "In the struggle for advantage among world powers, it is not military or economic might that makes the crucial difference but the fundamental qualities of a society: the characteristics of a nation that generate economic productivity, technological innovation, social cohesion, and national will."

Mazarr notes that most competitive societies "place a strong social emphasis on learning and adaptation. They are fired by the urge to create, explore, and learn. Instead of being shackled by orthodoxy and tradition, they embrace adaptation and experimentation and are open to innovations in public policy, business models, military concepts and doctrines, and art and culture."

Mazarr stresses the benefits of a diverse society. He states that "most dynamic and competitive nations embody a significant degree of diversity and pluralism. A broad range of experiences and perspectives helps generate more ideas and talents that in turn sustain national power."

Why then is America so polarized? In his thought-provoking book, "The Great Experiment; Why Diverse Democracies Fall Apart and How They Can Endure," Yascha Mounk argues that "the rise of populist politicians who denounce their opponents as corrupt or illegitimate is the most important proximate cause to the new era of polarization." Efforts to delegitimize the opposition are tantamount to avoiding a democratic contest and to winning by default. Consequently, the electorate is deprived of the benefit of a proper ventilation of the issues.

In his excellent book, "Lincoln and the Fight for Peace," John Avlon stresses the importance of Lincoln's reconciling leadership style, one that seeks to unify rather than to divide. The importance of good leadership cannot be overstated in meeting both domestic and global challenges. While great leaders are critical to a nation's destiny, an enlightened public is also necessary, which is why great leaders are great teachers. Eleanor Roosevelt, an early supporter of the Foreign Policy Association, remarked, "You cannot be a great leader unless the people are great."

Civil society also has a role to play in shoring up a consensus on the importance of civil discourse to a vibrant democracy. Indeed civil discourse is a civic responsibility and an informed pubic is the best antidote to those who seek to poison our democracy with disinformation.

Facts underpin democratic processes. The *New York Times* columnist Michiko Kakutani observes: "Without reliable information, citizens cannot make informed decisions about the issues of the day, and we cannot hold politicians to account. Without commonly agreed upon facts, we cannot have reasoned debates with other voters and instead become susceptible to the fear-mongering of demagogues. When politicians constantly lie, overwhelming and exhausting us while insinuating that everyone is dishonest and corrupt, the danger is that we grow so weary and cynical that we withdraw from civic engagement. And if we fail to engage in the political process—or reflexively support the individual from our party while reflexively dismissing the views of others—then we are abdicating common sense and our responsibility as citizens."

Sadly, many overlook the responsibility of citizenship in a democracy. Yascha Mounk writes: "As citizens of democratic countries, we do, collectively, hold a lot of political power- and have a corresponding obligation to make our voices heard in moments of crisis. It's incumbent on us to vote for parties that are committed to making the great experiment succeed, to advocate for policies that would realize the promise of diverse democracy, and of course to protest when governments target minorities or deepen discrimination." In the current environment, the backlash against Asian Americans due to the Covid pandemic that originated in China must be condemned.

At the 2022 Foreign Policy Association Annual Dinner, Dr. Ashish Jha, White House Coordinator for the Coronavirus Response, asked what is the most important word in times of pandemic. The high school teachers participating in the Judith Biggs Great Decisions Teacher Training Institute immediately gave the correct answer: trust. In my closing remarks at FPA's Annual Dinner, I underscored the importance of three more words that capture FPA's mission. They are: truth, knowledge, and vision. These are more likley to prevail when education is valued and perceived as a high calling. Without a capacity for critical thinking, social media presents a minefield that bodes ill for our collective future. H.G. Wells put it succinctly: "Civilization is in a race between education and catastrophe."

We must empower future generations to be effective global citizens. This will require a deep understanding of current, as well as emerging global challenges. From the ongoing competition between authoritarian ideology and democratic values, to climate change, economic recession and pandemics, we must educate the inhabitants of our fragile planet for a sustainable global order.

Noel V. Lateef
President and Chief Executive Officer
Foreign Policy Association

Energy security
by Carolyn Kissane

Firefighters conduct work after a Russian attack targeted energy infrastructure in Kyiv, Ukraine, on October 18, 2022. Strikes by Russia continued on Ukrainian infrastructure. (STATE EMERGENCY SERVICE OF UKRAINE /UPI/NEWSCOM.)

It was 50 years ago when the world experienced its first full blown oil shock with the 1973 Arab oil embargo. Then it was all about oil. It was a crisis when much of the Arab oil-producing countries stopped selling to Western countries in response to the West's support of Israel in the Yom Kippur War. The oil embargo became a rallying cry for the need to create energy security through greater energy independence. It also motivated the creation of the International Energy Agency (IEA), an institution that, among other things, required member countries to hold 90 days of oil in strategic reserves, an action taken to avert a repeat of the disruptions of 1973–74. That crisis also motivated energy insecure countries to consider different sources of energy, turning away from dependence on imported fossil fuels. For instance, it propelled Japan to develop domestic nuclear power, which up until the Fukushima disaster in 2011 provided 30% of the country's energy. Likewise, Denmark, a country with under 5 million people, felt the impacts of the crisis and wanted to find a way to cushion itself from the

disruption and fiscal vulnerabilities of the oil price spike that resulted from the embargo. In response, Denmark began developing wind energy, first onshore and eventually offshore, and today holds the position as a green energy innovator and a leader in offshore wind.

Fast forward to 2022, and energy security goes far beyond reliable and affordable access to oil, or to gas, and today includes a more diversified mix of energy, from hydrocarbons to renewables. What hasn't changed in the five decades since the oil crisis, though, is the critical role energy

Carolyn Kissane *serves as the Assistant Dean of the graduate programs in Global Affairs and Global Security, Conflict, and Cybercrime at the Center for Global Affairs. She is the Director of the SPS Energy, Climate Justice and Sustainability Lab, Coordinator of the Energy and Environment concentration at the Center, and is faculty adviser to the Energy Policy International Club. She was named Breaking Energy's Top Ten New York Women in energy and Top Ten Energy Communicator.*

Wind turbines rotate in the Baltic Sea between the islands of Rügen and Bornholm (Denmark). The wind farm, about 35 kilometers northeast of Rügen, has a capacity of 385 megawatts, which is mathematically sufficient to supply 400,000 households. (JENS BÜTTNER/ PICTURE ALLIANCE VIA GETTY IMAGES)

plays in the global economy. For countries, energy plays a fundamental role in national security decisionmaking, and shapes relationships between both allies and enemies. Energy is critical to human well-being and without enough of it, development becomes almost impossible. The global economy and growth has been driven by access to abundant energy.

Covid-19, the Russian invasion of Ukraine, and fears of growing inflation have upended predictions about the future. The ongoing conflict in Ukraine, the horrors that Vladimir Putin is inflicting on the country, and the impacts and consequences for the wider world, especially rising insecurities around energy and food, provide a stark reminder at how vulnerable countries are to conflict that happens even thousands of miles from their own borders. As the catastrophe of war continues to unfold, we can expect energy insecurity to be an ongoing theme and challenge. 2022 saw a massive disruption to energy security with Russia's re-invasion of Ukraine in February, exposing to the

Before you read, download the companion **Glossary** that includes definitions, a guide to acronyms and abbreviations used in the article, and other material. Go to **www. fpa.org/great_decisions** and select a topic in the Resources section. (Top right)

world the massive vulnerabilities of energy dependencies. The geopolitics of energy returned in 2022, not that it ever went away. Suddenly, the reality of energy security and its connections to geopolitics moved from specialized analyst reports to become front page news. The weaponization of energy now includes not only withholding supply, as was the case in 1973, but also the destruction of infrastructure, as Putin has demonstrated across Ukraine and in the Baltic Sea. Russia appears to be seeking to inflict maximum damage – using its energy resources as weapons, while also targeting Ukraine's energy system, forcing blackouts and taking out critical energy infrastructure. President of the European Commission Ursula von der Leyen calls the attacks on Ukrainian infrastructure "war crimes." Today energy security is not only a national security concern but also a personal one, individuals feel today's energy insecurity when they fill their cars and heat their homes, and those in energy poor regions experience heightened pain from inaccessibility and the harder to achieve economic growth and stability.

Doubts abound about the ability of countries to effectively respond to such shocks, especially when they are happening so quickly and at the same

time. That said, security, while still a vital concern, is not the only one. While fossil fuels continue to underpin economies, providing more than 75% of all energy, the contours of the energy landscape are radically transforming. Demands for deep decarbonization are growing, countries and companies are setting ambitious net-zero targets, and renewable energy proliferates globally. It is important to note the rapid growth of renewable energy, which is making bigger impacts and is expected to take up a larger share of overall energy supply. In some countries, renewables already represent 50% or more of the electricity portfolio. In the United States, in a turn-around from the previous administration, U.S. President Biden and his administration have adopted major climate policies--the Inflation Reduction Act is the most recent--that should speed the transition toward a low-carbon economy, expand future technological options, and enhance the United States' ability to be a global climate leader. Be that as it may, while the COVID pandemic collapsed oil and gas demand for much of 2020, it quickly bounced back in 2021 along with a price recovery. The question is whether the world given its current energy mix and outlook can meet the targets and bold ambitions for radically cutting greenhouse gases by mid-century to mitigate against the catastrophic impact of climate change.

Even with the increasing role of renewable energy in the global energy space, the geopolitics of energy still matter, and disruptions are becoming the new normal; a future of greater uncertainty in which energy and the security of its supply and the environmental security of the mix is certain to be a decades long challenge. Energy insecurity will likely be the new normal for the next decade and beyond. Today energy security is in the spotlight due to Russia's re-invasion of Ukraine, but that's only one reason the world is in the throes of multiple energy crises. And there are no easy solutions. Energy, the economy, the climate: they are all interdependent. Movements in any one of those fields leads, inexorably, to changes in all the others. This is due to the fact that all of those seemingly separate, technical domains are underpinned by, and in turn shape, politics, both domestic and international. If we fail to recognize these interdependencies, we will fail to see the ways in which they often overlap and contradict each other. We need to adopt a comprehensive approach to energy, one that appreciates not only short-term stability, but equally long-term sustainability and a just transition.

This article aims to examine energy security, using both historical and contemporary lenses to define what it is, explore how the ongoing energy transition is impacting and influencing energy security, and anticipate the prospects for the years ahead. In doing so it asks whether or not the world's attention has been pulled too far towards security at the expense of dealing with the consequences of climate change, both in terms of mitigation and adaptation. Do today's energy security challenges further lock countries into carbon pathways that exacerbate the need for alternatives, while at the same time curbing our ambitions to abate emissions.? As often mentioned in other spheres of global affairs, there can be no development without security. What does that mean with regard to energy? Are the current energy crises forcing us to mortgage our future in our haste to achieve a degree of stability for the present?

What is energy security?

The term "energy security" evokes scenes of securing fuel supplies during war or oil tankers being sabotaged. There is indeed a connection between international security and securing energy supply, which is a critical component for economic growth and building a modern society. A number of factors determine a country's relationship to securing its energy resources. The IEA definition of energy security: ensuring the availability, affordability, and accessibility of energy supply for a country. Is that definition holistic in 2022? What else should be considered as the international energy trade landscape

shifts, especially in light of the changing climate and Russia's invasion of Ukraine?

Energy security in the 21st century is different from 20th century energy security. The 20th century focused on access to fossil fuels and the quest to supply enough fossil fuels to meet demand and, at the same time, make access reliable and affordable. Today, energy security goes beyond access to hydrocarbons, and security is but one part of what is referred to as the energy trilemma, finding the balance between current and future security, equity and affordability, and sustainability.

Being energy secure means something different than it did even two decades ago. Especially prior to the U.S. shale revolution, the term "energy independence" was in vogue in an effort to emphasize the need to stop importing oil from unreliable or turbulent places, such as the Middle East, in order to insulate consumers from price volatility and was actually the name of a key piece of legislation from that era. However, because of the nature of the

global energy market, consumers in one country cannot be protected from supply shocks due to events half a world away. Indeed, the Russian invasion of Ukraine is a perfect example of how supply shocks can disrupt global energy markets and cause economic pain around the world. The United States is now the world's largest petroleum producer, but even that didn't prevent American gas prices from spiking to historic levels in 2022. Since energy independence no longer equates to cheap gas prices, the term "energy security" is a more accurate term.

Daniel Yergin, author of the Pulitzer Prize winning book on oil, *The Prize,* defines energy security as "the capability to assure adequate, reliable energy supplies at reasonable prices in ways that do not jeopardize major national values and objectives." This definition integrates economic, security, and ideological elements in addition to the core necessity of ensuring access to adequate supplies. However, energy security today is about more than access, supply, and affordability. Meghan

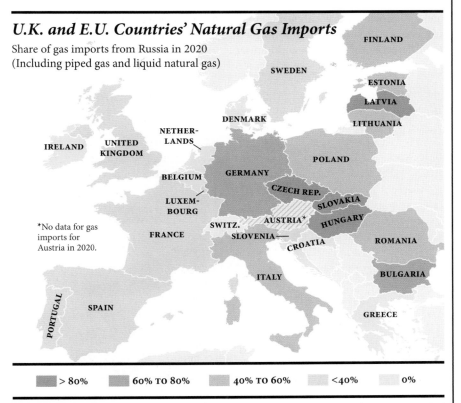

U.K. and E.U. Countries' Natural Gas Imports

Share of gas imports from Russia in 2020
(Including piped gas and liquid natural gas)

*No data for gas imports for Austria in 2020.

Legend: > 80% | 60% TO 80% | 40% TO 60% | <40% | 0%

SOURCE: Eurostat, British Dept. for Business, Energy, and Industrial Strategy   Lucidity Information Design, LLC

O'Sullivan, author of *Windfall*, goes further with her definition of energy security. She integrates how countries can account for things beyond energy access into their foreign policy. She defines energy security as "having access to affordable energy without having to contort one's political, security, diplomatic, or military arrangements unduly." While the mid-20th century version of energy security centered on access and supply, the 21st century is moving towards O'Sullivan's more nuanced and multi-layered understanding of energy security. A bit of background helps to illustrate the difference.

Today's energy security crises are coming in the midst of multiple global challenges, one of which is climate change. Mitigating against climate change (reducing carbon emissions) requires energy shifting and specifically a reduction in the sources of energy that have historically been at the heart of achieving and maintaining energy security: oil, gas, and especially coal. Energy security today has become an emergency for many countries, in Europe it's about making up for the loss of Russian gas and even Russian oil, and for other regions it's about addressing energy poverty which continues to stifle economic growth and human

development. It's a massive challenge to provide education, adequate health services, and attract foreign investment when energy access is unreliable, not present or extremely volatile.

In the beginning

Petroleum and foreign policy have been intimately linked in the United States since the Second World War. Starting in 1945, three major events have dramatically altered the trajectory of American energy and foreign policy. In the closing days of the war, American security interests led President Franklin Delano Roosevelt (FDR) to travel from the Yalta Conference in Crimea to meet with the first king of Saudi Arabia, Abdulaziz ibn Abdul Rahman ibn Faisal ibn Turki ibn Abdullah ibn Muhammad Al Saud, also known as ibn Saud. The meeting was intended to forge a relationship between the United States and Saudi Arabia that would secure American energy needs for the coming decades. The close rapport established between FDR and ibn Saud has indeed shaped American Middle Eastern policy for the last eighty years. Though this relationship has endured as presidents and kings have come and gone, it has not been without strain. In 1973, following U.S. support for Israel during the Arab-Israeli War, the Arab

members of OPEC suspended oil shipments to the United States and a number of Israeli allies. It was one of the earliest examples in which energy was deployed as a weapon. The embargo ushered in an era of new Western energy policy; driving government investment and research in oil exploration, contingency plans, and alternative energy technologies. As oil prices per barrel climbed by over 400 percent, the 1973 crisis led the United States to establish the Strategic Petroleum Reserve (SPR). Today the U.S. SPR is the world's largest reserve of crude oil, with a capacity of over 713 million barrels. It has been used to ease pressure in the oil market on three occasions, most recently in 2022, when Russia's re-invasion of Ukraine caused a price hike in the price of oil, the Biden administration released the largest amount of oil to date from the SPR.

The last two decades have brought about significant shifts in the global energy landscape, and the United States is a case in point. Consider the following: in 2004, the United States was the largest importer of crude oil and preparing to import liquefied natural gas. Plans were underway to build natural gas liquefaction import terminals, and supply would come from Qatar and other gas-rich countries. At the same time, China's demand picture was moving into overdrive. Rapid industrialization and a growing middle class meant China required more oil and gas to meet its energy demand. In response to this growing demand challenge, China launched its "Going Out Strategy", which involved China buying high equity stakes in overseas oil and gas projects. The search for new oil and gas finds took on an urgency when the world thought it was running out. The fear of insecurity of supply drove oil prices to record levels, but by 2015 with the shale oil revolution, or what some referred to as the U.S. energy renaissance, the United States became a top oil and gas producer and by 2015 was exporting oil and on its way to becoming a net oil exporting country. Saudi Arabia, rather than see a weakened hand in the market, brought a group of other countries in to join OPEC not as members but as

An aerial view of the Strategic Petroleum Reserve storage at the Bryan Mound site in Freeport, Texas. (BRANDON BELL/GETTY IMAGES)

additional suppliers, OPEC +. OPEC + now manages almost 40% of global oil production and includes Russia, one of the world's largest producers. Saudi Arabia and Russia are the two most important de facto leaders of this alliance. The formation of OPEC+ was an implicit admission that their previous go-it-alone strategy had failed. This move was a recognition that the fundamentals of oil geopolitics had changed and going forward, the Saudis, Russians, and other large producers would need to work together to confront the challenges of a more complex and complicated oil market and one in which the United States is a major producer.

Technological innovations and disruptions in exploration and extraction techniques catapulted the United States into becoming one of the largest crude oil and natural gas producers in the world, surpassing Saudi Arabia and Russia in energy production. The United States moved from touting energy independence to energy dominance, and its foreign policy shifted along with this new position.

Feelings of energy dominance, though, have proven themselves to be destabilizing. In 2008, Russia went into Georgia, and in 2014 it annexed Crimea and invaded the Donbas region of Ukraine. Russia didn't pay a high price for these transgressions then and believed their natural resource endowments and the countries that depended on those resources would act as a protective shield against retaliation for their violation of Ukraine's sovereignty. In 2014, the West decided against military action and instead used economic statecraft. Sanctions were meant to slow Russia's future energy growth, specifically around developing new oil and gas fields, which required Western expertise and technology. But despite the fact that sanctions were in place for more than seven years, Russia managed to increase its reserves and built what some called an economic fortress. Russian oil production reached over 11 mbd (million barrels a day) in 2016 and the first half of 2017, almost surpassing the all-time high of 11.7 mbd set in 1987. A provocative counterfactual is

Secretary-General of OPEC Haitham al-Ghais (R) and Saudi Arabia's Minister of Energy Prince Abdulaziz bin Salman Al-Saud (2nd L) hold a press conference after the 33rd OPEC (Organization of Petroleum Exporting Countries) and non-OPEC ministerial meeting, which was held to evaluate the market conditions and to discuss the production amount to be applied as of November, in Vienna, Austria on October 5, 2022. (ASKIN KIYAGAN/ANADOLU AGENCY VIA GETTY IMAGES)

to consider what would have happened if Europe in 2014 recognized Russia's status as an unreliable bad actor, and began to wean itself then off of Russian gas. The EU could be much more energy secure today if it had. Instead, not only did the EU continue to be the largest buyer of Russia's gas, Germany even agreed to work with Russia on a second pipeline, Nordstream 2. The Russian economy remains heavily dependent on resource extraction. As of 2018 more than 80% of Russian exported goods relied on mineral extraction, including petroleum products, coal, lumber, and metals. Germany believed an increased level of trade interdependence would play to Russia's rational side, but that belief only lasted for so long.

In 2022 Russia went too far, further invading Ukraine in February and unleashing the wrath of the West. Rather than letting Russia continue to play in the global market, the sanctions and response of the West are aimed at stifling Russia's growth, degrading its military industrial complex and its overall war effort, and making it an energy pariah, aiming to limit its ability to sell its oil and gas on the global market. At the same time, the war has exposed Europe's dependency on Russian gas leaving it vulnerable to a

severe energy crisis as it seeks to replace Russian gas. Germany canceled the Nordstream 2 project, and now the continent is scrambling to counter Russia's use of the energy weapon, specifically its gas and oil. In response to the crisis, the EU has looked to the United States to send liquefied natural gas to Europe. Germany has gone so far as to extend the life of three of its remaining nuclear power plants, a thought once impossible to imagine, and the region has seen an increase in the consumption of coal to make up for the shortfall in Russian gas. All of these measures illustrate why energy security matters, because without it, economies are under threat, and people expect to be able to keep the lights on, heat homes, and power factories, and when that is in question, there's a need for dramatic policy action.

Europe's response to the energy crisis hasn't only involved leaning on hydrocarbon sources from beyond Russia, the region is also increasing renewable energy. Wind and solar generated a record 24% of EU electricity from March to September in 2022 up from 21% of EU electricity in the same period last year. Nineteen EU countries achieved a wind and solar record, including France (14%), Italy (20%), Poland (17%) and Spain (35%).

What does it all mean?

■ Energy is political

Energy and politics go hand in hand–they can't be separated or disconnected. The U.S. Department of Defense, "the world's largest energy consumer," spends significant amounts of money researching how to "ensure that energy is reliable, affordable, and sustainable." The most recent U.S. National Security Strategy mentions climate 63 times and treats climate change and the risks it poses as a significant national security threat, both at home and abroad. The United States continues to spend billions to protect the free flow of oil and the transit of gas, through maritime security agreements.

It is not just foreign actors that pose threats to American energy security, though. Just keeping the lights on has posed a challenge to millions. Over 200 people died in 2021 during the Texan "Deep Freeze" and California has, likewise, struggled to provide electricity to its residents during periods of extreme heat. Extreme cold and heat are challenges for utilities and grid operators; as Alice Hill from the Council on Foreign Relations argues, our energy infrastructure was built for a different climate. The bad news doesn't end there. A changing climate means that the winter of 2022–23 will see a "triple dip" La Niña (the colder counterpart of El Niño), making draughts even more likely. This poses an especially critical challenge for the already dry Western part of the United States. When water levels in dams get low, there are issues with the reliability of hydropower dams, reducing the availability of a low-carbon energy source. Addressing climate change is not merely a 'nice to have': it is a key ingredient in any search for energy security.

Other countries understand this, too. As mentioned above, Germany has made a bold move, and is extending the life of three of its remaining nuclear power plants. It was a reversal the government had to make, even in the face of severe opposition from the

Green party. France's recent experience with the Yellow Vest Movement was triggered by the government's move to remove subsidies on diesel; it is again facing public discontent over inflation, energy price spikes, and loss of economic opportunities. Such challenges are not limited to France, fuel price spikes were a significant trigger to the overthrow of the government in Sri Lanka earlier in 2022.

■ Energy security must be seen as part of the larger context of Great Power Competition

Long before Russia invaded Ukraine in February 2022, the world was beginning to come to terms with a return to competition amongst the so-called Great Powers. President Trump, for example, declared a 'trade war' on China in 2017. Covid exacerbated the desire to "decouple" from China and for countries to increase their self-reliance over their supply chains, in everything from medical supplies, to microchips, to food, to energy.

China seeks regional and possibly global primacy and is building out its manufacturing of the energy technologies the world is scrambling for – giving it partial hegemony over trajectory of the energy transition. Lack of cooperation and willingness to work together on international challenges is prevalent, the one area where there was potential was climate change, but even that cooperation is disintegrating with the fallout between China and the United States.

What is more, achieving energy sustainability will be difficult without China. China is positioning itself as a global manufacturer of green technology. It is the world's leading producer of solar panels, wind turbines, batteries, and electric vehicles (EVs). China has been the top investor in clean energy projects for nine of the last ten years, according to the Frankfurt School of Finance and Management. Over the last two decades China has invested billions in energy projects across the globe. China

and domestic entities have produced, engineered, financed, and developed renewable energy projects from Argentina and Brazil to Mexico, Scotland, Ethiopia, and Turkey. These and other programs have been rolled out as part of a deliberate effort to rebrand China as the world's green energy champion. The continued growth of renewable energy and China's role in being the largest manufacturer of the majority of renewable energy technologies has helped boost Chinese power and reorient existing trade relationships. Beijing is also pushing to assume the mantle of global nuclear energy power.

President Xi Jinping on energy security and climate change: "Based on China's energy and resource endowments, we will advance initiatives to reach peak carbon emissions in a well-planned and phased way, in line with the principle of getting the new before discarding the old."

A potent and increasing challenge in ensuring reliability and accessibility is that of infrastructure security. And growing insecurity is not only because of bad actors hacking the grid to cause a disruption to a pipeline, but also due to extreme weather. Extreme heat, flooding, wildfires, sea level rise and more are causing significant damage to critical energy infrastructure. Furthermore, the networked nature of energy infrastructure means that it is exposed to cyber threats directed at infrastructure, as demonstrated in the Colonial Pipeline attack in the spring of 2020 by a Russian non-state actor. The hack crippled fuel transit along the East Coast and it took almost a week to get the pipeline returned to full operational mode. The attack exposed pipeline vulnerabilities and the lack of alternatives when a critical vein of the energy infrastructure chain is broken.

The targeting of energy infrastructure is a tactic in Russia's invasion of Ukraine, Javier Blas calls it, "an electricity war." Moscow has been systematically targeting power stations and the electricity grid with missiles, forcing parts of Ukraine into rolling blackouts, while at the same time threatening Ukraine's 15 nuclear power plants, a definitive breach of international law. Subsea infrastructure is also at risk, the Nord Stream One pipeline was sabotaged illustrating how infrastructure once thought protected and secure is open to sabotage leading to heightened energy insecurity.

Global maritime chokepoints are also an area where energy security is important, over 60% of the world's petroleum and other liquids production moves through maritime routes; where any disruption can threaten security of supply. A most recent example is the Ever Given, one of the world's largest container ships that found itself stranded and lodged sideways in the Suez Canal. Over 10% of global trade, one million barrels a day of oil and 8% of liquefied natural gas pass through the canal. Lloyd fond estimated that the standing of the Ever Given was disrupting $9.8 billion in trade per day, with resulting higher prices for many impacted commodities and goods.

Combined, these threats are leading to calls for a change in strategy. U.S. Treasury Secretary Janet Yellen has stressed the need for 'friendshoring': the sourcing of key supplies—including energy—from those countries who are considered to be allies. While some, such as Canadian Finance Minister Chrystia Freeland, have been quick to pick up on this, keenly emphasizing both their friendliness and their capacity to provide both energy and other essentials, it must be recalled that "two can play at this game." Will such calls merely exacerbate feelings of "us vs them," further complicating global moves towards greater energy security and sustainability? China and India, for instance, have increased their purchases of Russian oil and coal. Perhaps more critically, though, where does it leave those countries, many who suffer from energy poverty, who are not so easily identified as 'friends' of one side or the other of the growing Great Power divide?

■ Security and sustainability are interrelated, but often contradictory

While we are unquestionably at the beginnings of an energy transition, it is important to note that there are multiple possible pathways to achieving low emission or emission-free generation, none of which have been firmly decided upon by most stakeholders. In the short term, natural gas producers like the United States, Russia, and Qatar will continue to leverage their gas resources in the global energy trade.

Energy and addressing climate change are not mutually exclusive, and they can't be when we consider the reality of global energy supply and demand. The world remains a major consumer of fossil fuels. Russia's invasion of Ukraine catapulted energy security front and center, and is upending the geopolitics of energy in new and unexpected ways. Coal is making a comeback and with significant carbon emission consequences. Many analysts and energy forecasts had predicted coal use would be on the decline with more plants seeing early retirement, but the new landscape of high gas prices and shortage of supply is providing coal with a second act, in some places we are actually seeing the unretiring/shifting of shut down timelines.

Curative effective policies are criti-cal. The United States is positioned to contribute to enhancing global energy security through its abundant energy sources, and can and must lead the way in addressing the urgency of climate change. It's possible to do both. The recently released Power Transition Trends 2022 by BloombergNEF shows that a profound change in the energy sector is underway. As found by the energy research firm, wind and solar now make up 11% of global power generation. Of the new power-generation capacity added in 2021, solar covered half, and wind took up a 25% share. While the green energy uptake is positive, the report echoes last year's unprecedented spike in coal-fired power generation. Up 750 terawatt-hours from 2020, the power sector's carbon dioxide emissions rose 7% year-on-year – a development likely to continue with the world confronting an ongoing energy crunch and a looming economic downturn. Lastly, the data also reveals that new power-generation assets are concentrated in a small range of markets. In numbers, the top 10 countries for wind power have accounted for 89% of all new capacity installed between 2012 to 2021. Hoping for the spike in coal-fired power generation to be nothing but a detour, numbers underline the vast and continuously untapped poten-

Maxar new high-resolution satellite imagery of the Suez canal and the container ship (EVER GIVEN) that remained stuck in the canal north of the city of Suez, Egypt. (SATELLITE IMAGE (C) 2020 MAXAR TECHNOLOGIES/GETTY IMAGES)

Environmentalists demonstrate during the World Climate Change Conference 2015 (COP21) on December 12, 2015, in Paris, France. The first universal agreement on the climate was proposed at the United Nations conference on climate change COP21 in Le Bourget, France. (CHESNOT/GETTY IMAGES)

tial for renewables to expand in size, scale, and across territories.

With the effects of climate change becoming more visible, achieving "energy security" must reflect that reality. Clean energy sources, ones that are ideally localized and can insulate countries from global shocks, are increasingly a necessary component of "energy security." Being able to generate clean and renewable energy without relying on energy supplies from outside your border is a necessary component of "energy security" in 2022. It allows citizens to live with less of a threat of external forces disrupting everyday life. Energy sources with lower emissions also have localized impacts by improving air quality. Countries' ability to scale up their clean power generation helps with another aspect of "energy security."

There is growing geopolitical competition in the hydrocarbon space as the world grapples with a need for a more decarbonized future, and growth in the renewables industry. New policies promoting greater amounts of non-fossil fuel sources in the energy mix may prove disrupting to the current geopolitical landscape, which continues to be dominated by oil, gas, and coal. Climate action is changing this dynamic and unleashing a paradigm shift which threatens future hydrocarbon demand with implications for international relations and security. The reality is, however, that these twin drivers—energy independence and energy transformation—are often in opposition to each other.

The next decade is considered pivotal. What we do or don't do will determine whether the world meets its climate goals or if we cross the 1.5°Celsius (the equivalent is 2.7° Fahrenheit) threshold, which most experts believe is inevitable given the current climate crises. Energy related carbon emissions increased in 2018 and 2019, fell in 2020 due to COVID induced lockdowns and reduction in global energy demand, but rebounded in 2021 and 2022. For many, the pace of the global energy transition is not fast enough. The 2015 Paris Agreement was viewed as a success by many; but seven years later, emissions continue to rise and countries are moving away from the commitments and action plans they submitted, mostly because of reactive policies to today's energy challenges. China and the United States agreed to ambitious carbon reduction targets, and every country submitted nationally determined contributions (NDC) outlining their actions to reduce carbon emissions by 2030. As a non-binding agreement, the results, as of 2022, remain lackluster and most analysts argue countries are not on track to meet the 1.5°C threshold. What this inaction has resulted in is a rise in social movements targeting the impacts of climate change. Across Europe there have been Extinction Rebellion protests. In March 2019, 1.5 million children across 112 countries protested against climate change. The leader of that School Strike, Greta Thunberg, became a household name, appeared at Davos, the UN, and around the world calling on governments and corporations to do more and to stop carbon emissions from rising. Her message in 2019 to Davos participants: "I don't want you to be hopeful, I want you to panic. I want you to feel the fear I feel every day and then I want you to act." For all of these movements, climate change is a global emergency threatening human existence and survival as we know it.

The emergence of EVs, more advanced battery storage technologies, cheaper production and use of renewable energy, enhanced energy efficiencies, and a growing awareness around the need to reduce fossil fuel energy consumption are all part of what's happening and will continue to drive peak demand. With the world looking to decarbonize and new technologies emerging to challenge the supremacy of oil and gas, the question is not if but when demand peaks. There is disagreement over when it will happen; some forecast as early as 2025, while Exxon Mobil and the IEA move it to 2040. The growing pressures around climate change action and capital may move the demand peak up, and the repercussions will be great, especially for countries heavily reliant on fossil fuel revenues to support their budgets.

The move to EVs, though, raises other concerns, especially around rare earth or critical minerals. There are a number of minerals deemed critical to the technologies and products that are important to the economy, especially for the energy transition. EVs, batteries, computers, smart phones, and high-level military technology, all require critical mineral inputs in their production. The problem with critical minerals is similar to that for hydrocarbons, they are not available everywhere in the world, and a handful of countries

currently command the majority of production and processing.

Addressing climate change/through the addition of renewable energy and displacement of the internal combustion engine vehicles requires a massive amount of critical minerals and metals, all of which require mining and processing, this is an emerging area in the geopolitics of energy and security landscape and one that is both necessary and challenging. The threat of the resource curse which has plagued some countries endowed with oil, think Venezuela and Angola, becomes the green resource curse in places like the Democratic Republic of the Congo which is one of the world's largest producers of cobalt, an integral component in batteries for EVs and a host of other products that are part of the energy transition.

As with hydrocarbons, manufacturing capacity and distribution of the resources needed for renewable energy generation varies greatly. An entirely new class of resources, sometimes called Critical Minerals may replace fossil fuels as the main source of geopolitical leverage. REES, the vast majority of which – more than 80%–are processed in China. All renewable energy technologies depend on criti-

cal minerals like lithium, cobalt, nickel and manganese. Not only are rare earth minerals critical components for renewable energy technology but also in computer and defense technology. Similarly, lithium, a component in the most widely available type of battery storage is produced by Chile, Argentina, Australia, and China. For electric vehicles to meet future targets, lithium output alone must grow almost six times its current production levels. China is already way ahead of the United States in EV battery production and market share, and even with a dedicated push in the United States to increase critical mineral mining and processing, and "out-compete" with China, however, China continues to surge ahead in the race for batteries and across much of the energy transition supply chain. The United States has arrived later to the critical mineral mining and processing game, and increased dependency on supply chains, making the United States more insecure when it comes to acquiring inputs.

As the countries move to increase the number of electric vehicles, deploy more solar power and electrify their economies there is a need for more copper, cobalt, and a host of other neces-

A man sorts through cobalt ore ahead of its sale to Congo Dongfang International Mining Sprl, a subsidiary of Zhejiang Huayou Cobalt Co. Ltd., at the market place at the Kasulo township in Kolwezi, Democratic Republic of the Congo, in February 2018. So-called artisanal mining is as commonplace as farming in many parts of the Congo. (WILLIAM CLOWES/ BLOOMBERG VIA GETTY IMAGES)

sary inputs in the manufacturing of the technologies essential for the energy transition. Just as countries have sought to ensure adequate access to oil and gas, for economies to decarbonize the need to procure minerals and metals is a new part of the geopolitics of energy.

Cobalt and coltan, another set of crucial elements are produced primarily in the Democratic Republic of the Congo, which has recently declared Cobalt a Strategic Element in an effort to increase domestic revenues. As states recognize the increasing value that these minerals have to the global economy, what actions will they take? Similar questions from the geopolitics of oil and gas re-emerge with critical minerals; will producer countries cooperate to act in a cartel-like fashion like OPEC? Or will they demand concessions from other states or the private sector? There are no clear answers as it is still early in the rare earth and critical resource energy transition, but it is clear that the race to secure—including through 'friend-shoring'—and deploy critical minerals and metals will be a central theme in the geopolitics of energy for the years and decades to come.

■ **Energy: diversity is key to both security and sustainability**

The global energy mix consists of a large portfolio of different energy sources, from hydrocarbons (oil, natural gas, and coal) to lower carbon and renewable energy sources, (wind, solar, hydropower, geothermal, biofuels and battery storage). There is also nuclear energy which is a non-carbon emitting source of power, but not without its controversies. The global landscape for nuclear energy illustrates the countries that view nuclear as a critical part of its mix, to those that are either shutting nuclear down to prohibiting any nuclear power plants from future construction. Hydrocarbons, make up more than 75% of the overall global energy mix, and have been at the forefront of the history of the geopolitics of energy. Not every country in the world is endowed with natural resources, nor the critical

energy resources required to power economic growth and development. Most countries import hydrocarbons, and it is important to understand both the production and consumption side of hydrocarbons. The world today consumes almost 100 million barrels a day of oil. An oftentimes overlooked aspect of contemporary energy security is the ownership of the resources. National oil companies, (NOCs) or what the International Monetary Fund (IMF) call, "hidden giants," control the majority, more than 70% of the world's oil and gas assets. Countries with NOCs include, Saudi Arabia, the Islamic Republic of Iran, Mexico and many others. All of the countries that make up OPEC have national oil companies. OPEC, the organization of oil producing countries had for many years wielded significant power over oil markets, being able to increase or decrease production depending on market and global conditions. The organization (some call it a cartel) provided more than 30% of global oil supply, giving it an important role in global energy security.

The future energy mix will be diverse, and include hydrocarbons, oil and gas, and even coal, especially in parts of the developing world where alleviating energy poverty is a priority. Renewables, comprising wind, solar, biofuels, hydropower, and geothermal energy will grow at the fastest rate, and see the largest increase in growth around the world. It is important to highlight, fossil fuels, oil and natural gas, and in some places, coal, will continue to play a significant role. Natural gas demand rises, as we see today, the most of any individual fuel source, to meet the needs for electricity and lower emission industrial heat. The inclusion of hydrocarbons in 2050 will perplex and frustrate many, but the reality of our complex global energy mix and a demand outlook that continues to show growth, especially in Asia and Africa, means that we are less likely to see a source of energy retiring and more likely to see more efficiency and less carbon intensity associated with its use, but also a more robust and competitive

landscape for a host of renewable energy technologies. The quest for energy will be a central theme in the energy transition, and the geopolitics of energy will continue to be a driver of both energy cooperation and emerging tensions as countries seek greater security. We are sure to see more energy crises in the years to come that keep the geopolitics of energy at the forefront.

As a corollary to the "availability" pillar, a key element of "energy security" in 2022 may also come in diversity. Relying on a small number of energy sources is increasingly risky as supply shocks become more common. These shocks could either be political, as is the case with Russia currently, or natural as could be the case if storms or floods knock energy sources offline. Diversity of energy supply can mean a couple of different things. First, it can mean a diversity of energy generation sources, such as varying between fossil fuels, renewables, or nuclear energy. It could also mean seeking a diverse source of energy suppliers, as energy importers like China and India try to do. Adding this component to the "energy security" conversation and definition will help countries navigate the inherent risks that are embedded in the global energy market and can help insulate countries from supply shocks and protect consumers from price spikes or rationing.

Electricity is the lifeblood of modern civilization and without it, we would backslide to an incomprehensible state of existence. Just imagine what life would be like in a world sans internet or instantaneous light and communication, to say nothing of the myriad other industries and modern amenities that would go away almost instantly if electricity were to be lost to us.

The key question in the energy transition is: what are the energy sources to push forward to achieve both energy security and decarbonization? Natural gas is abundant, less carbon intensive than coal, and has been considered an important bridge fuel in the energy transition. Unsurprisingly, the rise in natural gas is global and more countries are using gas due to its abundance and lower cost. For China it's a coal to gas to renewables story but some countries are pushing back against natural gas since it is still a carbon emitting source of energy.

Provision of reliable electricity is a critical step in helping to lift communities out of poverty. Access to power is important for agricultural production both in the global north and south, needed for food storage and overall economic productivity and development. Over 840 million people live without access to electricity, 55% of people living in Sub Saharan Africa have no access to electricity

Part of future energy security and achieving lower carbon emissions from the entire energy system will require a host of carbon capture technologies, starting with carbon capture utilization and storage. To achieve the right energy mix to meet current and future demand, acknowledging oil, gas, and maybe even some coal will continue to be used, the only way to get closer to net zero will be to deploy carbon capture.

Conclusion

Today we are in the midst of a period of massive global challenges, dealing with economic and development setbacks in the developing world where energy poverty remains a problem, how to mitigate against climate change while also adapting to its disruptions, and coping with the externalities of the ongoing Russian war. The world still lacks coordinated cooperation on climate change, the food and fuel crises hitting the world, use in the decades to come, even as we grapple with the impacts of climate change. A challenge is how the world manages energy; while advancing new technologies that can be deployed in the effort to decarbonize, battery storage, and more, and at the same time making sure we have the energy we need to keep our societies running, without energy shortages and contaminant economic disruptions.

The world's economy to date has been built on the exploitation of oil and other fossil fuels, and there's been an expectation that hydrocarbons must

Employees work on the assembly line of C01 electric sedan at a factory of Chinese EV startup Leapmotor on October 29, 2022, in Jinhua, Zhejiang Province of China. (HU XIAOFEI/ VCG VIA GETTY IMAGES)

also be readily available and affordable, but we're seeing that's a lot to expect in a time when we're also seeking to reduce demand for those same hydrocarbons. Energy security considerations are not new, and though sources of energy may change, achieving and maintaining energy security will be a central focus on the ongoing global energy transition, disruptions and discontinuity are and will continue to be the new normal. A challenge is to increase energy access designed with climate-smart energy systems and technologies that provide for a more energy secure future, while not exacerbating and contributing carbon emissions.

Why this energy crisis is different? There is no such thing as instant gratification – the world has been thrown into multiple crises, all of which connect back to energy and its security. 2022 will go down as a massive wake up call for energy security. How to achieve security, affordability, and be on the pathway to decarbonization – unintended consequences of policies/relationships. How not to mismanage the transition/ how to achieve a better match between investment and supply. With 8 billion people on the planet, and almost a billion who live in energy poverty, the challenge for meeting energy security today in the midst of what can be de-

scribed as the upending of traditional geopolitics - while aligning security with the realities of climate change, and how traditional approaches to energy security have exacerbated human contributions to a warming planet.

It is not an either or on energy security and the energy transition rather, it's both – but achieving and maintaining energy security during the energy transition is proving to be complex and messy, and depending on the region of the world the challenges are different, illustrating the common but still differentiated needs across the world. Achieving an energy secure place that's adequate to face crisis while recognizing being energy insecure perpetuates crisis.

There's no such thing as easy energy security, not that there ever was, but today's energy landscape is made more complicated due to radical shifts in the international order and more demands for cleaner and more sustainable energy sources to be part of the larger global energy mix. What is certain is that the course of the next decade will expose more and not less energy security challenges and dilemmas, requiring the new balancing of both energy and climate statecraft simultaneously, and it remains to be seen, if this is achievable.

discussion questions

1. Much of the current discourse on energy security is trending away from nuclear power towards renewable forms of energy like solar. In the article, we read that while we are trending away from hydrocarbons, they may always account for a portion of our energy production. Do you believe that nuclear power may have a similar future?

2. The article argues that climate mitigation requires energy shifting and a change in our primary sources of energy to cleaner forms. Do you believe that there is still hope in mitigation strategies, or should we move on and instead learn to adapt to climate change effects?

3. The war in Ukraine has exposed Europe's intense energy dependence on Russia. What do you believe is Europe's best option to gain energy security and move away from dependence on Russia?

4. China is increasingly the world manufacturing leader in green energy production. Given recent efforts by the Trump administration to decouple from China and create more independence in U.S. manufacturing, what do you believe is the best option moving forward? Should the U.S. attempt to cooperate with China in green energy manufacturing and production, or should we develop our own manufacturing capabilities independent from China?

5. While EVs are a helpful and popular step towards decarbonizing our daily lifestyles, the article argues that the REES that are crucial for the production of EVs are also harmful to the environment and create many energy security issues. What are some alternative options to EVs that are less harmful and more effective in decarbonization?

6. China has considerable leverage over the world's progress in reducing carbon emissions given its extreme manufacturing power and REES processing capabilities. What sort of leverage does the U.S. have? How can this leverage be used effectively to gradually move towards decarbonization?

suggested readings

Birol, Fatih, "Three Myths about the Global Energy Crisis." **Financial Times,** September 5, 2022. A short read from the Head of the International Energy Agency arguing the current crises in the energy space do not mean a shift away from clean energy, but rather, a possible expedited movement towards lower carbon energy.

Bordoff, Jason, "Why this Energy Crisis is Different." **Foreign Policy,** September 24, 2021. Bordoff looks at why Russia's invasion of Ukraine and the resulting energy crisis is different from past energy security events. He specifically argues this time it's not just about the oil, but also about natural gas, and other sources of energy. It's not an oil crisis but an energy crisis. The Russian invasion of Ukraine happened during a period of upheaval in energy, and only exacerbated by Russia's weaponization of its natural gas exports to Europe.

Gallagher, Kelly Simms, "The Coming Carbon Tsunami." **Foreign Affairs,** January/February 2022. Gallagher, in this **Foreign Affairs** piece looks at the developing world, and the rise in carbon emissions we can expect as countries, such as India and Indonesia, address domestic demand with more fossil fuels, and the resulting increase in expected carbon emissions. The developed world is decoupling economic growth away from rising emissions, but not yet in the developing world where energy poverty continues to persist.

Kissane, Carolyn, **The Upending of the Geopolitics of Energy: Disruption is the New Normal.** Palgrave Macmillan, 2021. Kissane looks at the changing nature of energy security and its impacts on the geopolitics of energy, and argues, disruption is the new normal as the world moves towards decarbonization. Countries that are dependent on natural resource revenues, especially oil and gas, will try to ensure their futures, and will seek to continue producing. She poses questions about stranded assets, and the geoeconomics competition between the US and China, and impacts on global energy security.

O'Sullivan, Meghan, **Windfall: How the New Energy Abundance Upends Global Politics and Strengthens America's Power.** Simon and Schuster, September 12, 2017. 496 pp. In the early 2000s the United States developed the technologies and capacities to unleash an energy revolution, shale oil and gas, and took the United States from being a net importer of oil and gas to a country that now exports oil and gas. The outcome of abundance and reduced domestic energy security would mean the United States could be more intentional on how it approached its foreign policy and could use oil and gas in its outreach abroad. It takes a lens of how energy has been and can be used in how a country approaches its foreign policy.

Don't forget to vote!

Download a copy of the ballot questions from the Resources page at www.fpa.org/great_decisions

To access web links to these readings, as well as links to additional, shorter readings and suggested web sites,

GO TO **www.fpa.org/great_decisions**

and click on the topic under Resources, on the right-hand side of the page.

War crimes: what are they? how can they be prosecuted?

by Francine Hirsch

Makeshift graves are seen at the Pishanske cemetery on September 23, 2022, in Izium, Ukraine. A total of 447 bodies were exhumed from the gravesite, including 22 soldiers and 5 children. The bodies will be examined by forensic experts for possible war crimes. (PAULA BRONSTEIN/GETTY IMAGES)

In the months since Russian President Vladimir Putin's brutal invasion of Ukraine on February 24, 2022, we've seen mounting evidence of Russian war crimes including the rape, torture, and murder of civilians, the bombing of schools and hospitals, and the abuse of prisoners-of-war. Horrifying stories about the kidnapping and deportation of Ukrainian children to Russia and shocking images of mass graves outside of Kyiv put the world on high alert. During a visit to Bucha in mid-April, the prosecutor of the International Criminal Court (ICC), Karim Khan, called Ukraine "a crime scene." World leaders, including U.S. President Joseph Biden and U.S. Secretary of State Antony Blinken, publicly accused Russia's leaders of committing war crimes in Ukraine and carrying out a genocide of Ukrainians. The discovery of burial pits in a birch forest outside the northeastern Ukrainian city of Izyum, after its liberation from Russian forces in September, prompted fresh calls for justice and accountability.

International lawyers and politicians have vowed that the criminal actions of Russian leaders and soldiers will not go unpunished. International institutions such as the ICC, along with dozens of national governments, have mobilized to investigate Russian war crimes and crimes against humanity in Ukraine. Ukraine's Prosecutor General's office has also launched its own effort to document Russian war crimes and has begun to prosecute Russian war criminals. In May, Ukraine held its first trial of a Russian soldier—a 21-year-old sergeant charged with fatally shooting an unarmed Ukrainian man. A Kyiv court found the soldier guilty of violating the laws and customs of war. Other trials have followed.

FRANCINE HIRSCH *is Vilas Distinguished Achievement Professor of History at the University of Wisconsin-Madison, where she teaches courses on Soviet history, Modern European history, and the history of human rights. Her most recent book,* Soviet Judgment at Nuremberg: A New History of the International Military Tribunal After World War II *(Oxford, 2020), has received several book awards including the George Beer Prize of the American Historical Association.*

At the same time, some international lawyers and world leaders, including Ukrainian President Volodymyr Zelenskyy, argue that these current efforts do not—and cannot—go far enough. They are calling for the creation of a "special tribunal," possibly on the Nuremberg model, to try Russian leaders for the "fundamental crime" of planning and waging an illegal war of aggression.

Back in March, just a few weeks after Russia's invasion, the editors of JusticeInfo.net, a website devoted to justice initiatives related to mass violence, observed that the war in Ukraine "has put into action the entire contemporary landscape of international justice, with a speed unprecedented in history." But what exactly is international justice—and what does its contemporary landscape look like? Put differently: What are the different categories of war crimes under international law? And what kinds of institutions are in place to investigate and prosecute them? How effective is our current system of international law and what are the chances of bringing Russian soldiers, officers, and leaders to justice? Finally, what kind of role could or should the United States, which is not a member of the ICC, play in these efforts?

Categories of war crimes

What exactly are we talking about when we talk about war crimes? The news media often uses "war crimes" as an umbrella term for a long list of transgressions, including violations of the rules of warfare, the mistreatment of civilians during a military conflict, the breaking of international treaties, and the waging of a predatory war of aggression. International lawyers and international organizations, however, generally use the term to refer more specifically to certain grave violations of the laws and customs of war elaborated in international law conventions such as the Hague Conventions, the

Before you read, download the companion **Glossary** that includes definitions, a guide to acronyms and abbreviations used in the article, and other material. Go to **www. fpa.org/great_decisions** and select a topic in the Resources section. (Top right)

Geneva Conventions and their protocols, and the Rome Statute.

The laws and customs of war were first codified in multilateral treaties in the late 19th and early 20th century—most notably the Hague Conventions of 1899 and 1907. These conventions prohibited certain methods of warfare, such as the use of poisons or dumdum bullets (that expand in the human body) and the attack or bombardment of undefended towns and cities. They forbade the pillaging of conquered territory, as well as the mistreatment and murder of civilians and prisoners of war. Special clauses in the Hague Conventions banned attacks on hospitals and the destruction of culture, stipulating that "all necessary steps must be taken to spare, as far as possible, buildings dedicated to religion, art, science, or charitable purposes, historic monuments, [and] hospitals" which were "not being used at the time for military purposes." The Hague Conventions also included the provisions of the Geneva Convention of 1864 (updated in 1906) for the treatment of sick and wounded soldiers.

The Hague and Geneva Conventions made major contributions to the development of international humanitarian law and initiated critical conversations about the role of international institutions in safeguarding and promoting the welfare of humanity. However, these conventions, while calling for peace, took as a given the legality and even the inevitability of war. The signatories to the Hague Convention of 1899 adopted a resolution on the peaceful settlement of international conflicts and created the Permanent Court of Arbitration, the first international body explicitly established to review and rule on disputes between states. But they did not give this body real power: it remained voluntary, not compulsory, and its decisions were not binding.

How then were war crimes to be punished? Significantly, these early international law conventions did not address the criminal responsibility of individual perpetrators, focusing instead on the rights and obligations of sover-

See p. 2 for a map of Ukraine.

eign states. The Hague Conventions stipulated that a state whose military violated the laws and customs of war owed compensation or reparations to its adversary. That adversary, the aggrieved state, could also formally respond with "proportionate" reprisals—temporarily lifting its own observance of the laws and customs of war. The Hague Conventions did not explicitly grant states permission to try captured enemy soldiers for breaching the laws and customs of war. But such trials by national or military courts in fact became commonplace during wars. After the conclusion of a peace treaty, states typically granted amnesty to enemy combatants. This would change with the First World War.

The question of individual criminal responsibility came to the fore during the First World War. The German military's massacres of civilians provoked international outrage and demands for justice. But what did justice look like and how could it be attained? Reparations were more or less a given and played a major role in the postwar settlement. But could individual leaders and soldiers be held criminally responsible for the murder of civilians and the mistreatment of prisoners of war? Could they be tried for these and other war crimes by an international body?

At the Paris Peace Conference in 1919, the victors set in motion plans to try German soldiers and generals as well as Germany's former leader, Kaiser Wilhelm II, as war criminals. The Treaty of Versailles called for a special tribunal to try the Kaiser—not for war crimes per se but for "a supreme offense against international morality and the sanctity of treaties." This was a bold move that pushed the bounds of international law. It challenged the prevailing belief that heads of state were immune from prosecution. It also introduced the idea of an illegal war and suggested that waging such a war was a criminally punishable act. The plan collapsed after the Dutch, who were sheltering Wilhelm II, refused to extradite him for trial.

Plans for an international tribunal of German soldiers and generals also fell apart. When the victors sought to extradite almost nine hundred German soldiers and generals (as agreed to in the Treaty of Versailles), Germany's new government protested that this infringed on its sovereignty and would lead to domestic unrest. A compromise was reached. From May 1921, Germany's Imperial Court of Justice in Leipzig held a series of war crimes trials under German military law. The Leipzig Trials were a bust: only seventeen German soldiers were actually brought before the court, and all either received light sentences or were acquitted. In one case, a soldier was excused for torpedoing a hospital ship on the grounds that he had been following "superior orders."

As efforts to punish individuals for war crimes floundered, world leaders and international lawyers looked for ways to establish a more robust system of international law that could preserve the peace. The Charter of the new League of Nations established a Permanent Court of International Justice to mediate disputes between states. Unlike the Permanent Court of Arbitration set up by the Hague Conventions, participation was compulsory for member states, who were required to take part in dispute resolution before (ideally, instead of) resorting to war. Like the Permanent Court of Arbitration, this court did not have the jurisdiction to try individuals. Proposals by international lawyers to create a separate international court under the League to try individuals, including leaders, for war crimes were shot down. For many countries, concerns about state sovereignty were paramount. In fact, in spite of the tireless efforts of President Woodrow Wilson (who had first proposed an "association of nations"), the Senate voted against U.S. membership in the League, wary of any institution that might serve as a world government.

The effort to expand the bounds of international law gained new momentum in the 1920s as delegates to the League of Nations challenged the very legality of war. Newly proposed treaties sought to pin down the difference between a lawful and an unlawful war, but none were ratified. Then in Septem-

8/27/1928, Washington, DC: President Calvin Coolidge signs the Kellogg-Briand Pact in his office. Secretary of State Frank B. Kellogg is seated to the left of the President. Also pictured are: Andrew Mellon; Charles Dawes (seated R); and Senator William E. Borah (R, behind President Coolidge). (BETTMANN/GETTY IMAGES)

ber 1927 the League's Assembly unanimously adopted a resolution stating that "a war of aggression can never serve as a means of settling international disputes, and is in consequence an international crime." The resolution conferred an obligation on League members but was not legally binding.

These deliberations in the League of Nations were shaped by, and also shaped, a broader conversation in many countries about how to prevent future wars. Lawyers and politicians from non-League countries, including the United States (which had its own "outlawry of war" movement), participated in these discussions and also addressed key questions: Should all wars be declared illegal? Or only wars of aggression? What should be the consequences for waging aggressive war? These discussions helped pave the way for an ambitious multilateral peacekeeping agreement: the Kellogg-Briand Pact. Led by the United States and France, representatives from twelve countries signed the pact in Paris in August 1928. Dozens of other countries soon came on board; by late 1929 there were 62 signatories, including the Soviet Union. The pact condemned "recourse to war for the solution of international controversies" and renounced war "as an instrument of national policy." It required signatories

to resolve their disputes "by peaceful means" but (like the League's resolution of a year earlier) did not set legal consequences for states or rulers that refused or failed to do so. Could war really be considered a crime if there was no clearly stipulated punishment? Notably, the Geneva Conventions of 1929 demanded the humane treatment of prisoners of war, but took war itself as a given.

By the mid 1930s it had become clear that neither the League of Nations nor the Kellogg-Briand Pact could do much to stop a country set on war, and that the international community could not be counted on to respond decisively after the fact. Japan's invasion of Manchuria in 1931 and Italy's invasion of Abyssinia in 1935 were cases in point: both withdrew from the League after being rebuked for their actions, but faced no meaningful consequences. Meanwhile there were other developing dangers to world peace. Adolf Hitler withdrew Germany from the League in 1933 and remilitarized the Rhineland in 1936 in violation of the Treaty of Versailles.

Wasn't it time for international organizations to do more to deter and punish those who planned and waged aggressive war? The Soviet Union had joined the League in 1934, and its international lawyers soon began to explore

2

A.N. Trainin (center with mustache), head of the Soviet delegation to the War Crimes Executive Committee, speaks to his colleagues. To his right sits I.T. Nikitchenko, who later represented the U.S.S.R. on the International Military Tribunal. This body worked out the Allied agreement to create the International Military Tribunal to prosecute German war criminals at Nuremberg.
(CHARLES ALEXANDER/COURTESY OF HARRY S. TRUMAN LIBRARY / UNITED STATES HOLOCAUST MEMORIAL MUSEUM)

this question in depth. In a 1937 book, *The Defense of Peace and Criminal Law,* the Soviet lawyer Aron Trainin argued that the League of Nations and the Kellogg-Briand Pact had both fallen short by not making the waging of war a criminally punishable offense. He called for the creation of an international criminal court to try "persons violating peace." Trainin's proposal was prompted by the combined threat of Germany and Japan, who had joined together in November 1936 to sign an Anti-Comintern Pact that was clearly directed against the Soviet Union. Meanwhile, Soviet leaders and diplomats were working behind the scenes to secure an agreement with Nazi Germany. The Soviet and German foreign ministers signed a Treaty of Non-Aggression on August 23, 1939, pledging their countries to "desist from any act of violence, any aggressive action, and any attack on each other."

The Soviet-German non-aggression pact paved the way for the conquest of Poland. On September 1, 1939, German forces invaded Poland from the west. Two weeks later, on September 17, Soviet forces invaded Poland from the east. The Soviet Union did not declare war on Poland, but cynically claimed that it had launched a campaign of liberation to protect Belarusians and Ukrainians within Poland's borders. By October 6, Poland was defeated and divided (along

lines that Stalin and Hitler had agreed to in the non-aggression pact's secret protocols). The Second World War was well under way. For the first twenty-one months of the war the Soviet Union supported Germany with exports of grain, oil, and other resources. During that time Norway, Denmark, Belgium, the Netherlands, Luxembourg, France, Yugoslavia, and Greece all fell to Germany. Then, on June 22, 1941, Hitler launched Operation Barbarossa and violated his treaty with Stalin by invading the Soviet Union. By the time the United States entered the war six months later, some fifty countries had become involved in the conflict and most were actively fighting.

The Second World War was the deadliest military conflict in history, bringing unimaginable suffering and destruction to Europe. Nazi forces occupied huge swaths of the continent, committing mass atrocities and implementing plans to wipe out entire peoples. The deportation and murder of civilians was on a scale no one could quite believe—but the evidence kept coming in, thanks largely to the efforts of the European governments-in-exile. International organizations and treaties had not been able to stop the war or prevent the commission of horrific war crimes. But as people throughout occupied Europe dreamed of vengeance and restitution, some leaders and international lawyers pinned their hopes on a robust program

of postwar justice. Their efforts to hold Nazi leaders and soldiers accountable for war crimes would lead to a revolution in international law, as ideas about individual criminal responsibility and individual human rights were finally put into action.

While the Americans and the British vowed that Nazi perpetrators would be brought before courts in the countries they were oppressing, the Soviets set their sights on an international tribunal. On October 15, 1942, Soviet Foreign Minister Vyacheslav Molotov proclaimed the criminal responsibility of the Nazis for atrocities in occupied Europe and invited the other Allied governments to cooperate in bringing Hitler, Herman Goering, and other Nazi leaders before a "special international tribunal" to be punished with "all of the severity of criminal law." The United States and Britain opposed such an approach. The U.S. government worried about reprisals against Allied prisoners of war. The British maintained that the crimes of Hitler and Goering were far too serious for a trial and argued instead for punishment by an executive decree of the Allied governments. The Soviets went down their own path. They created their own war crimes commission, the Extraordinary State Commission, and asked Soviet lawyers to assess the criminal responsibility of Nazi leaders for invading other countries in pursuit of "predatory goals."

As the war raged on, Allied lawyers found themselves sharply debating the definition of "war crimes." The United Nations War Crimes Commission (UN-WCC) began meeting in London in October 1943. All of the Allies except for the Soviet Union participated. The chair of the commission, the British judge Sir Cecil Hurst, wanted to define "war crimes" as a violation of the laws and customs of war as set out in the Hague Conventions. But representatives from occupied Europe fought for a broader definition. The Belgian lawyer Marcel de Baer and the Czechoslovak lawyer Bohuslav Ečer argued that the commission must extend its reach to acts that fell outside of the Hague Conventions, such as the persecution of Germany's Jews. The U.S. delegate

Herbert Pell agreed and introduced a motion to treat crimes committed because of the religion or race of the victims, and crimes against stateless persons, as war crimes. He called such acts "crimes against humanity"—reviving a term that the Russians, French, and British had used in a declaration in 1915 to condemn the Ottoman slaughter of Armenians. Pell's proposal received a mixed reception in the UN-WCC (and criticism from within the U.S. State Department), but the idea that certain abuses were crimes against humanity soon took hold.

De Baer and Ečer also urged their colleagues in the UNWCC to expand the definition of war crimes to include "the crime of war." They argued that "without the crime of aggressive war there would be no war crimes" and deemed it "illogical" to "punish the products of the crime and not the crime itself." Soviet lawyers had come to the same conclusion. In the summer of 1943, Trainin completed a report for Soviet leaders titled "The Criminal Responsibility of the Hitlerites," which the Soviets published as a book the following year. Trainin argued for the criminal responsibility of perpetrators at all levels. Calling the plea of superior orders a "saving bunker" for war criminals, he maintained that soldiers should face punishment for breaches of the laws and customs of war. But the greatest degree of criminal responsibility, he suggested, belonged to Germany's leaders. He argued that Hitler and his circle should be tried not only for traditional war crimes but also for waging the war—committing a "crime against peace"—in the first place. Trainin coined the term "crimes against peace" and defined it as: acts of aggression; propaganda of aggression; the conclusion of international agreements with aggressive aims; the violation of peace treaties; provocations designed to stir up trouble between states; terrorism; and the support of fifth columns. To try Nazi leaders for crimes against peace, he called, not surprisingly, for an international tribunal.

Trainin's arguments spread across Europe to London. In October 1944, his ideas were discussed by the UNW-CC. Ečer continued to insist that Nazi leaders be held responsible for launching an illegal war. He further argued that defining the war as "criminal" made it possible to see acts like "the extermination of foreign races" not "as simple 'violations of laws and customs of war' but as instruments of a general criminal policy." Ečer noted that Soviet jurists strongly supported "the opinion that the preparation and launching of this war are crimes for which the authors must bear penal responsibility." Using Trainin's term, he proclaimed that the war "must be punished as a crime against peace." In the wake of the October meeting, Ečer presented the UNWCC with a detailed report on Trainin's book. Many of the delegates brought copies of the report back to their governments; in November it was forwarded to the State Department, which sent it on to the White House with a copy of the book in translation.

In January 1945 two lawyers from the U.S. War Department's Special Projects Branch, Murray Bernays and D. W. Brown, wrote a secret report for President Franklin D. Roosevelt on the question of whether starting the current war was a crime for which Nazi leaders could be tried and punished. They answered yes. International law evolves with "the public conscience" and it could no longer "be disputed that the launching of a war of aggres-

sion today is condemned by the vast majority of mankind as a crime," they argued. They noted that a number of Allied lawyers, including Trainin and the British lawyer Hersch Lauterpacht, shared this view. An Allied declaration calling out the criminality of aggressive war would "rest on solid grounds," and would itself take on the power of "valid international law."

As Allied victory began to seem all but certain, American and British leaders came to embrace the idea of bringing Nazi leaders before an international tribunal. After the Nazi surrender in May 1945, plans to organize the International Military Tribunal (IMT) began in earnest. Representatives from the United States, Great Britain, the Soviet Union, and France met in London that summer to discuss the IMT's framework. Among the participants were prominent lawyers such as French law professor André Gros, Supreme Court Justice Robert H. Jackson, and the Soviet lawyer Trainin. Much of the discussion centered on the charges, which comprised Article 6 of the Nuremberg Charter. It was agreed that the defendants would be charged with traditional war crimes (violations of the rules and customs of war) as well as the crime of waging an illegal war. The latter was labeled "crimes against peace" and included the "planning, preparation, initiation, or waging of a war of aggression,

1946: The International Military Tribunal in Nuremberg. The four judges and their four alternates (left) preside in the courtroom of the Palace of Justice. From left to right are Alexander Volchkov (USSR), Iona Nikitchenko (USSR), Norman Birkett (Britain), Geoffrey Lawrence (Britain), Francis Biddle (USA), John Parker (USA), Henri Donnedieu de Vabres (France), and [not visible] Robert Falco (France). (HULTON ARCHIVE/GETTY IMAGES)

or a war in violation of international treaties, agreements or assurances." The idea of an illegal war no longer seemed quite so controversial.

The most heated discussions about Article 6 centered on crimes against civilians, labeled in an initial draft as "atrocities, persecutions, and deportations on political, racial or religious grounds." All the participants agreed that these crimes should be tried and punished—but once again questions about state sovereignty came into play. Could the IMT address Germany's treatment of its own citizens? The charge of crimes against civilians was soon renamed "crimes against humanity" and defined as "murder, extermination, enslavement, deportation, and other inhumane acts" committed against civilian populations as well as "persecutions on political, racial or religious grounds." But it was ultimately limited to crimes committed "in execution of or in connection with" the planning or waging of aggressive war. Germany's persecution and extermination of its Jewish population would only be prosecutable as a crime against humanity if it could be tied to the Nazi war of aggression.

In November 1945, the United States, Great Britain, France, and the Soviet Union convened the IMT at the Palace of Justice in Nuremberg, Germany, to try 22 former Nazi leaders for war crimes, crimes against peace, crimes against humanity, and conspiracy. Those in the dock included members of Hitler's inner circle as well as government ministers, military leaders, and propagandists. For ten months, the world learned in shocking detail about the horrors of the concentration camps and the crematoria, the mobile killing squads and gas vans, and the death pits of Babi Yar. The word "genocide" was introduced to the world, thanks to the efforts of Raphael Lemkin, a lawyer with the U.S. War Department (and a Polish-Jewish refugee) who coined the term. It appeared in Count Two of the Indictment—War Crimes—and was defined as the intentional destruction of "particular races and classes of people and national, racial, or religious groups." During the trials the

Raphael Lemkin (© ESTATE OF ARTHUR LEIPZIG, COURTESY OF HOWARD GREENBERG GALLERY, NEW YORK/NATIONAL PORTRAIT GALLERY, SMITHSONIAN INSTITUTION)

term came to be used more broadly to describe a "deliberate and systematic plan" to wipe out peoples and cultures. British chief prosecutor Sir Hartley Shawcross argued in his closing speech that the Nazis had pursued genocide "in different forms" against different peoples, and that the methods had included deportation, death by starvation, forced assimilation, and outright murder.

In many ways Nuremberg was a success. The Allies had put their differences aside and had worked together to create a comprehensive record of the crimes of the Third Reich and to bring the former Nazi leaders to justice. The vast majority of those tried (nineteen defendants) were convicted, most on multiple charges. The IMT established the criminal responsibility of those who waged aggressive war and committed crimes against humanity. It served as a precedent for further trials, such as the Tokyo Trial of 1946-48 and the subsequent U.S.-led Nuremberg Military Tribunals of 1946-49, and it opened up a new era in international law. Ideas about justice and human rights that were articulated during the trials fed into a broader discussion about the role that new institutions like the United Nations (established in October 1945) could play in preserving the peace.

The Charter of the United Nations required member nations to resolve their disputes "by peaceful means" and to refrain from "the threat or use of force against the territorial integ-

rity or political independence of any state." The United Nations' court of arbitration, the International Court of Justice (ICJ), began operations in April 1946 in The Hague. But after a second devastating world war, many lawyers and leaders were hoping for something more ambitious than a reboot of the Permanent Court of International Justice. In December 1946, two months after the Nuremberg verdicts, the United Nations General Assembly passed a resolution affirming "the principles of international law" recognized in the Nuremberg Charter and judgment and asked the United Nations Codification Committee to incorporate these "Nuremberg principles" into a new international law code of "crimes against the peace and security of mankind." In the same session the General Assembly declared genocide an international crime and asked the United Nations Economic and Social Council to draft a genocide convention.

Nuremberg also had its limitations—and these too shaped the postwar discussion about war crimes. The IMT had been circumscribed from the start by concerns about state sovereignty. Crimes against humanity had been defined particularly restrictively, as only prosecutable in the context of an aggressive war. As work began on the new international law code, some lawyers called for a broader definition that would extend to a state's persecution of its own subjects or citizens during both wartime and peacetime. The IMT had also been dogged by the criticism that as a court of the victors it had no hope of being impartial. After the trials, the French judge on the IMT, Henri Donnedieu de Vabres, revealed that he had been deeply troubled at Nuremberg by such allegations of victor's justice. He argued that the creation of a permanent international criminal court would remedy this problem. Unlike the ICJ, which could only arbitrate disputes between sovereign states, this court would be able to try individuals for war crimes, crimes against humanity, and crimes against peace. It would eliminate the need for ad hoc tribunals like the IMT in the future. But as the Cold

War set in, concerns about state sovereignty only intensified. By 1952 efforts to draft a new international law code and establish an international criminal court had both run aground.

Work on the Genocide Convention went more smoothly, but only with serious compromises. In December 1948, the United Nations General Assembly unanimously approved the convention, declaring genocide (as well as inciting genocide or attempting genocide) a crime under international law. The convention defined genocide as one of several acts committed "with intent to destroy, in whole or in part, a national, ethnic, racial, or religious group." These acts included: killing or inflicting serious physical or mental harm to the members of the group; preventing births within the group or forcibly transferring the group's children to another group; and deliberately inflicting conditions "calculated to bring about the group's physical destruction." The intent of the perpetrator was key to the crime. Drafts of the convention had included "political groups" as a category and had also covered cultural genocide (the intentional destruction of a group's identity and culture). But these clauses had provoked significant controversy and were dropped. The convention treaded carefully around the question of enforcement. It stipulated that persons charged with genocide could be tried by a national tribunal or by an international tribunal—provided that the contracting parties accepted the latter's jurisdiction. The idea of an international genocide tribunal also proved controversial and was soon scrapped. Even so, some states worried about infringements on their sovereignty: the United States signed the treaty but did not ratify it until 1988.

During the Cold War, the Nuremberg principles shaped the international community's understanding of criminal responsibility and war crimes, even as plans to create a new international law code and an international criminal court came to naught. Terms like "crimes against humanity," "crimes against peace," and "genocide" became central to discussions about interna-

Three hundred skulls sit in lines outside a chapel in Rwanda on November 6, 1994, as authorities investigate the genocide that resulted in the death of one million Tutsis in April 1994. (SCOTT PETERSON/HULTON ARCHIVE/GETTY IMAGES)

tional law and human rights, as did a greater awareness of the need to protect civilians in war zones. The Geneva Conventions of 1949 contained specific provisions on providing humanitarian relief to the civilian populations of occupied territories. At the same time, though, this Nuremberg-inspired language of human rights and international law quickly became highly politicized: the Soviet Union and the United States began to regularly denounce one another's foreign and domestic policies as "crimes against peace" and "crimes against humanity."

As Europe was becoming divided into east and west, Western European lawyers and politicians also created their own postwar institutions, such as the Council of Europe, a human rights organization founded in 1949, and its European Court of Human Rights (ECtHR). The latter, which began operations in 1959 in Strasbourg, France, adjudicated complaints submitted by states or individuals concerning abuses of civil and political rights. It did not deal with war crimes per se, but ruled on a wide range of human rights violations, including the rape, torture, and murder of civilians as well as attacks against protected civilian sites such as hospitals, schools, and residential buildings. Council of Europe members were expected to enact the ECtHR's decisions, as the court had no

enforcement mechanisms of its own.

Cold War politics had made an international criminal court untenable. After the collapse of the Soviet Union in 1991, the United Nations gradually revisited the possibility of a more robust system of international justice. In the 1990s, the Yugoslav Wars and the genocide in Rwanda brought questions about war crimes, international law, and individual criminal responsibility back into the spotlight. The absence of a permanent court to try atrocity crimes meant that there was still a need for ad hoc tribunals. The United Nations Security Council established such tribunals for Yugoslavia and Rwanda: in 1993 it created the International Criminal Tribunal for the Former Yugoslavia (ICTY) and in 1994 the International Criminal Tribunal for Rwanda (ICTR). Both tribunals successfully prosecuted individuals, including leaders, for crimes against humanity, genocide, and other grave violations of international humanitarian law. Both were inspired by the IMT and gave new force to the Nuremberg principles and to the international law conventions that the horrors of the Second World War had inspired.

The ICTY and the ICTR both adopted the definition of genocide from the Genocide Convention. But they differed in other respects. The ICTY statute defined "war crimes" as grave breaches of the Geneva Conventions of 1949 as well as "other violations of the laws and customs of war." The ICTR statute did not use the term "war crimes," but instead spoke of "war victims" and listed prosecutable violations of the Geneva Conventions of 1949 (and their 1977 Additional Protocol) such as murder, torture, pillage, the taking of hostages, rape, and enforced prostitution. Both tribunals based their understandings of crimes against humanity loosely on the Nuremberg Charter—as "inhumane acts" committed against civilians, including murder, extermination, enslavement, deportation, imprisonment, torture, rape, and persecutions on political, racial and religious grounds. The ICTY restricted crimes against humanity to acts committed during military conflicts, but allowed that such conflicts could be internal. The ICTR limited crimes against humanity to crimes committed during internal armed conflicts (reflecting the situation in Rwanda); it stipulated that such crimes had to have been committed "as part of a widespread or systematic attack" against civilians "on national, political, ethnic, racial or religious grounds." The ICTY and the ICTR had something else in common: neither had the authority to prosecute the crime of aggression (crimes against peace).

The work of these ad hoc tribunals gave new life to the idea of a permanent international criminal court. In 1994 the United Nations International Law Commission set to work on a new statute for such a court and worked with fresh momentum on a Draft Code of Crimes Against the Peace and Security of Mankind. The draft code was completed in 1996, but never ratified. The International Criminal Court (ICC), on the other hand, after intense negotiations and numerous compromises, actually came into being. In July 1998, at a United Nations conference in Italy, 120 states adopted the Rome Statute, the ICC's founding treaty. The Rome Statute created the ICC as an independent judicial body separate from the United Nations. The court began operations in July 2002 in The Hague. The Rome Statute did not grant immunity to state leaders, recognizing that they are often

"at the root of war crimes." Nor did it exempt military officers from responsibility for crimes committed by their subordinates. The ICC has the jurisdiction to investigate crimes committed on the territory of member states, crimes committed by the nationals of member states, and crimes that were referred to it by the United Nations Security Council—opening the way to the possible prosecution of leaders of countries that had not ratified the Rome Statute.

The ICC was authorized from its start to investigate and rule on three categories of crimes: genocide, crimes against humanity, and war crimes. The definition of genocide in the Rome Statute was lifted directly from the Genocide Convention. The definition of crimes against humanity built upon previous understandings of the term—but went significantly further. It included the persecution of "any identifiable group" on "political, racial, national, ethnic, cultural, religious, gender, or other grounds that are universally recognized as impermissible under international law." It also included murder, extermination, enslavement, unjust imprisonment, torture, deportation, sterilization, forced pregnancy, rape, and other sexual crimes when committed as part of "widespread or systematic attack against any civilian population" (regardless of whether the victims are part of an identifiable group). Finally, the definition included conduct that had come to be recognized as criminal well after Nuremberg, such as apartheid and enforced disappearances. The ICC's understanding of crimes against humanity also differed from the Nuremberg (and ICTY) definition in another important respect: it allowed that such crimes could occur during peacetime.

The "war crimes" category in the Rome Statute was the most extensive, with a long and detailed list of offenses. These included grave breaches of the Hague and Geneva Conventions, such as the mistreatment of civilians and prisoners of war, as well as other violations of the laws and customs of war, such as the use of prohibited weapons and the bombing of undefended towns and villages. Like the

Hague and Geneva Conventions, the statute specifically called out attacks on hospitals, schools, historic monuments, and places dedicated to religion, art, science, or charitable purposes. The Rome Statute's list of war crimes also included "outrages upon personal dignity" such as rape, sexual slavery, forced prostitution, forced pregnancy, and forced sterilization. And it included more recently recognized war crimes, such as the conscription of children into military service.

The fourth possible category of crimes included in the Rome Statute was preparing and waging a war of aggression. However, the signatories could not agree on the meaning of "aggression" (which the Nuremberg Charter had left undefined) and the court's jurisdiction over this crime was put on hold. Finally, at a 2010 conference in Uganda, an agreement was reached. The Kampala Amendments (codified as Article 8bis of the Rome Statute) defined the "crime of aggression" as "the planning, preparation, initiation or execution" of "an act of aggression which, by its character, gravity, and scale, constitutes a manifest violation" of the Charter of the United Nations. An "act of aggression" was then defined as "the use of armed force" by one state to attack "the sovereignty, territorial integrity or political independence" of another state with or without a declaration of war. Examples could include invasion, bombardment, occupation, and annexation.

Aggression was defined specifically as a leadership crime. The ICC could investigate and prosecute "the planning, preparation, initiation or execution" of "an act of aggression" committed by someone with the authority "to exercise control over or to direct the political or military action of a state." The language "control or direct" was intended to be significantly limiting; the IMT, by contrast, had applied a broader "shape or influence" standard. The ICC's power to prosecute leaders for aggression was further constrained by limitations on its jurisdiction that were added to appease states concerned about their sovereignty. Non-ICC states (their leaders and citizens) were exempted from prosecution for aggression even if they invaded an ICC member state. Member states were given the choice to opt out of ICC jurisdiction for "aggression crimes." The Kampala Amendments went into force in 2018. But to date, only a modest number of ICC member states—43 out of the 123 parties to the Rome Statute—have agreed to accept the court's jurisdiction over the crime. These are significant limitations on the ICC's jurisdiction, as we are now seeing very clearly in the context of Russia's war against Ukraine.

The current landscape of international justice

So, what are the international institutions currently in place to investigate Russian war crimes in Ukraine, and how much can each actually do? What are the chances of bringing Russian soldiers, officers, and leaders to justice? The ICC and the Council of Europe's ECtHR have both embarked on investigations. Each has a different jurisdiction and different limitations. Only the ICC can try individual war criminals. The ECtHR's mandate is to resolve disputes between states pertaining to the European Convention of Human Rights; it can deal with war through the lens of this convention. But it has long been stymied by Russia's refusal to heed its rulings. In February, the Council of Europe expelled Russia; in June, the Russian State Duma passed a bill ending the ECtHR's jurisdiction in the Russian Federation.

The ICJ has also been involved in trying to quell the conflict. Ukraine brought a case against Russia to the ICJ in late February. It argued that Russia had invaded on false pretenses, with a phony claim that Ukraine was carrying out a genocide against Russian speakers within its borders. The ICJ made a significant ruling in Ukraine's favor in March, issuing an emergency order directing Russia to stop the war and cease all military operations in Ukraine. The vote was 13-2, with the Russian and Chinese judges dissenting. The ICJ ruling was a moral victory—but it had no teeth. The ICJ counts on the promise of states to follow its rulings. It has no

A playground in front of a school that was shelled and destroyed by Russian forces on July 21, 2022. (IVA ZIMOVA/PANOS PICTURES/REDUX)

enforcement mechanism of its own, but must rely on the United Nations Security Council, where Russia (one of five permanent members) has a veto which it has used to oppose any actions against its leaders.

The fact is that Russia has shown no interest in adhering to international law or in abiding by any international institution's decisions. Putin has been cynically manipulating the language of international law to make bogus accusations against Ukraine, while acting with impunity. Investigations into Russia's war crimes have been continuing and fact-finding missions have been launched nonetheless—even as the mechanisms for justice remain uncertain.

In April the United Nations General Assembly voted to suspend Russia from its Human Rights Council. A few weeks later, the Human Rights Council set up a Commission of Inquiry which has been gathering evidence of human rights abuses and international humanitarian law violations carried out by Russia in Ukraine. It has pledged to focus on violations of the rights of children and other vulnerable populations, as well as sexual crimes. It has been interviewing local authorities and victims. At the end of its investigation, the Commission of Inquiry will make recommendations toward the goals of holding perpetrators accountable and ensuring justice for victims. But it can only do so much. The commission can

publicize information about Russian war crimes and share its findings with governments (as the UNWCC did during the Second World War), but it does not have a mandate to organize trials. Once again, it would likely be up to the United Nations Security Council to act—and Russia's veto means that this won't happen.

A number of other organizations have also been gathering evidence of Russian war crimes and crimes against humanity in Ukraine. These include the Office for Democratic Institutions and Human Rights (ODIHR) of the Organization for Security and Co-operation in Europe (OSCE), which has documented numerous human rights violations including the torture, deportations, and targeted killing of civilians, and the enforced disappearances of local Ukrainian officials. None of these organizations have their own mechanisms for accountability.

The international institution best positioned to bring at least some Russian perpetrators to justice may very well be the ICC. Russia and Ukraine are not members of the ICC. But back in 2014 Ukraine accepted the ICC's jurisdiction to investigate war crimes committed on its territory. As a result, the ICC can investigate allegations of genocide, crimes against humanity, and war crimes committed in Ukraine "by all parties to the conflict." The ICC opened such an investigation in early

March, with support from dozens of member states—and has sent a large team of detectives to Ukraine to gather evidence. The European Union Agency for Criminal Justice Cooperation (Eurojust) has been supporting this effort. In March, Eurojust established a Joint Investigation Team, bringing together the ICC Prosecutor's Office and Ukrainian, Polish, Lithuanian, Estonian, Latvian and Slovakian judicial authorities. Its mandate is to "collect, analyze, and preserve evidence in relation to core international crimes" and to share this evidence with the ICC and other relevant international and national institutions.

As the ICC and Eurojust continue their work of gathering evidence, Ukraine has been preparing its own investigations of Russian soldiers for murder, rape, the bombing of schools and hospitals, and other breaches of the laws and customs of war. In August, Ukraine's Prosecutor General's office announced it was looking into more than 25,000 possible war crimes and was receiving hundreds of new reports every day. Ukraine has already tried several cases in its own national and regional courts. The ICC is also working with Ukraine's Prosecutor General's Office to decide how to coordinate their work. International lawyers point out that that ICC is meant to be a court of last resort. And ICC prosecutor Khan has affirmed that Ukraine has "the first right and indeed the first responsibil-

ICC prosecutor Karim Khan speaks on July 14, 2022, during an ICC-hosted conference in The Hague about pursuing justice for the victims of Russian war crimes in Ukraine. Representatives from forty countries, including Ukraine, agreed to coordinate their efforts to investigate crimes and hold perpetrators accountable. (SELMAN AKSUNGER/ANADOLU AGENCY VIA GETTY IMAGES)

ity to investigate and prosecute crimes" committed within its borders. But Khan has also suggested that given "the scale of criminality, which is absolutely massive," Ukraine cannot do this alone. He has proposed that the ICC and Ukraine might coordinate their efforts and decide on a case-by-case basis whether the best forum is the ICC or Ukraine's national court system.

At least a dozen European countries (including Lithuania, Germany, and Sweden) have also launched independent investigations into Russian war crimes, under the principle of "universal jurisdiction"—which allows states to investigate and prosecute certain grave international crimes regardless of where they were committed. The idea of universal jurisdiction (which has its roots partly in the Geneva Conventions of 1949) remains controversial and has been used sparingly in the past. (It was used by Israel in 1961 to try Adolf Eichmann.) Some international lawyers believe that it holds great promise for bringing Russian perpetrators to justice. Here too, ICC prosecutor Khan has spoken of the need for coordination and for the international community to adopt "an overarching strategy." Other international law experts and United Nations officials have agreed, warning that the overlapping efforts of different states and institutions may lead to "the re-traumatization of victims arising from being interviewed multiple times by different investigators."

What role should the United States have in these and other efforts? The United States never ratified the Rome Statute, and its role in the ICC's efforts will necessarily be limited. U.S. Ambassador for Global Justice Beth Van Schaack has met with ICC prosecutor Khan to discuss U.S. support for the ICC's work in Ukraine. The Biden administration has also been considering ways to support Ukraine's own investigations. In May, the United States joined the European Union and the United Kingdom to establish the Atrocity Crimes Advisory Group for Ukraine, which, according to Secretary of State Blinken, will directly support Ukraine's efforts "to document, pre-

serve, and analyze evidence of war crimes and other atrocities committed by members of Russia's forces in Ukraine, with a view toward criminal prosecutions." It will assist in a number of areas including forensic investigations. Also in May, the State Department launched the online platform Conflict Observatory as a central hub to preserve and share satellite images and other evidence of Russian atrocities in Ukraine for use in future possible trials.

The ICC is moving forward with plans to try Russian war crimes, but cannot try Russian leaders for aggression—since Russia is not a state party to the Rome Statute (or its Kampala Amendments). There has been growing momentum among world leaders and international lawyers to create an ad hoc tribunal that could try Russia's leaders specifically for preparing and waging an aggressive war. One possible option is a special international tribunal established by a treaty among interested states or by an agreement between Ukraine and the United Nations or by the European Union. Various draft indictments have been drawn up for a special international tribunal; they all imagine Russian President Vladimir Putin as the chief defendant.

Another proposed option is the creation of a special Ukrainian court to prosecute aggression in close collaboration with the European Union, comprised of Ukrainian and other European judges. Some lawyers have argued that such a court would have to be international in order to prosecute Putin; they maintain that leaders have immunity from prosecution before any national court under customary international law. In the meanwhile, Ukraine is poised to prosecute lesser figures for aggression on its own. Ukraine's Prosecutor General's office announced this summer that it had already identified over six hundred Russians to indict and try for this crime; its list includes government officials, military officers, police chiefs, and Kremlin propagandists.

Where do we go from here?

The international community has come a long way since the Hague Conventions when it comes to defining and punishing war crimes. Nuremberg was a critical turning point, fully affirming the idea that individuals—including leaders—could be held criminally responsible for atrocities and breaches of international law. At the same time, our understanding of international law greatly expanded as a result of Nuremberg to include important new categories of crimes: crimes against humanity, genocide, and crimes against peace. It is now generally agreed that waging a predatory war of conquest against another state is a punishable criminal act. Nuremberg, and the new international conventions it inspired, brought hope for enduring peace and the vision of a permanent international criminal court, even as the Cold War created new fault lines and tensions.

That international court, the ICC, finally became a reality after the end of the Cold War. And yet we still find ourselves living in the shadow of the postwar moment. We have numerous international institutions that have been established to protect individual and collective human rights and to punish those who violate them. But concerns about yielding sovereignty to these institutions have remained a huge issue for a number of powerful states. The United States, China, Russia, and India are among the 70 or so United Nations member states that have opted not to join the ICC, limiting its power and reach. The United Nations has been similarly constrained. Russia took the defunct Soviet Union's place on the Security Council and has been using its veto to prevent that institution from effectively functioning. Could international outrage over the war in Ukraine and the United Nations' limited ability to act ultimately lead to a rethinking of the purpose and utility of the Security Council? Might this outrage at Russia be powerful enough to lead the United States to consider joining the ICC? What role should the United States play in supporting international human rights and bringing war criminals to justice—in Ukraine and more generally?

Russian soldiers and leaders can be held individually criminally respon-

Ukraine's former Prosecutor General Iryna Venediktova (C) and ICC prosecutor Karim Khan (R) visit a mass grave on the grounds of the Church of St. Andrew and Pyervozvannoho All Saints in Bucha, on the outskirts of Kyiv, on April 13, 2022. (FADEL SENNA/AFP VIA GETTY IMAGES)

sible for war crimes. There are mechanisms in place to prosecute Russian soldiers and officers for violations of the laws and customs of war and for crimes against civilians; such trials can be held by Ukraine and by the ICC. Some lawyers have argued that this is, and should be, enough. The crimes of genocide and aggression will be much harder to prosecute. Genocide is notoriously difficult to prove because of the need to show intent. Aggression poses its own set of challenges because of the conditions set out in the Kampala Amendments and other international-law restrictions on trying heads of state. But these crimes are also arguably the most important to prosecute and to talk about, for reasons that de Baer, Lemkin, Ečer, and Trainin well understood. Holding Russian leaders and officers accountable for aggression and genocide helps get at the purpose behind the war—something that is critical for making sense of things in the present and for posterity, something that is essential for justice. It makes it possible to see the murders, deportations, rapes, disappearances, and other terrible crimes being carried out by Russian forces in Ukraine not "as simple 'violations of the laws and customs of war'" but as instruments of a "general criminal policy" and as an

all-out assault on the Ukrainian people.

In their 1945 memo, War Department lawyers Bernays and Brown told President Roosevelt that international law evolves with "the public conscience." Where are we today with regard to international law? We have well-defined categories of war crimes. We have international organizations and international courts devoted to international humanitarian law and human rights. But international law, like all law, loses meaning without enforcement. For war crimes to be punished, for our international legal system to work, states must be willing to get behind international principles, join international institutions, and pursue enforcement. States, even large and powerful ones, must be willing to cede some degree of sovereignty. In order to prosecute Russian leaders for the crime of aggression some kind of ad hoc tribunal will be necessary. But maybe someday in the future the dream of de Vabres and others will come true and we won't need ad hoc tribunals. For this to happen we would need a permanent international criminal court with a much broader mandate. Is this in America's interest or not? This is something that Russia's war of aggression against Ukraine and Putin's threats to the rest of the world might help us to decide.

discussion questions

1. What is more important, the establishment of an international law code or the preservation of state sovereignty? Explain why.

2. Are rulings by international courts valuable even if they have no enforcement mechanisms of their own? Why or why not?

3. Russia's veto power on the UN security council allows it to avoid any actions against its leaders. Is it time to restructure international organizations such as the United Nations?

4. What is the best course of action to hold Russian soldiers and leaders responsible for war crimes committed in Ukraine?

5. Many argue that the current international courts do not have enough power to deter war crimes from occurring. If an international court with a broader mandate is introduced, what would this mean for the U.S. and would we be likely to support it?

suggested readings

Bosco, David, **Rough Justice: The International Criminal Court in a World of Power Politics**. Oxford University Press, January 16, 2014. 312 pp. Analysis of the give-and-take involved in the creation of the International Criminal Court. Insightful discussion of the crime of aggression and the negotiations that led to the Kampala Amendments.

Crawford, Julia and Thierry Curvellier, **Ukraine Responds to Warfare with Lawfare**. Justiceinfo.net, March 25, 2022. Discussion of Ukraine's strategic use of the international legal system to fight back against Russian aggression. Maps out possible pathways to justice.

Fadel, Leila interview with Leila Sadat, **Why genocide is difficult to prove before an international criminal court**. NPR Morning Edition, April 12, 2022. Interview with international law professor Leila Sadat on the difference between "crimes against humanity" and "genocide" and on the need to prove intent for the prosecution of genocide. Also discusses possible U.S. cooperation with the ICC.

Heller, Kevin Jon, **Options for Prosecuting Russian Aggression Against Ukraine: A Critical Analysis**. Journal of Genocide Research, July 6, 2022. Discussion and assessment of possible mechanisms for prosecuting Putin and other Russian leaders for waging a war of aggression against Ukraine. Evaluates international as well as domestic options and looks at the question of immunity.

Hirsch, Francine, **Soviet Judgment at Nuremberg: A New History of the International Military Tribunal after World War II**. Oxford University Press, July 8, 2020. 560 pp. Retells the story of the Nuremberg Trials, bringing in the positive and negative contributions of the Soviet Union. Reveals the unexpected critical role of Soviet lawyers in the postwar development of international law.

Hull, Isabel, **Anything Can Be Rescinded**. London Review of Books, April 26, 2018. Thoughtful critique of Oona A. Hathaway and Scott J. Shapiro's *The Internationalists* (2018). Argues that the Kellogg-Briand Pact should be seen not as the product of "ideas and thinkers" but as the result of "a long, halting and uneven process by which European states tried to limit war among themselves."

Don't forget to vote!

Download a copy of the ballot questions from the Resources page at www.fpa.org/great_decisions

To access web links to these readings, as well as links to additional, shorter readings and suggested web sites,

GO TO www.fpa.org/great_decisions

and click on the topic under Resources, on the right-hand side of the page.

China and America: back to the future?
by David M. Lampton

Chinese President Xi Jinping speaks at the podium during the meeting between members of the standing committee of the Political Bureau of the 20th CPC Central Committee and Chinese and foreign journalists at The Great Hall of the People on October 23, 2022, in Beijing, China. China's ruling Communist Party revealed the new Politburo Standing Committee after its 20th congress. (LINTAO ZHANG/ GETTY IMAGES)

For the last decade-plus the core issue in U.S.-China relations has been: Could Beijing and Washington make room for one another in Asia and the broader international system as mutual stakeholders? Or instead, would each follow its instincts and seek regional and international system dominance and take actions to weaken and deter one another, thereby running risks of conflict?

Unfortunately, the jury has reached a verdict—the governments of the United States and China now are turning to strategies to deal with each other reminiscent of earlier periods of intense big power competition. The minimal goal of each is to deny dominance to the other; the maximum goal of each is to achieve dominance for itself. How long this period of increasing tension will last is unclear but it is unlikely to be short. It will be expensive—certainly in dollars and quite possibly in lives, unless both sides change course, soon.

As this contest sharpens, the new era into which we are moving has echoes with two past foreign policy periods—the Cold War of the second half of the 20th century and the world of "spheres of influence" in the 19th century and much of the 20th.

DAVID M. LAMPTON *is Professor Emeritus at Johns Hopkins University's School of Advanced International Studies (SAIS), where he headed China Studies and was Hyman Chair until 2018. Now he is Senior Research Fellow at the School's Foreign Policy Institute. He also has been President of the National Committee on U.S.-China Relations in New York and Chairman of the Asia Foundation in San Francisco. Author of numerous books and articles, his most recent volume, with Professors Selina Ho and Cheng-Chwee Kuik, is entitled:* Rivers of Iron: Railroads and Chinese Power in Southeast Asia *(Oakland, CA: University of California Press, 2020).*

3

One pristine example of the spheres of influence world was the Monroe Doctrine of 1823 warning Europeans that Washington would not countenance their intervention in the Western Hemisphere. Another example is the Kennedy administration's absolute rejection of the Soviet Union's attempt to place nuclear weapons in Cuba in the early 1960s. In similar fashion, by defining the South China Sea and Taiwan as "core interests," linking these areas to the national security of the People's Republic of China (PRC), Beijing is saying that its interests take precedence in this region over the claims and interests of distant powers, notably the United States. Beijing's *Global Times* graphically indicated its claims in the wake of House Speaker Nancy Pelosi's (D-CA) August 2022 stop in Taiwan.

Similarly, Russia's invasion of Ukraine, and before that Crimea and Georgia, are yet other expressions of the same sphere of influence impulse. Big powers try to establish buffer zones.

To be sure, the context in which America and China now are operating has some important differences from these earlier eras, three in particular: 1) The degree of global, economic interdependence is greater than ever before, seen in intricate supply chains upon which everyone depends. Today it is harder than ever to inflict damage on one's adversary without harming oneself and friends. 2) The big powers, and many second-tier powers, have weapons of mass destruction or soon could develop them if they were to determine their security required them to do so. Escalation and proliferation are enormous present dangers. And 3), the world faces existential global issues that could extinguish or severely disrupt life as we know it if cooperation is not forthcoming, particularly Sino-American cooperation. One need look no further than climate change and environmental deterioration.

Looming decisions in a new era

All this requires Americans to make decisions, including:

What fraction of national wealth are Americans willing to spend on this new contest? At the height of the Cold War, U.S. defense spending averaged about 10% GDP, generally falling to the 3–5% range thereafter—"the peace dividend." What is the United States willing to spend in a contest with China (and Russia) given its own competing domestic needs? The PRC is economically and intellectually more dynamic than the Soviet Union ever was (or Russia is). Nonetheless, their combined weight is deeply disconcerting.

How does the United States forge sufficient domestic cohesion to be effective abroad? A majority of Americans—Democrats, Independents, and Republicans alike—believe it is important that America remain the only superpower, but they are sharply divided on how to maintain primacy—through what mix of diplomacy, the exercise of military might, and the use of economic levers? There are voices calling for cutbacks in military and other assistance to Ukraine, for instance.

Now, China is a global power with extraordinary reach, influence, and ambition. It's the second largest economy, with world-class cities and public transportation networks. It's home to some of the world's largest tech companies and it seeks to dominate the technologies and industries of the future. It's rapidly modernized its military and intends to become a top tier fighting force with global reach. And it has announced its ambition to create a sphere of influence in the Indo-Pacific and to become the world's leading power. U.S. Secretary of State, Antony J. Blinken, "The Administration's Approach to the People's Republic of China," May 26, 2022.

How can the United States win the support of a critical mass of friends and allies in the international system to offset the dynamism and mass of China? Is ever more foreign aid, direct investment abroad, and military assistance required? If so, what are the implications for the domestic agenda? How far will America's friends and allies go if Washington wants to impose ever more sanctions and export controls on the PRC?

As competition with China becomes more intense, Washington is responding by adopting industrial policy focusing on R&D and investment in priority areas. What role do Americans wish their government to play in their domestic economy?

As the United States competes strenuously on so many fronts, is it realistic to expect meaningful cooperation from the PRC on world health, environmental and climate issues, counter-proliferation, and global economic system management?

! Before you read, download the companion **Glossary** that includes definitions, a guide to acronyms and abbreviations used in the article, and other material. Go to **www.fpa.org/great_decisions** and select a topic in the Resources section. (Top right)

What does "dominance" even mean in a world falling apart?

It is possible that alternative futures will emerge, including a China that greatly adjusts course and gets back on the more accommodative path of Xi Jinping's predecessors. This could happen if China's internal weaknesses became maximal constraints and/or if elite solidarity in Beijing splinters due to the rising opposition of those dissatisfied with the domestic and international costs of President Xi Jinping's current course. However, this is not the future for which the United States or like-minded countries can plan. The United States and China have set out on dangerous intersecting courses and it is hard to foresee a probable scenario that has them changing their headings any time soon. That China is a problem is one of the few things Americans agree about. Among many Chinese the feeling is mutual.

Xi Jinping has just been anointed the maximal leader for what could prove to be life at the October 2022, 20th Party Congress of the Chinese Communist Party and managed to stack the Standing Committee of the Politburo with close allies. Secretary of State Antony Blinken's May 26, 2022, speech on China policy quoted above was a clear indication of the direction in which American policy is moving. The rising tensions are most evident in the Taiwan Strait, but by no means limited to that strategic strip of water.

How have both nations incrementally created an early-stage cold war world in which sphere of influence thinking plays a significant role? Beijing is doing so to expand its power, assure natural, trade, and financial resource flows to itself, and to push its defense perimeter further from its shores. America is trying to constrain the PRC by sanctions, export controls, and diplomacy, secure its own economic future, and maintain global leadership, all the while trying to maintain its expansive defense perimeter and keep friends and allies under its security umbrella.

If this is the future into which we are moving, how did we get to this point?

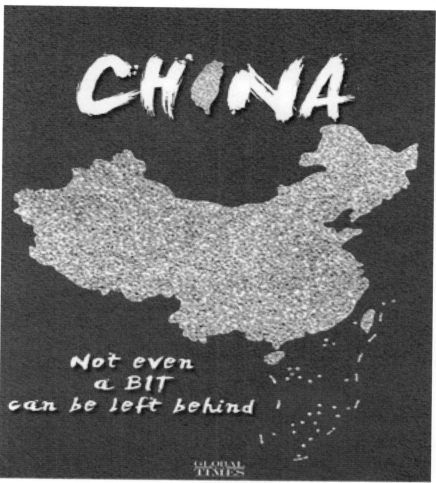

GLOBAL TIMES

How did we get here?

Fifty-one years ago Richard Nixon met Mao Zedong in Beijing's imperial residential compound, thereby initiating the "week that changed the world."

From the 1970s until about 2010, the U.S.-China relationship went through two phases. In about 2010 the two countries began to enter the third phase in which they now are ensnared. The first two phases occurred under the broad banner of "engagement" and the third, today's crystallizing policy frame, is "competition." In moving from engagement to competition, we have simultaneously moved from a world of mutual reassurance to one of increasingly dangerous mutual deterrence. Deterrence is based on threat.

The first phase was initiated by President Nixon and Henry Kissinger and pursued with variations by four administrations thereafter (Ford, Carter, Reagan, and George H. W. Bush)—joining with China to offset what was seen as surging Soviet power. This led Wash-

In this Feb. 21, 1972, photo, Chinese communist party leader Mao Zedong, left, and U.S. President Richard Nixon shake hands as they meet in Beijing. Nixon's visit marked the first time an American president visited China. (AP IMAGES)

A Chinese man stands alone to block a line of tanks heading east on Beijing's Changan Blvd. in Tiananmen Square on June 5, 1989. (AP IMAGES)

ington to see an interest in helping Beijing create greater comprehensive national power to be a more muscular adversary to Moscow and to help achieve other objectives such as arms control agreements with Moscow, and to extricate Washington from Vietnam. In this endeavor, the U.S. citizenry was supportive. Over time this strategic phase involved transferring selected weapons to the PRC, trading some intelligence, cooperating to defeat Soviet troops in Afghanistan, and looking favorably on working with the PRC to increase its human and technological capacities. In the Carter administration, the economic opportunities provided by a reforming China became a growing, positive consideration for Americans.

Then, in the 1989–91 period, a new, more-difficult-to-manage phase of engagement began. With the 1989 violence in Tiananmen Square, human rights was powerfully injected into bilateral relations. Then, in 1991, the Warsaw Pact and the Soviet Union imploded, removing the common threat that had proven a strong adhesive in U.S.-China relations previously. And shortly thereafter, the 1995–96 missile crisis in the Taiwan Strait, and Beijing's retreat in the face of the U.S. response, convinced President Jiang Zemin and the Chinese military to accelerate defense modernization markedly.

Since 1989 there has been continual contention on trade and human rights issues and growing concern that as Chinese power grew Beijing would become less observant of the post-World War II order. Every U.S. administration, from Clinton through Obama, sought to gradually shape the international environment and otherwise induce Beijing to become what U.S. Trade Representative Robert Zoellick in 2005 called a "responsible stakeholder" in the post-World War II order and more observant of legal principles and norms.

Following China's 2001 entry into the World Trade Organization, the PRC's comprehensive national power mounted rapidly and its confidence grew as America struggled with economic calamity (2008–9) and was bogged down in conflicts in the Middle East and Central Asia. By 2010, China had become noticeably more assertive in the South and East China Seas and Secretary of State Hillary Clinton upbraided Beijing for its activities in those waters at the Regional Forum meeting of the Association of South East Asian Nations (ASEAN) in Hanoi in July of that year, in turn eliciting a sharp verbal response from the PRC. In late 2011, the Obama administration initiated its "pivot to Asia," signaling a more muscular turn in U.S. policy in the region.

With a new leader in China in 2012–13, Xi Jinping, and Donald Trump moving into the White House in January 2017, each country had in place a leader willing to change the frame of relations from "engagement" to "competition." Xi was not only more assertive and ambitious than his three predecessors, he also was more worried about the Chinese Communist Party (CCP) losing internal control. His growing fear of instability at home, married with new tools of surveillance, created the specter of the "surveillance state."

When Joseph Biden entered the White House in January 2021, he changed much about Donald Trump's domestic and foreign policies, but he maintained, indeed strengthened, some of the main contours of Trump's China

U. S. Military Expenditure in 2012–2022

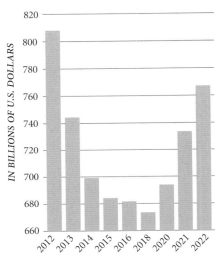

SOURCE: tradingeconomics.com, SIPRI

China Military Expenditure in 2012–2022

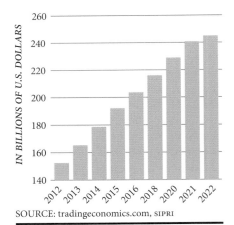

SOURCE: tradingeconomics.com, SIPRI

Lucidity Information Design, LLC

policies, from tariffs, to investment and export controls, to reduced dialogue. With respect to Chinese students coming to the United States, the number has fallen by more than half since prior to the pandemic, for a variety of reasons, not least Covid, anti-Asian sentiment creating an unwelcoming environment, tightening of U.S. visa issuance policy, improved quality of Chinese institutions so not so many Chinese students feel the need to go abroad, and other factors.

In one important respect, however, Biden strengthened America where Trump had undermined it—alliance and partnership relations. President Biden has built a security relationship known as AUKUS (Australia, the UK, and the U.S.) and strengthened security coordination within the Quad (India, Japan, Australia, and the U.S.). In the case of AUKUS, the United States and Britain are cooperating to deliver a fleet of nuclear-powered (not nuclear-armed) submarines to Australia.

In another respect, Biden's China policy also was a departure from Trump's—he emphasized that the contest between China and the United States was importantly about autocracy versus democracy.

This, therefore, is the era in which we now are embroiled. The mechanisms of dialogue and exchange that in the engagement era were used to try to smooth-out rough patches have either become moribund due to Covid, or terminated by one side or the other in retaliation for various actions. A major PRC countermeasure in this respect was the August 5, 2022, cancellation or suspension of eight consultative and cooperative activities taken in retaliation for Speaker Nancy Pelosi's trip to Taiwan.

In today's era defined by competition, leaders and publics in China and the United States have now adopted a deterrence posture against one another. Mutual threat is the core of mutual deterrence, and an arms race is underway between the two countries, involving conventional weapons, weapons of mass destruction, space, and cyber. A steep upward climb in military expenditures in both countries is well underway. Whereas in the past China seemed content to have a hundred or so nuclear warheads to feel secure in its deterrence, today Beijing could be headed toward a thousand by 2030.

In short, we have, step-by-step moved into a world in which both Beijing and Washington are using a Cold War tool box. The August 2022 military show of force in the Taiwan Strait has brought the relationship to a new and more dangerous stage.

The Cold War frame

Starting with the Obama administration (2009–17), then moving to the Trump and Biden administrations, gradually Washington has adopted serial measures to try to get its own house in order, increase economic capacity, achieve greater self-reliance in key technologies, rebuild and expand alliance and friendship relationships, seek to reallocate military assets in the direction of Asia, adopt a greater degree of industrial policy, and begun to use economic inducements and foreign aid (including infrastructure) to compete with the PRC's global Belt and Road Initiative (BRI). Emblematic of this entire process was the bipartisan, overwhelming, passage of competitiveness legislation in Congress (The Chips and Science Act), signed into law by President Biden on August 9, 2022. When it passed the Senate, the *New York Times* headline of July 28, 2022, was concise: "In Bid to Counter China, Senate Passes a Sweeping Industrial Bill."

Predictably, these U.S. moves trigger Beijing's propensity to see neo-containment. In turn, the PRC strengthens its efforts to consolidate security all along its enormous periphery, including becoming more assertive in Xinjiang, Hong Kong, the Taiwan Strait, and the South and East China Seas, pushing its defense perimeter as far offshore as possible, and building an economic network placing Beijing at its center in order to secure its economic lifelines and external markets. The PRC accelerates its development of cyber and space capabilities as well as its basic and applied research in new technologies. A central feature of Chinese General Secretary Xi Jinping's report to the 20th Party Congress on October 16, 2022, was the emphasis on investing in R&D, cultivating science and technology talent, and emphasizing industrial policy.

For Washington, all of this constitutes what Secretary Blinken said was Beijing's "ambition to create a sphere of influence" and to "become the world's leading power." It triggers in America the reasonable conviction that the post-World War II institutional order is being challenged by the PRC.

For their part, PRC leaders observe the past and current behavior of other powers, and indeed China's own historical dynasties, and conclude that China is no less entitled to the greater sway in its region than other great powers have claimed in their backyards.

■ **The Biden Administration Gradually Codifies Its Strategy Toward China, 2021–22.**

The Biden administration had been in office two months when in March 2021 it issued *Interim National Security Strategic Guidance*. Donald Trump had been such a large departure from past U.S. practices and current needs that the new American president felt compelled to course correct quickly even before his National Security Council had a chance for the standard, comprehensive review characteristic of presidential transitions. About a year and a half later, in October 2022, the Biden-Harris administration finally issued its long-awaited *National Security Strategy,* the central points of which hewed closely to what it had said previously in its *Interim Guidance.* Even Russia's invasion of Ukraine in February 2022 did not displace Beijing as the primary long-term strategic challenge facing the United States in the White House view.

The main features of the *Interim Guidance* were: 1) We will not engage in "forever wars" and "we will right-size our military presence" in the Middle East. 2) We will deter adversaries, notably China, Russia, and Iran. 3) "Our presence will be most robust in the Indo-Pacific and Europe." 4) Washington will be more mindful of allies and the need to win their cooperation and financial support for dealing with China, as well as other issues. 5) America's external capacities depend on a revitalized American economy and democracy, starting with renewal of infrastructure, particularly clean energy, based on augmented R&D. 6) "We must join with likeminded allies and partners to revitalize democracy the world over." 7) The U.S. will "defend trusted critical supply chains and technology infrastructure." Toward the end of the document, in **bold type,** the following was the overall summary: **"This agenda will strengthen our enduring advantages, and allow us to prevail in strategic competition with China or any other nation."**

So, from the very opening days of the Biden administration its strategic guidance made clear that China was at the top of Washington's worry list. Trump-imposed trade tariffs continued and a "Summit of Democracies" was soon held in Washington. The *Interim Strategic Guidance* could not have been clearer: "China, in particular, has rapidly become more assertive. It is the only competitor potentially capable of combining its economic, diplomatic, military, and technological power to mount a sustained challenge to a stable and open international system."

The final strategically central aspect of the *Interim Guidance* showed how far both sides had come from the underlying strategic logic of the

Nixon-Mao move against Moscow in the early 1970s. Now Russia and the PRC were seen as collaborating against America: "Both Beijing and Moscow have invested heavily in efforts meant to check U.S. strengths and prevent us from defending our interests and our allies around the world."

Fast forward to almost a year after the *Interim Guidance* was issued, Russia was poised to attack, and then invade, Ukraine in February, 2022. Thereafter, the United States urged China to separate itself from Moscow, and not materially support the Russian aggression. But, by then, Beijing was operating in an environment in which Washington and Beijing were each other's biggest adversaries, making Moscow a more attractive partner of convenience for the PRC. Beijing also has sought to position itself as "an honest broker" fostering an end to hostilities while continuing to trade with Moscow in selected areas and to assert that "NATO enlargement" and a growing NATO presence all around Russia's western periphery was a principal precipitating cause of the Ukraine conflict. As one Chinese official affiliated with China's military put it to this author on February 17, 2022, "War in Europe would divert the U.S. [from China]." As of this writing, Washington says it has no evidence that Beijing is trading in military goods with Moscow as it pertains to the war in Ukraine.

■ The Joint Statement of Russia and China.

On February 4, 2022, with President Putin in Beijing for the opening of the Winter Olympic Games which relatively few other world leaders attended, Xi Jinping and the Russian leader took the opportunity to issue a "Joint Statement." Though not having the status of a treaty, coming less than three weeks before Moscow's invasion of Ukraine, this document carried with it faint echoes of the February 1950 Sino-Soviet Treaty of Friendship and Alliance that solidified the Truman administration's hardline posture toward China in the early stages of the Cold

War. That treaty preceded North Korea's invasion of South Korea.

The February 4, 2022, "Joint Statement" deeply affected Biden administration thinking. Several aspects of the Joint Statement caught American eyes. First was the assertion that there is an ongoing "transformation of the global governance architecture and world order" — read, the post-World War II U.S.-led world order is crumbling. Moscow and Beijing now vowed to "protect the United Nations-driven international architecture…seek[ing] genuine multipolarity with the United Nations and its Security Council playing a central coordinating role." The UN Security Council is a forum in which Moscow and Beijing each have a veto.

Second and notably, China and Russia articulated their mutual support for each other's sovereignty claims: "The Russian side reaffirms its support for the One-China principle, confirms that Taiwan is an inalienable part of China, and opposes any forms of independence of Taiwan. Russia and China stand against attempts by external forces to undermine security and stability **in their common and adjacent regions**…and will increase cooperation in aforementioned areas." [Emphasis added]

Third, the two sides equated western support for Ukrainian unity with fascism: "The sides will strongly condemn actions aimed at denying the responsibility for atrocities of Nazi aggressors, militarist invaders, and their accomplices, besmirch and tarnish the honor of the victorious countries."

Fourth, stating that their new relationship is "superior to political and military alliances of the Cold War era," they go on to say, "there are no 'forbidden' areas of cooperation…."

While it would be important to understand exactly how much Xi Jinping understood about Putin's invasion plans prior to late-February, beyond desiring that no Russian military operations disrupt Beijing's Winter Olympic Games, the sequence of developments has made clear that the sovereignty of nations no-longer occupies the same space in Chinese for-

Russian President Vladimir Putin speaks to China's President Xi Jinping during the Shanghai Cooperation Organisation (SCO) leaders' summit in Samarkand on September 16, 2022. (SERGEI BOBYLYOV/AFP VIA GETTY IMAGES)

eign policy that it used to going back to the mid-1950s. If sovereignty does not constitute the unshakeable foreign policy principle to which Beijing used to be committed, on what principle could cooperation with Beijing be based? How could Beijing expect its sovereignty claims with regard to Taiwan to be respected if it does not speak out for Ukrainian sovereignty?

■ **The Biden Administration's Increasingly Defined Approach to China, May 26, 2022.**

On May 26, 2022, three months after the Sino-Russian Joint Statement, U.S. Secretary of State Antony Blinken delivered a speech that reflected the main contours of the Biden administration's long-in-coming review of China policy and the initial impacts of the Sino-Russian "Joint Statement" and the invasion of Ukraine.

Comparing Blinken's speech with the "Conclusions and Recommendations" section of NSC 68 ("United States Objectives and Programs for National Security," April 1950) is illuminating. NSC 68 was an initial Cold War strategic document shaping the U.S. response to the Soviet Union and China for the following two-plus decades. There are numerous and im-

portant similarities between NSC 68's analysis and recommendations of the early 1950s and the key points of Secretary Blinken's speech more than 70 years later.

Though the U.S. Secretary of State emphasized that Washington was putting "diplomacy back at the center of American foreign policy," one can fear that what initially is being sold as a diplomatic strategy will morph into

U.S. Secretary of State Antony Blinken speaks on China at George Washington University May 26, 2022, in Washington, DC. Blinken delivered a speech on the Biden administration's policy toward China during the event hosted by the Asia Society Policy Institute. (ALEX WONG/GETTY IMAGES)

a militarily top-heavy approach (as George Kennan believed happened to his concept of containment in the 1950s and 1960s).

In 1950, NSC 68 said: "The gravest threat to the security of the United States within the foreseeable future stems from the hostile designs and formidable power of the USSR, and from the nature of the Soviet system." Blinken said: "China is the only country with both the intent to reshape the international order and, increasingly, the economic, diplomatic, military, and technological power to do it." He went on to proclaim, "We will remain focused on the most serious long-term challenge to the international order—and that's posed by the People's Republic of China." Near the conclusion of his remarks Secretary Blinken laid out the implications: "President Biden has instructed the Department of Defense to hold China as its pacing challenge, to ensure that our military stays ahead."

In terms of strategic objectives, NSC 68 said that: "Soviet domination of the potential power of Eurasia, whether achieved by armed aggression or by political and subversive means, would be strategically and politically unacceptable to the United States." Blinken said: "It's [China] rapidly modernized its military and intends to become a top-tier fighting force with global reach. And it has announced its ambition to create a sphere of influence in the Indo-Pacific and to become the world's leading power....Under President Xi Jinping, the ruling Chinese Communist Party has become more repressive at home and more aggressive abroad." NSC 68 said that the purposes of U.S. policy were: "To create situations which will compel the Soviet Government to recognize the practical undesirability of acting on the basis of its present concepts and the necessity of behaving in accordance with precepts of international conduct, as set forth in the purposes and principles of the UN Charter." Blinken said: "But we cannot rely on Beijing to change its trajectory.

So we will shape the strategic environment around Beijing to advance our vision for an open, inclusive international system." NSC 68 said: "Strengthen the orientation toward the United States of the non-Soviet nations; and help such of those nations as are able and willing to make an important contribution to U.S. security, to increase their economic and political stability and their military capability." Blinken said: "The second piece of our strategy is aligning with our allies and partners to advance a shared vision for the future. From day one, the Biden administration has worked to re-energize America's unmatched network of alliances and partnerships and to re-engage in international institutions."

It needs to be said clearly that if the

American public had access to Beijing's equivalent policy documents, directives, and decisions, U.S. citizens almost certainly would be justifiably alarmed. The point here, however, is that Beijing sees Washington's policy as "containment" and the U.S. Government views the PRC as trying to surpass American dominance, promote an authoritarian approach to development and governance, and to change the character of post-World War II economic and security systems not only regionally, but also globally. The goal each ascribes to the other is unacceptable. Each side is developing its military, economic, and diplomatic toolboxes of coercive means to deal with each other. Deterrence is the name of the game, not reassurance.

The rising salience, and danger, of the Taiwan issue

Speaker of the U.S. House of Representatives Nancy Pelosi (D-CA), center left, speaks to Taiwan's President Tsai Ing-wen, center right, after arriving at the president's office on August 3, 2022, in Taipei, Taiwan. Pelosi arrived in Taiwan as part of a tour of Asia aimed at reassuring allies in the region, as China made it clear that her visit to Taiwan would be seen in a negative light. (CHIEN CHIH-HUNG/OFFICE OF THE PRESIDENT VIA GETTY IMAGES)

A further parallel with the first Cold War is that as Washington and Beijing diverge strategically, each attaches increasing weight to Taiwan, the single most volatile flash point in the U.S.-China relationship since 1950. On May 23, 2022, President

Biden articulated his personal commitment (there is no legal requirement under the 1979 Taiwan Relations Act, or TRA, to defend Taiwan militarily if it is attacked). Beijing reacted by joining with Russia to send a joint flight of six bombers near Japan and South

Korea, and southward into South China Sea airspace immediately after Biden's remarks. The U.S. president was still in Asia.

Then the day after Army Day 2022 on the Chinese Mainland, House Speaker Nancy Pelosi, in the face of oblique pressure from the Biden administration not to visit the island at that time, landed in Taipei. Beijing immediately responded by announcing military, live-fire exercises, creating a ring around the entire island consisting of six exercise areas. The PRC military display immediately was followed by a *White Paper* threatening prosecution of Taiwan leaders, reeducation of its people, and equating Taiwan's reunification with the national security of the PRC. As the *White Paper* put it,

"National reunification is the only way to avoid the risk of Taiwan being invaded and occupied again by foreign countries, to foil the attempts of external forces to contain China, and to safeguard the sovereignty, security, and development interests of our country."

Washington had already moved naval assets, including the carrier USS Ronald Reagan, into the region to the east of Taiwan. Immediately after Beijing said its exercises were over for now, it issued the *White Paper*.

This sequence of developments more than faintly echoes the trends that produced a Korean War, two Taiwan Straits crises in the 1950s, and two decades of Cold War with China. The point is not that the two eras are identical, but rather that they are similar and perilous. Among the dangers is the fact that the norms and practices that the United States and China observed concerning Taiwan over eight successive administrations from Nixon through Obama have steadily eroded. And while China was not a nuclear power until late-1964, today it bristles with a growing number of nuclear and conventional warheads and delivery means. To date, the United States has never launched a direct attack on a nuclear weapons power.

The year 2022 was the 50th anniversary of the Nixon trip to China. The strategic core of the Nixon-Mao rapprochement of the early 1970s and thereafter was using the combined strategic weight of China and the United States to offset the USSR. Today, Beijing and Moscow are cooperating ever more closely to America's detriment. The question is, what will the generations coming to policy dominance in Washington and Beijing do now? Coming out of the 20th Party Congress of

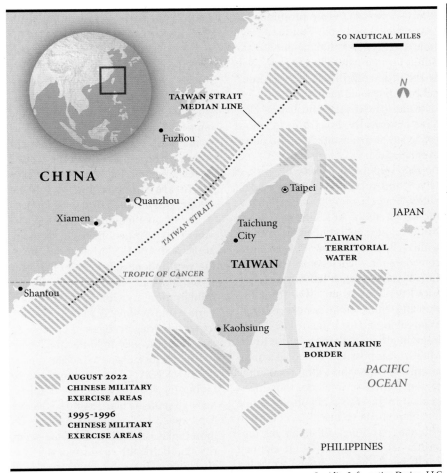

Lucidity Information Design, LLC

October 2022, the old, familiar faces in the making of Chinese foreign and economic policy are largely gone. The most familiar faces on the Standing Committee of the Politburo are Xi Jinping himself, and an ideologue named Wang Huning. Nationalism in both countries is on the rise.

Spheres of influence thinking and action

The definition of "sphere of influence" is: "A field or area in which an individual or organization [or state] has power to affect events and developments." In international relations discourse this term is associated with the practice of the principal big powers in the 19th and 20th centuries trying to cordon off reliable markets for exports, dependable sources of resources, and to be assured that strategically consequential real estate was not in the hands of unfriendly powers. Taken in this general sense, irrespective of whether or not it is explicitly acknowledged by great powers today, sphere of influence thinking is evident as China and the United States view each other's actions and as each sets its own strategic course.

In his May 26, 2022, remarks cited at the outset of this article, the U.S. Secretary of State attributed to China the "ambition to create a sphere of influence in the Indo-Pacific and to become the world's leading power." The United States was not prepared to accept a Japanese attempt to create such a sphere in the late-1930s and early 1940s, and has declared that the ambitions it sees China pursuing are unacceptable today. Whatever we want to call the current situation, China is trying to extend its regional sway, engaging in efforts to reduce American prominence in the area. The United States reacts in ways we have seen before—building security relationships, augmenting military might, and reducing reliance on strategic commodities and industries under Chinese control.

Great powers like to have buffer zones, reliable areas in which they feel relatively secure in placing economic assets and building their most reliable security relationships. Sometimes this kind of thinking is less prominent, as it was at the height of globalization. But, at other times, when security concerns become severe among the powers, sphere of influence thinking and behavior become more prominent. A prime recent example was the PRC's June, 2022, declaration that the Taiwan Strait, an international waterway, was under PRC control, contrary to international law and practice.

America, Russia, and China each have historically thought in sphere of influence terms, as noted at the outset of this article.

This impulse is clearly at work in U.S.-China relations today, as evident with China claiming historic rights to the South and East China seas to, in part, exclude naval challenges from the United States and Japan. It is a central consideration when it comes to Taiwan. China wants to push the American security presence as far away from Taiwan and China's long eastern seaboard as possible, and the United States wants to maintain its toehold as close to the Mainland as possible, and to, at a minimum, keep open this vibrant economic region. Sphere of influence thinking is evident in the PRC's impulse to define its comprehensive maritime control to 200 nautical miles off its shores (coterminous with the UNCLOS-defined Exclusive Economic Zones) while the United States tries to limit territorial waters to 12 nautical miles.

In pursuit of consolidating its sphere of influence impulses and claims, explicit or otherwise, each power seeks to bring in reliable allies to bolster its claims and help it fight if it must. So, the United States enlists Japan, South Korea, Australia, and others in its Indo-Pacific strategy, and China enlists Russia and strives to keep as many small countries unaligned as possible. In Europe, as Putin seeks to extend his buffer zone to Ukraine, he simultaneously seeks support from China, and uses Belarus and others to help extend his sphere.

An early, unmistakable indication that China under Xi Jinping was thinking in this way came on May 21, 2014, when China's then new leader gave a speech at a conference on security cooperation, saying: "In the final analysis, let the people of Asia run the affairs of Asia, solve the problems of Asia and uphold the security of Asia." Most re-

cently a muscular version of this sentiment was articulated by the PRC's Foreign Minister, Wang Yi, when he spoke to the ASEAN Secretariat in Jakarta, on July 11, 2022, saying: "We should insulate this region from geopolitical calculations and the trap of the law of the jungle, from being used as chess pieces in major-power rivalry, and from coercion by hegemony [read the United States] and bullying. **Our future, and the future of our region, should be in our own hands."** [Emphasis added]

Less than a month later U.S. Secretary of State Antony Blinken, speaking at the ASEAN-U.S. Ministerial Meeting with Indonesian Foreign Minister Retno Marsudi, laid out the Biden administration's vision of a "Strategic Partnership" with ASEAN, one that fits under the broader regional concept of the "free and open Indo-Pacific."

"As we look ahead to the November [2022] ASEAN-U.S. summit, we're laying the foundations for a comprehensive strategic partnership so that we can expand our cooperation into even more areas, including maritime security, public health, cybersecurity. We also hope to increase cooperation with ASEAN throughout the broader region. For example, with the Quad [Japan, India, Australia, and the United States] and within the Indo-Pacific Economic Framework [inaudible] for your ideas to advance that kind of cooperation and collaboration."

In short, the United States and China each are defining geographic regions as key to their economic and security futures and seeking, within those regions, to augment technological and economic integration with themselves and to diminish the economic and technological dependence on the competing power.

Predictably, some countries try to avoid tight alignment with either, seeking to play the United States and China off against one another to their own benefit. Southeast Asia is one region where the competition is intense, with the Chinese Foreign Minister and the U.S. Secretary of State each expending considerable time and effort traveling in this region. Islands in the South

Pacific have become one area of Sino-American competition.

In thinking about this competition in East and Southeast Asia, Beijing believes it has three very strong cards to play:

Economic: Since 2020, China and ASEAN have been each other's largest trade partner. The China-sponsored Regional Cooperative Economic Partnership (RCEP) involving 16 Asian economies came into force in January 2022 (for ten of those countries) and the PRC's imports and exports are growing rapidly—the United States is not part of this grouping.

Geographic proximity: Geography confers advantages on China in terms of achieving a high degree of economic integration, high levels of trade and investment, and large human flows. China is taking advantage of this proximity by expanding rail connectivity, cross-border power grid hookups, and port development. In December 2021, Beijing completed the high-speed rail line from China to the Thai-Laos border at Nongkhai, with the PRC's *Global Times* reporting:

"[The] China-Laos Railway is also a convenient logistics channel between China and ASEAN, and a number of provinces and cities in China have started cross border freight trains on [the] railway. In the first quarter [2022], the import and export by railroad transport between China and ASEAN increased significantly by 3.5 times...."

Military and maritime power: Because almost all of the economically significant countries of South and Southeast Asia are maritime nations, naval and merchant marine fleets are key national assets. While just counting ships is an imperfect measure of power, it is indicative of trends. By ship count, China is the largest navy in the world and in terms of maritime fleets it is enormous, particularly if you count the Hong Kong Special Administrative Region and PRC merchant fleets together as one. Predictably, China is building ports and acquiring access rights (in some cases military) extending from its own coast all the way to the Persian Gulf. Its shipbuilding industry is now the world's largest as measured by deadweight tons completed per year. Two of the top four shipbuilding companies in the world are PRC.

Top 10 Largest Navies in the World (by total number of warships and submarines—2020)
China - 777
Russia - 603
North Korea - 492
United States - 490
Colombia - 453
Iran - 398
Egypt - 316
Thailand - 292
India - 285
Indonesia - 282

Because Southeast Asia is a massive, rapidly growing market, embraces geographically strategic real estate, and has enormous human resources, both China and the United States are competing in this region. Nonetheless, America is playing catch-up.

One indication of the importance of the region is the fact that in the days preceding Russia's invasion of Ukraine, Secretary Blinken was making the rounds in the Asia-Pacific. At a February 7, 2022, press briefing, the State Department spokesperson was asked why the secretary was making this trip when war was imminent in the heart of Europe:

Question: "Considering that we are in that window now and there's talk of a potentially imminent invasion [by Russia into Ukraine], was there ever a discussion about postponing the Australia trip? Is now the right time to be crossing the world, going to Fiji, when this invasion could happen at any time?"

Part of the State Department's response was that the PRC was rapidly expanding its foothold in Pacific Islands that had been aligned with Washington since the Second World War and that Vladimir Putin and Xi Jinping had met three days earlier in Beijing.

In short, strategically, the United States finds itself stretched, facing one Pacific-oriented great power dissatisfied with the post-World War II order,

President Joe Biden arrives to deliver remarks at a new Intel semiconductor manufacturing facility site in New Albany, Ohio, Sept. 9, 2022. The plant is part of Biden's efforts toward rebuilding American manufacturing through the CHIPS and Science Act. (PETE MAROVICH/ THE NEW YORK TIMES/REDUX PICTURES)

China, and a Europe-facing power, Russia, dissatisfied with the post-Cold War order in Europe and Central Asia. As the State Department spokesperson put it: "What we have seen over the course not of days, not of weeks, but of years…is an increasing closeness between Russia and China."

The growing American response

Washington's response has thus far had three central components, the first of which is the most fundamental and would be a foundation upon which any sound strategy must be built—increase American comprehensive national power and get America's own governance house in order. To this end, one sees bi-partisan adoption of legislation to increase U.S. R&D funding, gigantic efforts to renew America's aging infrastructure, massive investment in critical technologies (notably silicon chips), new investments in clean energy technologies (batteries and solar panels, for example), in part to compete with China, in part to boost American manufacturing, reduce reliance on the Middle East, and in part to meet greenhouse gas emission reduction targets.

A second component of the American response in the Biden era is to enlist friends and allies and broaden comprehensive cooperation. U.S. policy now refers to the "Indo-Pacific" rather than the Asia-Pacific. America is putting new effort into the Pacific Islands and seeking to improve relations with India, as well as reduce tensions between Japan and South Korea. Even the U.S.-Philippine Security Pact, weakened since 1992, is being revivified.

And third, militarily, the United States is animating new, and strengthening pre-existing, military undertakings, as noted earlier. The U.S. also is considering several arrangements for basing missile defense assets in the region, something Beijing has long adamantly opposed and a subject that already has caused considerable friction between Beijing and Seoul.

These moves already are deeply embedded in the American system and policy, and China's current policies and actions are equally deeply anchored. While there are forces in each society that would like to see a different direction, their numbers do not seem large, and the actions each side takes toward the other undermine more moderate elements in each society.

discussion questions

1. Given trends toward a Cold War frame for U.S.-China relations and sphere of influence thinking, is it likely we will be able to secure the cooperation that Washington wants, and the world needs, on global and transnational issues? Beijing's recent unwillingness to address the North Korea problem is one example.

2. Historically, the United States has resisted the Eurasian landmass being dominated by a single, much less hostile, power, or coalition of unfriendly powers. The United States now finds itself in the position of facing a China and Russia working ever more intimately together. What policies are required to address this adverse circumstance? Is it possible to improve relations with China, to win cooperation in the struggle against Russia in Europe?

3. With increasing Sino-American friction, Taiwan is becoming a progressively more volatile issue. Beijing sees Washington weakening its commitment to the "One China Policy" and moving toward a "One China, One Taiwan Policy," which for about seventy years the PRC has said it will not accept. President Biden says he is personally committed to intervening militarily in the Taiwan Strait if the island is attacked. What dilemmas and policy issues do these circumstances create? What posture would Washington adopt if China seizes smaller, offshore islands currently occupied by Taipei?

4. To what degree does U.S. policy place sufficient emphasis on multilateral economic relationships to effectively compete with Beijing? Was it a mistake by the Trump Administration to pull out of efforts to build the Trans-Pacific Partnership (TPP) in 2017?

5. In the event that China continues to strengthen bonds with Russia and U.S. relations with China continue to sour, what steps should the U.S. take to balance power in a region characterized by Sino-Russian cooperation? Aside from U.S. allies such as Japan and South Korea, which nations should the U.S. look to improve relations with to strengthen its presence in the region?

suggested readings

Blinken, Antony J, **The Administration's Approach to the People's Republic of China**. U.S. Department of State, May 26, 2022. A comprehensive look at how the Biden Administration plans to engage China.

The Executive Secretary, **A Report to the National Security Council**. U.S. Objectives and Programs for National Security, April 14, 1950. On U.S. national security policy at the beginning of the cold war. Includes an assessment of the conflict between the United States and the Soviet Union, as well as U.S. and Soviet nuclear weapons capabilities.

Lampton, David M, Selina Ho, and Cheng-Chwee Kuik, **Rivers of Iron: Railroads and Chinese Power in Southeast Asia**. Oakland, CA: University of California Press, October 13, 2020. 336 pp. What China's railway initiative can teach us about global dominance.

Rudd, Kevin, **The Avoidable War: The Dangers of a Catastrophic Conflict Between the U.S. and Xi Jinping's China**. New York: Public Affairs, March 22, 2022. 432 pp. A war between China and the United States would be catastrophic, deadly, and destructive. Unfortunately, it is no longer unthinkable.

Silver, Laura, Christine Huang, and Laura Clancy, **Negative Views of China Tied to Critical Views of Its Policies on Human Rights**. Pew Research Center, June 29, 2022. Large majorities in most of the 19 countries surveyed have negative views of China, but relatively few say bilateral relations are bad.

Thurston, Anne F. ed, **Engaging China: Fifty Years of Sino-American Relations**. New York: Columbia University Press, 2021. 472 pp. Multidisciplinary and comprehensive, *Engaging China* is a vital reconsideration for a time when the stakes of U.S. policy toward China have never been higher.

To access web links to these readings, as well as links to additional, shorter readings and suggested web sites,

GO TO **www.fpa.org/great_decisions**

and click on the topic under Resources, on the right-hand side of the page.

Economic warfare and U.S. policy
by Jonathan Chanis

People line up at Moscow's Rostokino IKEA on March 3, 2022, after the Swedish company announced plans to close its Russian stores.
(VLAD KARKOV/GETTY IMAGES)

After the second Russian invasion of Ukraine in February 2022 and the imposition of U.S. and allied sanctions, Russians lined up to purchase western consumer goods and remove dollars and rubles from their bank accounts. Although the panic did not last long, the imposition of harsh sanctions prompted the Kremlin to accuse the United States of waging economic war. Over the years, this accusation has been made against the United States by many states including Venezuela, Cuba, and Iran. Even China now wonders if it will be the next U.S. target.

Economic warfare is a persistent feature of international politics and many states, including the United States, utilize it. China regularly employs sanctions against countries deemed hostile, including Australia, Japan, Lithuania, Mongolia, Norway, South Korea, and especially now Taiwan. After House of Representative Speaker Nancy Pelosi's August 2022 Taiwan visit, China limited trade with Taiwan and even temporarily blockaded Taiwan's ports and airspace. More significantly, many view China's foreign economic policy as disguised economic warfare. China steals foreign industrial secrets, extorts proprietary technologies from foreign multinationals, discriminates against non-Chinese companies in their domestic market, and ensnares less-developed nations with subsidized loans and aid packages in order to compel favorable political and military agreements.

JONATHAN CHANIS *has worked in investment management, emerging markets finance, and commodities trading for over 25 years. Currently he manages New Tide Asset Management, a company focused on global and resource trading. He previously worked at Citigroup and Caxton Associates where he traded energy and emerging market equities, and commodities and currencies. He has taught undergraduate and graduate courses on political economy, public policy, international politics, and other subjects at several education institutions including Columbia University.*

Russia also utilizes economic warfare against, among others the Baltic states and Ukraine. In Ukraine, it blockades seaports, destroys transportation and communications networks, obstructs food production, attacks or occupies power plants, and cyber-attacks Ukrainian government and business operations. Besides economic warfare measures during combat, Russia has long practiced energy-economic warfare. According to a Baker Institute estimate, Russia has used energy as a weapon against European countries at least 22 times between 1990 and 2017 alone.

Even lesser powers such as Iran, Saudi Arabia, and Israel utilize economic warfare. Iran intermittently and covertly attacks Israeli and Saudi Arabian ships and infrastructure, and Israel and Saudi Arabia regularly reciprocate. Often these attacks are kinetic (e.g., missiles and sea mines), but increasingly they occur in the cyber domain.

Economic warfare is attractive because it is a "gray-zone" or "below threshold" type of warfare. States or non-state actors can engage in hostilities that constitute low intensity warfare while minimizing the risk of escalating violence. The key is not to provoke a full military confrontation or meet the definition of belligerency under international law.

The primary rationale for using economic warfare is that it is a "better alternative than going to war," and even if it is less effective than desired, it can "signal" disapproval of another's actions. However, there is disagreement about the role economic warfare should assume in U.S. policy, and this disagreement is reflected in the academic and policy communities, and in Congress and the Biden administration. Critics argue that the most prominent form of economic warfare, sanctions, "don't work," and often just strengthen a state's resolve to resist U.S. demands. Others argue that the policy aims sought often do not justify the enormous humanitarian disasters economic warfare often entails. They see the strategy as immoral and a violation of international law. Civil libertarians also raise concerns over the unchecked power economic warfare gives the U.S. president and federal bureaucrats.

In order to better understand these deliberations and decisions, this essay will 1) define economic warfare and provide historical context 2) provide an overview of U.S. sanctions programs 3) delineate the case for and against economic warfare, and 4) examine current economic warfare programs against Russia and China.

Definitions and context

Defining economic warfare is complicated because it describes both the target or ends of a strategy, and a means of coercion. As an end, it entails attacking an adversary's economy with all tools deemed appropriate, including militarily. As a means, it focuses on economic ways to undermine an adversary's military, political, or social organization. In both cases, the goal is to weaken the will or ability of an adversary to resist one's demands and coerce a behavioral change through regime change, or by forcing an elite or population to pressure its leadership to accept the initiating state's demands. Table 1 contains a typology of contemporary economic warfare tools.

Economic warfare has been a feature of global history since before the Peloponnesian War (431–404 BCE), and it increased in sophistication as people urbanized and supply chains became more complex. It evolved from burning an adversary's grain fields; to blocking a town, city, or country's food supply through armed siege or blockade; to restricting the natural resources necessary for industrial production, originally by surface ship interdiction but later by submarine and airplane; and now to interrupting the financial flows necessary for managing a modern economy in a globalized world.

Economic warfare usually has been a predecessor or adjunct to military operations, and during actual combat economic warfare is almost always utilized. Accordingly, the U.S. military integrates economic and infrastructural elements into most all U.S. strategic and operational plans. However, lethal force (e.g., sinking cargo ships or bombing factories), especially outside physical combat, need not be utilized for something to constitute economic warfare. The 19th and 20th centuries saw "pacific blockades" or naval coer-

Table 1: Economic Warfare Measures (Not Exhaustive)

OVERT

Conventional Measures – Sanctions

- Denial of foreign assistance, loans, and investments
- Trade embargoes and/or boycotts
- Shipping and insurance restrictions
- Freezing or seizing assets under U.S. or allied jurisdiction
- Restricting or prohibiting arms transfers
- Denial of credit, including by third parties
- Prohibiting economic transactions involving targeted countries, citizens, or businesses
- Travel restrictions
- Pressure on partner countries to also engage in the above ("secondary sanctions")

Extraordinary Measures

- Blockading ports and other transportation nodes
- Attacking / sabotaging national infrastructure
- Attacking / sabotaging others supporting the target
- Attacking industrial and agricultural production capabilities
- Interfering with government operations and communication networks through cyber-attacks
- Killing non-combatants to weaken morale and disrupt production

COVERT

All "Extraordinary Measures" Plus:

- Industrial espionage (state sponsored)
- Intellectual poverty theft (state sponsored)
- Fomenting labor unrest and strikes
- Counterfeiting currency
- Bribing / entrapping government officials or business leaders for favorable economic decisions
- Talent / labor recruitment or sponsoring defection

Lucidity Information Design, LLC

Before you read, download the companion **Glossary** that includes definitions, a guide to acronyms and abbreviations used in the article, and other material. Go to **www. fpa.org/great_decisions** and select a topic in the Resources section. (Top right)

cion with no or a minimum of violence. The Soviet Berlin blockade (1948–49) was not overtly violent, and, more recently (2016), Iran used cyberattacks—a new and distinct form of economic (and hybrid) warfare—to damage U.S. financial institutions and threaten U.S. financial stability. Particularly since 9/11 and increased sanctions use, the historic nexus between economic warfare and violence has weakened.

The term economic warfare was commonly used during the Second World War when the United States and others maintained boards, offices, and ministries of economic warfare. Since that time, and especially from the 1960s, the term was eclipsed by the word "sanctions," a specific type of economic warfare. Sanctions usually seek their objectives through bureaucratic manipulation of international trade and finance relationships and usually involve less use of force. The preference is to coerce change by limiting the economic gains available through global engagement. This reliance on bureaucratic measures creates the illusion that sanctions are a more sanitized form of warfare, or not even warfare at all. Governments utilizing sanctions often explicitly try to separate sanctions from economic warfare. As a senior Biden administration official said in response to Russia's economic warfare charge, "we need to stay sober with our rhetoric." The point was not that the Russia sanctions are not economic warfare, but that to publicly acknowledge it as such would legitimize an overt violent response from Russia.

Sanctions, especially trade sanctions, which are a type of blockade, do not rest exclusively on the use of economic tools in the absence of lethal force. Sanctions are predicated upon deterring violations through force, and the United States, like others, intermittently uses force to implement sanctions. Among other U.S. examples are the 1990s Iraqi no-fly zone, and the periodic stopping of Iranian and North Korean cargo ships by the U.S. Navy. As Vice Adm. Karl Thomas, commander of the U.S. Seventh Fleet recently said, "a blockade is less kinetic," it is

not non-kinetic; it only remains non-violent if it is not challenged.

Perhaps more important than the violence underlying sanctions, is the often equivalent results. U.S. use of sanctions has killed (at a minimum) hundreds of thousands of people, especially children. (See below.) From the perspective of the initiator, sanctions seem non-violent, but from the perspective of the target, sanctions can be extremely violent. It makes little difference to the target if someone dies of hunger or inadequate medical care, or from a bullet or bomb. Contemporary sanctions lethality stems from their post-World War I (WWI) evolution, when both Britain and Germany tried to destroy each other by precipitating social collapse through economic deprivation. The point, as historian Nicholas Mulder said, was to sever a country from the global economy and wait "…for it to exhaust itself or succumb to political revolution or social collapse. [The] effects on civilian society—immiseration, starvation, disease, bankruptcy…produce measures whose function and consequences are identical to war."

One of the longest U.S. economic warfare programs was the effort to restrict the acquisition of products and technologies by the Soviet Union and other Cold War adversaries. The aim was to restrain adversarial military power by limiting the ability to procure or produce weapons. From 1949 until 1994, the U.S. restricted exports of strategic products and technologies to communist countries through the Coordinating Committee on Multilateral Export Controls (CoCom). CoCom eventually included 15 NATO countries and Japan.

CoCom was replaced in 1996 by the Wassenaar Arrangement. However, unlike CoCom, Wassenaar does not give each member a veto over another country's sales, and its membership include a U.S. adversary, Russia, and three problematic states, India, Hungary, and Turkey. As a result, some in the U.S. Congress think that the Unite States and its allies are insufficiently vigilant about technology transfers, especially to China, and they are advocating for a

new version of CoCom to control multilateral exports.

Equally important as export controls was the management of Western European energy needs after World War II (WWII). As the world moved increasingly toward petroleum as the dominant transportation fuel, Western Europe needed ever larger amounts of oil, and the country that helped them obtain it was going to gain greater influence over European affairs. At that time, however, the United States was losing its capacity to export oil due to declining domestic production and rapidly increasing demand. Its solution was to promote Middle East oil development and guarantee the flow to Europe. This oil policy worked for two decades until the 1973 oil shock.

Even before the oil shock, West Ger-

California gasoline prices, June 2022. Crude oil and by extension gasoline has been a tool of economic warfare for over 100 years. Often, such as in the 1950s, the U.S. has successfully used this tool; In other instances, such as the 1970s and in 2022, the U.S. has been less successful. (PHOTO BY J. CHANIS.)

many began seeking closer economic and political ties with the Soviet Union. While there were many reasons for the country's new *Ostpolitik*, gaining access to Soviet energy was clearly one. With growing momentum for *Ostpolitik* and the 1973 oil shock, West Germany and others increasingly integrated Soviet energy into their economies. Despite U.S. opposition, beginning with the Kennedy administration, the Soviet Union succeeded in building a major oil pipeline in 1964 and a gas pipeline in 1978. By

European leaders symbolically turn Nord Stream 1's valve starting the flow of additional Russian natural gas to Europe in 2011. Then German Chancellor Angela Merkel and Russian President Dmitry Medvedev are in the photo's center (left and right). (PHOTO BY SASHA MORDOVETS/GETTY IMAGES)

the early 1980s, when the Soviet Union wanted to construct another major pipeline, U.S. policymakers became extremely alarmed. As a 1981 CIA report noted, the deepening energy relationship can "…provide the Soviets one additional pressure point they could use as part of a broader diplomatic offensive to persuade the West Europeans to accept their viewpoint on East-West issues". In response, the Reagan administration attempted to block the pipeline's construction by prohibiting American companies from selling necessary components. The prohibition eventually included European subsidiaries of American companies, and European products manufactured under U.S. license.

Given the priority this pipeline had for Europe, American sanctions were seen essentially as a declaration of economic war, and the dispute was one of the worst U.S.-European crises since the end of WWII. Unwilling to accept American "exterritorial laws," West Germany, Britain, France, and others passed laws prohibiting companies operating on their territory from complying with U.S. sanctions. Ultimately, the Reagan administration yielded and the pipeline was completed in 1983.

Around this time, the Reagan administration learned of a multi-year covert Soviet program to acquire products and technologies prohibited under CoCom. In response, the administration established a covert CIA program to sabotage these acquisitions by selling materials that "would appear genuine but would later fail." There even was an unconfirmed report that altered software caused a massive explosion on a Soviet pipeline in 1982. According to Thomas Reed, a former Air Force secretary, the explosion was just one

---

Box 1: Selected U.S. Economic Warfare Programs, 1960–84

Cuba: After the 1961 failed Bay of Pigs invasion, the Kennedy administration launched Operation Mongoose. This was an attempt, as a senior CIA official said, to conduct "…maximum possible sabotage of major Cuban industries and public utilities with priority attention being given to transportation, communications, power plants, and utilities." While many of the plans, such as using biological or chemical agents against Cuba's sugar crop never happened, numerous targets including petroleum and electric generating facilities were attacked. Even during the Cuban Missile Crisis, a CIA sponsored team attacked a Cuban copper mine. The CIA eventually lost control of several Cuban émigré groups that went on to attack numerous targets, particularly cargo ships. President Lyndon Johnson began phasing out the program in 1964. Some, including U.S. Army veteran and anti-war critic Andrew Bacevich, see Operation Mongoose as "…in effect…state-sponsored terrorism …."

Chile: While the U.S. may not have organized and directed the 1973 overthrow of Chilean President Salvador Allende, it helped create conditions that made the coup more likely. According to declassified documents, the United States launched an "invisible economic blockade" and clandestine war to "destabilize" Chile's economy. These efforts included curtailing or terminating credits and loans from U.S. and other lenders; fomenting labor discord and strikes; and making payments to local business leaders for purpose still unknown.

Nicaragua: Between September 1983 and April 1984, the CIA and local proxies conducted at least 21 direct attacks on Nicaraguan oil facilities and pipelines, grain storage facilities, bridges and ports, and ultimately placed mines in Nicaragua's harbors. The CIA trained and armed the rebels, selected the targets, and supervised the attacks. After the covert economic war became public, the U.S. Congress prohibited the use of any funds for overthrowing Nicaragua's government." In order to evade this restriction, the Reagan administration sold arms to Iran and used part of the proceeds to fund the Nicaragua war. After the operation was disclosed and multiple investigations, 14 senior administration officials were convicted of various crimes including destroying government documents and lying to Congress.

example of "cold-eyed economic warfare" waged by the CIA against the Soviet Union.

It is difficult to gauge the effectiveness of Reagan's covert economic warfare program, but some believe it to have been successful. In any event, the current European energy crisis demonstrates that the United States lost this multi-decade energy-economic struggle.

Compared to U.S. overt economic warfare efforts against the Soviet Union, the U.S. program against China was even more hostile. Rather than just limit the supply of products and technologies that could strengthen China's military capabilities, the U.S., beginning with the Korean War (1950–53), attempted to bring about the internal collapse of China by restricting all products that could help it industrialize. Accordingly, the U.S. created the "China Differential," an extra list of CoCom items that all communist countries could buy, except China. The aim was to cause sufficient economic pain in China to compel regime change, or if this failed, to split the Sino-Soviet alliance because of China's rising economic aid needs.

While the China export sanctions were the template for later U.S. sanctions on Cuba, Iraq, Iran, and North Korea, it is difficult to know what role they played in turning China toward economic reform. However, both the Eisenhower and Kennedy administrations thought the denial of U.S. trade caused great harm to China, including worsening periodic famines. Under this policy, additional Chinese starvation deaths were not collateral policy damage, they were central to it. As Walt Rostow, a prominent development economist then at the State Department said: "We maintained...a position tantamount to economic warfare" aimed directly at the Chinese people. In the 1970s as the two countries drew closer in order to combat growing Soviet power, the China Differential was phased out.

Before the end of the Cold War, there were other programs particularly in Cuba, Chile, and Nicaragua that changed how the U.S. conducts covert warfare, including economic warfare. (See Box 1.) After they were revealed, these programs undermined public trust in the CIA and executive branch, and resulted in Congress limiting the executive branch's ability to conduct covert actions, including economically. The permanent establishment of House and Senate oversight committees, the creation of a CIA Inspector General, stronger executive branch internal vetting procedures, and mandatory congressional reporting requirements curtailed unaccountable and often extreme covert actions.

Since U.S. covert programs generally are not disclosed for 50 years, it is difficult to know how significantly the intelligence reforms of the 1970s and 1980s reduced covert economic warfare programs. However, given the lack of strong contrary evidence, it is probable that the most aggressive U.S. economic warfare programs, such as covert physical attacks on vital economic infrastructure during peacetime, are less common than they were in the 1970s and 1980s. While it might be coincidence, after the last major covert action reforms took effect under the George H.W. Bush administration, sanctions use by the subsequent Clinton and George W. Bush administrations began to increase. Consequently, one can posit that the difficulty of mounting covert economic operations led to sanctions becoming the dominant form of U.S. economic warfare.

U.S. sanctions program overview

While most countries do not acknowledge the weaponization of economics for national security purposes, the United States indirectly did when it said (in the U.S. Treasury Department *2021 Sanctions Review)* that since the 9/11 attacks, economic and financial sanctions have become a "tool of first resort" that "allow U.S. policymakers to impose a material cost on adversaries." When effective they "...disrupt, deter, and prevent actions that undermine U.S. national security."

According to Drexel University's "Global Sanctions Data Base," the United States imposed more than 35% of all global sanctions between 1950 and 2019, and sanctions use increased significantly after 9/11 (see Graph 1.) Currently there are 37 separate U.S. Treasury sanctions programs, each sanctioning multiple individuals, companies, or entities. Most of these sanctions can be grouped into programs for: nuclear arms proliferators; international terrorism support; threatening regional stability; human rights and democratic governance violations / corruption, and; fulfillment of United Nations Security Council resolutions.

Between 2000 and 2021, the United States increased sanctions use by a factor of ten, from 912 designations to 9,421. (See Graph 2.) The Treasury's list of "Specially Designated Nationals and Blocked Persons" (SDN) contains more than 20 countries, approximately

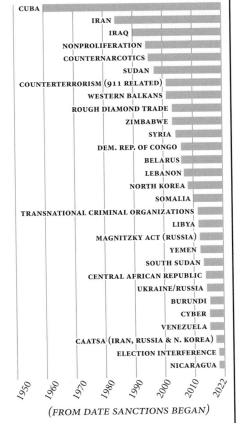

Graph 1:
U.S. Sanctions Programs

CUBA
IRAN
IRAQ
NONPROLIFERATION
COUNTERNARCOTICS
SUDAN
COUNTERTERRORISM (911 RELATED)
WESTERN BALKANS
ROUGH DIAMOND TRADE
ZIMBABWE
SYRIA
DEM. REP. OF CONGO
BELARUS
LEBANON
NORTH KOREA
SOMALIA
TRANSNATIONAL CRIMINAL ORGANIZATIONS
LIBYA
MAGNITZKY ACT (RUSSIA)
YEMEN
SOUTH SUDAN
CENTRAL AFRICAN REPUBLIC
UKRAINE/RUSSIA
BURUNDI
CYBER
VENEZUELA
CAATSA (IRAN, RUSSIA & N. KOREA)
ELECTION INTERFERENCE
NICARAGUA

1950 1960 1970 1980 1990 2000 2010 2022

(FROM DATE SANCTIONS BEGAN)

SOURCE: Council on Foreign Relations

Lucidity Information Design, LLC

6,300 individuals, and thousands of companies. U.S. persons are prohibited from dealing with an SDN, and all SDN assets accessible to the U.S. government are frozen. Prohibited transactions include supply of any product or services to a specified country, regime, or foreign national; importation of products originating from a subject nation or produced by an SDN; transfering money to or from financial accounts located in a designated nation, or in which an SDN has an interest; and provision of credit or financial services to an SDN.

Over 60% of sanctions are authorized under the National Emergencies Act. The president simply declares that an "unusual and extraordinary threat" exists and then typically invokes the International Emergency Economic Powers Act to craft a sanctions program. Other programs are legislated by Congress and they either authorize or require the President to act.

Violating U.S. sanctions laws can have draconian consequences. Fines can exceed $330,000 per violation, or twice the violation transaction value. In the event of willful criminal violations, violators may face fines up to $1 million, and/or 20 years' imprisonment. The Justice Department also may use forfeiture authorities to seize proceeds or assets connected to the conduct,

even in the absence of a criminal conviction. U.S. law also allows the Office of Foreign Assets Control (OFAC) to penalize foreign entities trading with sanctioned entities. These "secondary sanctions" are a powerful incentive for non-U.S. parties to comply with U.S. sanctions since the government can stop an entity from transacting in U.S. dollars. The largest sanctions penalty, almost $9 billon, was levied in 2014 when French bank BNP Paribas pleaded guilty to processing payments for Cuba, Iran, and Sudan.

More than a dozen other government departments and agencies are involved in managing U.S. economic warfare programs. Most important are the Commerce and State Departments. Besides supporting Treasury's financial efforts, these departments are involved in more traditional economic warfare programs such as restricting exports of military and dual use products, and controlling arms sales and military and foreign aid disbursements.

The case for and against economic warfare

Although the case for and against economic warfare needs to be broken down into sanctions and more traditional economic warfare, it is useful to recognize that both are hostile, often violent acts that can and have dis-

rupted or destroyed millions of lives. Their utilization must therefore be approached with as much seriousness as a decision to use force. Given that U.S. policy uses economic and financial sanctions as "a tool of first resort," it is legitimate to ask if the U.S. government has approached sanctions with sufficient deliberation. Regarding the use of overt economic warfare, such as blockading ports or sabotaging a country's infrastructure, U.S. policymakers do appear to approach the use of such measures with more thoughtfulness. An example was the Obama administration's consideration and rejection of blockading Iranian ports in 2009–10. Regarding covert economic warfare, it is difficult to know what U.S. government deliberations or actions occurred over the past few decades. However, given the general absence of suspicious incidents, and the ability of unlimited (i.e., "maximum pressure") sanctions to functionally replace much previously sought through covert economic warfare, perhaps one can assume that the U.S. is extremely good at these types of operations, and they remain secret, or fewer have occurred. One major exception probably is covert cyber warfare, where there are repeated public hints that a good deal more occurs than is being publicly disclosed.

The criticism of sanctions can be broken down into: 1) effectiveness / cost 2) humanitarian concerns, and 3) constitutional abuses.

Effectiveness / Cost

The empirical evidence of sanctions' effectiveness is sufficiently ambiguous to make the case for supporters, as well as opponents. According to Drexel University's database, when considering all types of sanctions, the objectives were achieved approximately 35% of the time, and partially 14% of the time. Only in 22% of the cases did sanctions completely fail. The remaining cases have yet to generate an outcome. This means that most cases with outcomes were either fully or partially successful. Additionally, proponents note that in many cases when sanctions are threatened, the target "pulls back" and does

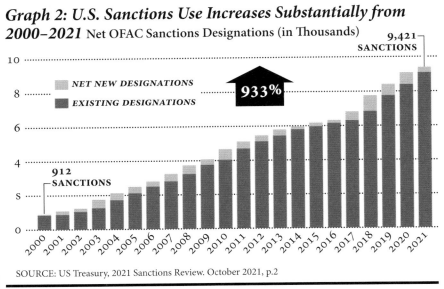

Graph 2: U.S. Sanctions Use Increases Substantially from 2000–2021 Net OFAC Sanctions Designations (in Thousands)

9,421 SANCTIONS

NET NEW DESIGNATIONS
EXISTING DESIGNATIONS

933%

912 SANCTIONS

SOURCE: US Treasury, 2021 Sanctions Review. October 2021, p.2

Lucidity Information Design, LLC

not continue with the action(s) that precipitated the sanctions threat.

There were notable differences in outcomes depending on the objectives. As illustrated in Graph 3, the sanctions with the highest probability of success were those related to promoting democracy and human rights. Those least successful related to combating terrorism, destabilizing a regime, and resolving a territorial conflict.

In pioneering research, Gary Hufbauer and his colleagues identified the conditions necessary for sanctions to be effective. Accordingly, a target is more vulnerable when it has a small economy with a large foreign trade sector; little possibility for substitution or conservation of the sanctioned products or services; weak alliances and inconsequential military power; and an inability to block third party compliance or mount counter-sanctions. The chances of sanctions succeeding increase when they are undertaken multilaterally, and when the initiating state is willing to incur substantial domestic economic costs.

If one considers failed cases (22%) and those without an outcome (29%), then sanctions' effectiveness seems more dubious, particularly since sanctions with "no outcome" can persist for decades (e.g., North Korea since 1950 and Cuba since 1960). Sanctions often fail because states adapt by making do with substitute products or technologies, or by using existing resources more productively. They often also evade sanctions with the help of others. Commodity producers, in particular, often find buyers for their sanctioned products who "backfill" the market vacated by companies from sanctioning states. These failures point to the "translation problem," i.e., sanctions can generate enormous economic pain, but still not coerce a policy change; they may succeed economically, but fail politically, and in some cases, they may even increase a target state's resistance to policy change.

Opponents say sanctions can make the world less safe by driving countries toward autarkic economic solutions that may encourage states to choose

Graph 3: Assessing the Effectiveness of Sanctions
An analysis of 1,100 sets of sanctions between 1949 and 2019

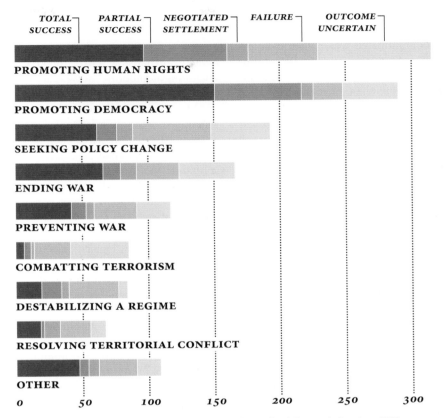

SOURCE: Drexel University's Global Data Base; Research Handbook Economic Sanctions, 2021; Bloomberg Economic News

Lucidity Information Design, LLC

war rather than risk seeing their power position degraded through sanctions. The prime historical example of this was Italy, Germany, and Japan before WWII.

Another concern is that efforts to reduce supply chain vulnerability by the U.S and China can accelerate deglobalization and bifurcate the global economy into U.S. and Chinese spheres. This can encourage U.S.-China decoupling and economic autarky. As a Chinese finance professor said: "The comprehensive economic sanctions against Russia after its invasion of Ukraine have only added urgency to [China] achieving self-sufficiency in technology, finance, food and energy. Self-sufficiency as a phrase has regained currency in the party's publications." Deglobalization and decoupling would slow global

growth, reduce economic efficiency, raise production costs, and stimulate inflation. Both China and Russia have developed alternative payment systems they hope will make SWIFT (the U.S. dominated global payment messaging system) obsolete. Russia and China, Saudi Arabia and China, and Russia and India increasingly seek and often find ways to minimize U.S. dollar use in bilateral trade, especially for oil.

Humanitarian concerns

Some argue that a policy that often deliberately targets civilians is immoral and illegal. The most prominent example of this is the U.S 1990s Iraq sanctions. While the Iraqi sanctions death toll is not precisely known, and the original Saddam Hussein inflated figures have been disproven, a study by Columbia University's Richard Garfield estimated a minimum of 100,000, and more likely 227,000, excess deaths of Iraqi children from August 1991 through March 1998. These deaths were attributed among other things to contaminated water, lack of high-quality food, and inadequate supplies in the curative health care system. Ethics and legal scholar Joy Gordon writes that the Iraq sanctions were "the worst humanitarian catastrophe ever imposed in the name of global governance...." Jeffrey Sachs and Mark Weisbrot cite Venezuela's devastation and argue that U.S. sanctions caused more than 40,000 deaths from 2017 to 2018. They assert that the sanctions fit "…the definition of collective punishment of the civilian population as described in both the Geneva and Hague international conventions [and are] illegal under international law [and U.S. treaties, and] appear to violate U.S. law...."

Without even criticizing the purpose of U.S. sanctions policy, many humanitarians aid organizations complain that the slow response of OFAC in granting humanitarian aid export licenses aggravates humanitarian crises by hampering the logistical and financial activity of aid organizations operating in sanctioned jurisdictions. As a result, innocent people suffer and die. Between OFAC's slow response and aid agencies and financial institutions "overcompliance" due to fear of falling afoul of the regulations, it is difficult to get humanitarian aid, including vaccines, to countries like Afghanistan, Burma, Iran, Somalia, Syria, and Venezuela.

Constitutional concerns

The constitutional critique argues that the executive branch uses the National Emergency Act (NEA) and the International Emergency Economic Powers Act (IEEPA) to evade congressional oversight. According to a review by the Brennan Center for Justice's Andrew Boyle, the issue is not the sanctions themselves, but a process that increasingly gives unchecked power to the executive. He argues that the process needs better transparency and more

considered deliberation, especially by Congress.

This critique also highlights how U.S. sanctions policy can violate designated Americans' constitutional rights, especially the Fourth and Fifth amendments (unreasonable seizure and due process). While the overwhelming number of individuals and entities sanctioned are foreign, dozens of U.S. citizens and entities also are sanctioned. According to Boyle, some of these designations have been made without evidence, and procedures for getting off the SDN list are essentially non-existent. Similarly, asset seizures have occurred without criminal convictions and there is no process to contest such seizures.

Boyle proposes legislative reforms such as separating the IEEPA from the NEA thereby making it more difficult to use IEEPA in non-emergency situations. He advocates making Congress affirmatively approve within 90 days every presidential sanction action and then renew such approval annually. Boyle wants OFAC to develop transparent, specific, written standards and regulations for granting licenses, and he wants a 60-day decision period for any such decision. He thinks Congress should consider restricting the use of IEEPA against U.S. persons to cases only involving criminal conduct.

Russia, China, and U.S. economic warfare

Despite economic warfare and especially sanctions' problems, after Russia invaded Ukraine a second time, U.S. policymakers immediately instituted an extensive sanctions response. Since the Biden administration determined that a direct U.S. military response was not (at least at that point) justified, economic warfare represented a third option between using military force and doing nothing. Moreover, four decades of increasing sanctions use conditioned the U.S. to use sanctions as a "first resort."

The U.S. now has a large bureaucratic interest, both in government and in the private sector, predisposed toward ever greater sanctions use. Be-

sides the institutional interests of the many departments and agencies now involved in sanctions policy, many people built careers in sanctions work, and this creates momentum for sanctions adoption regardless of any policy rationale. While comprehensive figures are unavailable, the sanctions economy easily employee tens of thousands of people. Besides the thousands working for multiple governments, most every major bank, corporation, and law firm has people dedicated to sanctions compliance, and there are numerous "sanctions experts" in academia and consulting.

With a low level of international trade relative to Gross Domestic Product (GDP), the costs of sanctions to the U.S. economy have been marginal, and the threat of economic retaliation by targeted states negligible. Heretofore, this relative invulnerability has allowed the U.S. to impose sanctions on others with minimal consequences for its own economy. This has allowed the U.S. to act with less concern that threatening another state's interests would precipitate a meaningfully punitive response by that state or its allies. The current cases of Russia and China, however, are different. Making economic war on these countries—the eleventh and second largest global economies—risks greater economic disruption and hostile counteractions.

Even before the second Ukraine invasion, the United States had substantial sanctions on Russia, including placing numerous individuals and entities on the SDN list; restricting Russian debt trading; and prohibiting certain oil and gas investments and equipment sales. After the second invasion, the United States vastly increased the number and types of sanctions imposed. A partial list is found in Table 2.

These actions constituted the most comprehensive sanctions against a country in decades. When these sanctions were imposed, the Biden administration said they would be "crippling" and deprive Russia of funds and components necessary for sustaining the Ukraine invasion. A senior official even suggested that Russia's GDP would de-

Table 2: Sanctions Imposed on Russia After Its February Invasion of Ukraine

- Denial of foreign assistance, loans, and investments
- Russian Central Bank asset freeze
- Add additional government and private persons/entities (including numerous "oligarchs") to U.S. SDN list
- Limit access to SWIFT
- Partial ban on Russian oil purchases
- Block most U.S. exports, including high-tech components
- Ban Russian airlines from U.S. airspace
- Prohibit U.S. investment in Russia
- Sanction Nord Stream 2 pipeline
- Prohibit Russian ruble and foreign denominated bonds trading

Lucidity Information Design, LLC

cline by 50%. The ruble and stock market would collapse (and stay down) and inflation would overwhelm the population. Mulder wrote: "The overall effect has been unprecedented…in all but its most vital products [Russia has been] decoupled from 21st-century globalization." Hufbauer wrote "…the sanctions have proven among the most powerful in modern history…. [T]he economic hardship now inflicted on Russia ranks among the brutal episodes of modern times…. [O]nly North Korea, Cuba, Iraq, and Iran have suffered comparable losses…." But Russia's economy has not collapsed and the sanctions, thus far, have not been nearly as effective as many first thought.

In a prescient *Wall Street Journal* op-ed, the historian Nicholas Lambert questioned the euphoric rhetoric and compared the Russia sanctions to WWI British sanctions. He wrote: "On a Richter scale of economic warfare, Britain aimed at a 10 and achieved an 8 before scaling back to a 5; what the West is doing to Russia now is maybe a 3…."

Ironically, one can use Hufbauer's criteria to discern why Russian is not an ideal candidate for sanctions: Russia has a large economy; it depends on few vital imports; there is substantial scope for conservation and substitution of sanctioned products and services; and it has significant ability to mount

counter-sanctions. Most importantly, the sanctions largely have not stopped Russia's oil exports and its attendant revenue generation because they are not fully multilateral.

Oil is the life blood of the Putin regime and if Russia can sell it and collect revenue, it has a good chance of avoiding truly catastrophic outcomes, at least in the near term, especially for its elite. Sanctions have been very inconvenient for Russia's oil trade and the total volume sold is down slightly, but according to International Energy Agency calculations, Russian oil export revenue is up 50% from pre-war levels. The higher global price more than offsets any volume decline. China, India, and others are more than willing to purchase Russian oil at discounted prices. Only half of the G-20 countries (which constitute approximately 85% of global output) are sanctioning Russia. Among the non-sanctioners are China, India, Turkey, South Africa, Saudi Arabia, Indonesia, Mexico, and Brazil. And several countries are also actively helping Russia evade the sanctions including Iran, North Korea, and Turkey.

The latest estimates for Russia's 2022 GDP see a decline of 4–8%, and

inflation is expected to be approximately 15%. This is hardly a catastrophic economic collapse and Russia has experienced higher inflation in the past and survived. There are reports of increasing consumer shortages and an inability to source critical parts for military equipment and civilian production, but it is unclear how severe these bottlenecks will become, or if they can be translated into a policy change. Some, such as Jeffery Sonnenfeld, think Russia already is in a desperate economic situation. Others think sanctions are a longer-term proposition that will wear Russia down over time. Some think no real policy change will occur until Russian oil exports are completely restricted.

Rich Goldberg of the Foundation for Defense of Democracies argues sanctions need to be intensified by removing *all* Russian banks from SWIFT and imposing secondary sanctions on any company buying or helping Russia sell oil. A "maximum pressure" campaign would steadily force global buyers to reduce Russian oil purchases and when combined with an escrow program, would deprive Russia of oil revenue. This would be a repeat of the "successful" 2011 and 2017 U.S. sanctions

Tugboats help an oil tanker dock at China Petrochemical Corporation's (Sinopec's) Zhoushan, China terminal. November 4, 2020. As the U.S. and Europe have reduced purchases of Russian oil, other states, particularly China and India, have vastly increased their purchases. (YAO FENG/VCG VIA GETTY IMAGES)

Vladimir Putin and Xi Jinping meet in Beijing just before the second Ukraine invasion and Xi declares that the Chinese-Russian partnership has "no limits." (LI TAO/XINHUA VIA GETTY IMAGES)

against Iran, and if Russia decided to withhold oil from the market in retaliation, the United States and its allies would win the "standoff" because Putin needs the revenue more than the world needs the oil.

Goldberg's logic is consistent, but some have argued that the risks in this approach are enormous. First, the global oil market today is very different than in 2011 and 2017. U.S. shale oil production was increasing substantially in 2011, and by 2017 it helped oversupply the market. Today, the world is desperately short of oil. The removal of Russian exports would have a dire price impact. According to a J.P. Morgan estimate, in the case of a total loss of Russian exports, prices would reach $380/barrel. This implies U.S. gasoline prices well in excess of $12/gallon. Even if one discounts the J.P. Morgan number by 50%, this still implies a deep U.S. and global recession. Coercing China, and especially India, to go along with what is close to economic suicide over Ukraine also would be problematic. A possible outcome might be a humiliating U.S retreat, like 1983, or the long-discussed destruction of the U.S.-dollar-based global financial system. Price cap schemes might avoid the

worst of these outcomes, but Chinese, Indian and others' self-interest is going to make it difficult to keep Russia from earning oil revenue, at least until the world no longer needs its oil.

Despite decades of heavy sanctions use, the United States has never stopped utilizing other forms of economic warfare. It has redoubled efforts to restrict sensitive technologies exports, especially to China (e.g., 5G telecommunication equipment), and in one of the more creative programs encouraged approximately 7,000 Cuban doctors and nurses on overseas assignments to defect. In 2020, Senator Robert Menendez tried unsuccessfully to revive this program. While efforts to lure Russian technology workers to the United States has yet to received much U.S. government attention, other countries such as Poland, Uzbekistan, Kazakhstan are actively recruiting these workers.

The United States also is taking steps to reduce its vulnerability to economic warfare by others, particularly China. This is defensive economic warfare includes: using the Federal Bureau of Investigation to thwart Chinese corporate espionage; identifying Chinese and other state sponsored hackers and

criminally charging them with attacking U.S corporations; curtailing Chinese recruitment of U.S scientists; and strengthening procedures for vetting inbound foreign investment with national security aspects.

A possible next step in U.S. offensive economic warfare is to limit outbound U.S. investment to "any country of concern," especially China. This is a reaction to the narrowing technical and industrial gap between the United States and China, and the de facto funding of China's military buildup by U.S. investors. According to a pending Presidential Executive Order, U.S. corporations and investors would be required to disclose certain outbound investments and seek authorization from a new interagency panel that could block any investment on national security grounds. The law would apply to greenfield investments including joint ventures, and private equity transactions funding Chinese companies. The requirement covers "critical and emerging technologies" including semiconductors, large-capacity batteries, rare-earth elements, pharmaceuticals, biotechnology, artificial intelligence, quantum computing, and financial technologies. According to an analysis by Rhodium Group, had this legislation been in affect over the last two decades, it would have covered up to 43% of all U.S. foreign direct investment in China.

Although economic warfare is central to interstate competition, it is a difficult tool to integrate into U.S. foreign policy. Economic warfare, even without extreme violence, is still warfare, and gaining widespread international support can be difficult. Most important economic warfare targets now also are major economic powers with better abilities to resist U.S. actions and retaliate. It also is unclear what the American public, businesses, and investors are willing to sacrifice in order to support any such measures. Regardless, a desire to avoid direct military force while at the same time pursing U.S. national interests continually pushes the country back toward the use of economic warfare.

discussion questions

1. How effective has U.S. use of economic warfare been in achieving U.S. foreign policy goals? Have the civilian deaths caused by sanctions been justified?

2. Has the sanctions process become unaccountable to the American public and the Congress? Is it in need of reform?

3. Are sanctions the best policy tool the United States has to use against Russia? If not sanctions, what policy should the United States pursue in response to Russia's invasion of Ukraine? Should the United States utilize other forms of economic warfare?

4. Should the U.S. design a CoCom like structure to deal with China? If yes, should it be limited to military product applications, or more expansive to retard China's growing economic power?

5. Should the United States take a more assertive role in limiting outbound U.S. investment to China?

suggested readings

Boyle, Andrew, **Checking the President's Sanctions Power**. Brennan Center, June 10, 2021. A comprehensive look at the libertarian and humanitarian problems with U.S. sanctions policy.

Funakoshi, Minami and Hugh Lawson and Kannaki Deka, **Tracking sanctions against Russia**. Reuters, Updated periodically. A comprehensive timeline of sanctions against Russian broken down by initiating country.

Gordon, Joy, **The Hidden Power of the New Economic Sanctions**. *Current History,* January 2019. The moral case against sanctions.

Hufbauer, Gary, Jeffrey Schott, Kimberly Ann Elliot, and Barbara Oegg, **Economic Sanctions Reconsidered**. Washington D.C.: The Peterson Institute for International Economics, June 15, 2009. 248 pp. The definitive empirical analysis of the efficacy of almost 200 economic sanctions cases.

Kirilakha, A. and C. Felbermayr, C. Syropoulos, E. Yalcin and Y. Yotov, **The Global Sanctions Data Base: An Update that Includes the Years of the Trump Presidency**. Drexel University. The Global Sanctions Data Base. A comprehensive review of over 700 sanctions cases.

Lambert, Nicholas, **What Real Economic Warfare Looked Like**. *Wall Street Journal,* March 18, 2022. A prescient first take on the Russia sanctions enthusiasm.

Hanemann, Thilo, Mark Witzke, Charlie Vest, Lauren Dudley, and Ryan Featherston. Two Way Street – An Outbound Investment Screening Regime for the United States? Rhodium Group. Jan 26, 2022. A deep dive into the merits of outbound investment restrictions.

Don't forget to vote!
Download a copy of the ballot questions from the Resources page at www.fpa.org/great_decisions

To access web links to these readings, as well as links to additional, shorter readings and suggested web sites,
GO TO **www.fpa.org/great_decisions**
and click on the topic under Resources, on the right-hand side of the page.

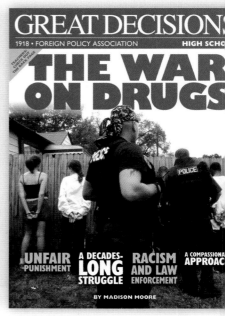
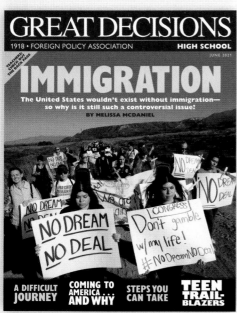

Political trends in Latin America
by Jorge Castañeda

Elected president of Brazil for the leftist Workers Party (PT), Luiz Inacio Lula da Silva speaks after winning the presidential run-off election, in Sao Paulo, Brazil, on October 30, 2022. Brazil's veteran leftist Lula was elected president by a hair's breadth, beating his far-right rival in a down-to-the-wire poll that split the country in two, election officials said. (NELSON ALMEIDA/AFP VIA GETTY IMAGES)

Electoral results in Latin America over the past four years have led many observers of the regional/political scene to discern a left-wing surge in the hemisphere. It evokes what occurred during the closing years of the last century and the first decade of the current one, when what was then labeled a "pink tide," or wave, swept through the area. Beginning with Hugo Chávez's 1998 election in Venezuela, by 2005 most of the region, with the exception of Mexico and Colombia, was governed by leaders who self-described themselves as from and of the "left." Regardless of the exact definition of the term, nearly all of these rulers were characterized by themselves and by most analysts as progressive, nationalist, popular-oriented: in a nutshell, left-wing or left of center.

After Chávez came Ricardo Lagos in Chile, Néstor and Cristina Kirchner in Argentina, Luiz Inácio Lula da Silva in Brazil, Evo Morales in Bolivia, the *Frente Amplio* in Uruguay, Rafael Correa, elected president of Ecuador in 2006, Daniel Ortega, brought back into power in Nicaragua in

JORGE CASTAÑEDA *is a renowned public intellectual, political scientist, and prolific writer, with an interest in Mexican and Latin American politics, comparative politics and U.S.-Mexican and U.S.-Latin American relations. Among his more than 15 books published in the United States and elsewhere are:* Ex-Mex: From Migrants to Immigrants *(The New Press, 2007),* Mañana Forever? Mexico and the Mexicans *(Vintage, Random House, 2012), and* America Through Foreign Eyes *(Oxford University Press, 2020). He was Foreign Minister of Mexico from 2000 to 2003. He taught at Mexico's National Autonomous University (UNAM) from 1978 through 2004, at Princeton University, and the University of California, Berkeley and (since 1997) at NYU. Jorge Castañeda is the Global Distinguished Professor of Political Science and Latin American Studies at New York University.*

5

2007, and in 2009, the FMLN in El Salvador. If one included the Cuban dictatorship, enthroned since 1959, a large share of Latin America´s population and GDP were governed on and by the left.

The 'two lefts' of the early 2000s

From the beginning, though, observers detected nuances and significant contrasts in this pattern. More than 15 years ago, I suggested in an essay published in *Foreign Affairs* that there were at least two lefts in the region: one, modern, democratic, globalized, pro-market, in a word, social-democratic; and another, nationalistic, authoritarian, statist, in a word, populist and anachronistic. Lumping them together in a single homogeneous group was, I argued, inaccurate and deceptive. I attempted to trace the differences among them to the origins of these two lefts. Those that came from a traditional socialist, communist, or labor union-based tradition (Chile, Uruguay, Brazil) had assimilated the lessons of the collapse of the Soviet Union and the socialist bloc, and had become in part indistinguishable from Western European social democracy. The best example of this strain was the Chilean *Concertación*, which one way or another governed the country from 1990 through 2018, with the exception of the four years from 2010 to 2014. Those that proceeded from classic, Latin American, populist currents—Argentina, Mexico, Ecuador, Venezuela, Bolivia—tended to be far more statist, nationalist, authoritarian, and anti-American. The best example was, of course, Hugo Chávez himself. He came from a military background, attempted to overthrow the democratically elected government of his country in 1992, and once in office, immediately proceeded to revamp

the country´s constitution. He and his successor, Nicolás Maduro, have now ruled Venezuela for 23 consecutive years.

The two lefts, or the pink tide, bequeathed a mixed heritage. Thanks to an exceptional commodities boom, fueled by insatiable Chinese demand for the types of raw materials produced by many South American countries, economies grew at higher rates than before. Thanks to the social commitment made by these progressive leaders, and their electorates' demands, a significant chunk of these extraordinary resources were plowed into social policies that reduced poverty, and to a lesser extent, inequality. Thanks to their own caution—not in all cases—and post-Cold War indifference in Washington, most of these governments got along decently with the United States, under both the Bush and Obama administrations.

On the opposite side of the ledger, authoritarian tendencies and perpetuation in office spread rapidly. In Venezuela, in Ecuador, in Bolivia, in Argentina, let alone in Nicaragua, rulers clamped down on the press, on the judiciary as well as on civil society, and rigged constitutions or elections to reelect themselves endlessly. After initial fiscal prudence, public expenditures ran out of control in Argentina, Brazil, Ecuador and, of course, Venezuela. And lastly, corruption, the traditional Latin American bane—that the left was supposedly destined to eradicate—reappeared, in spades. Presidents and ministers were accused, and sometimes prosecuted and jailed—more or less fairly, depending on the case—in Argentina, Brazil, Bolivia, Ecuador, Peru, El Salvador, and Nicaragua.

Finally, the first pink wave politicized foreign policy to a remarkable degree for a region that had undergone a period of relative unity in regard to world affairs. When President Bill Clinton hosted the first Summit of the Americas in 1994, most of his colleagues held similar views on many international matters: Fernando Henrique Cardoso of Brazil, Ernesto Zedillo from Mexico, Eduardo Frei Ruiz-Tagle in Chile, Carlos Menem in Argentina,

even Alberto Fujimori in Peru. But Chávez's arrival on the scene, given his charisma, boldness, and petrodollars, led to a deep division in the region. He created the ALBA, or Bolivarian Alliance of the Americas (**4**), largely to torpedo President George W. Bush's Free Trade Agreement of the Americas (ALCA, in Spanish). He nudged Lula and Kirchner (not members of ALBA) toward more anti-American, pro-Cuban stances, and re-introduced the classic, Latin American anti-imperialist rhetoric of years gone by. Countries like Mexico, Peru, Colombia, Costa Rica, sometimes Chile, were forced to take their distances from their neighbors in ALBA, for either ideological reasons or geo-political considerations.

The fact is that either because of corruption scandals, or the end of the commodity boom, or simply voter fatigue after many years of the same leaders or parties—Lula's Workers' Party or *Partido dos Trabalhadores* (PT) governed from 2003 through 2016—most of the pink wave regimes were voted out of office by the second half of the 2010s. They were largely replaced by right-of-center, or in some cases—i.e., Brazil—extreme right-wing presidents, who often tried to roll back many of the policies implemented by their progressive predecessors. There was a smattering of anti-incumbency bias in this process, but it also seemed that a stage of political development had come to an end. This was more apparently true in those cases where the left-of-center regimes were displaced in a context of corruption scandals.

Return of the Pink Tide

But 2018 changed this assessment. This was when the new pink tide emerged, although as we shall try to show, the term and the notion are even more misplaced than before. For the first time since 1934, a president who self-designated himself as a man of the left was elected to the presidency of Mexico. The country had suffered through strident, occasionally disruptive populist leaders in the 1970s, but never after Lázaro Cárdenas had it put at its helm a left-wing president, or at

Before you read, download the companion **Glossary** that includes definitions, a guide to acronyms and abbreviations used in the article, and other material. Go to **www.fpa.org/great_decisions** and select a topic in the Resources section. (Top right)

least one who considered himself as such, and whose supporters certainly saw him in that light. Andrés Manuel López Obrador was elected in 2018 with 53% of the vote, more than any president of Mexico since elections became relatively free and fair, that is, in 1994. This was to be the first difference between the first and second tides: Mexico was part of it.

In rapid succession, Peronist candidate Alberto Fernández, in the company of former President Cristina Fernández Kirchner, came to power in Argentina in 2019; in 2020, Luis Arce in Bolivia, in 2021 Pedro Castillo in Peru and Gabriel Boric in Chile were elected, and in 2022, Xiomara Castro and Gustavo Petro in Honduras and Colombia, respectively, also reached the presidency of their nations. Lastly, Lula was re-elected president of Brazil in a squeaker of a run-off election in late October. In some cases, particularly in Peru, it became increasingly difficult to continue to label rural school-teacher Castillo as a progressive leader. He opposed abortion, gay marriage, marijuana legalization, and other liberal demands vehemently, and most importantly, he mainly dedicated his first year in office to surviving a series of impeachments, without implementing any of his economic and social campaign promises. On substance, his bark is worse than his bite, but he shares much of the statist, nationalist, and populist ideology espoused by some of his colleagues. In other cases, such as Honduras, President Castro was chiefly seen as a woman of the left because of the role her husband, Manuel Zelaya, played in the first decade of the century, and the fact that she defeated a clearly right-wing candidate in the February 2022 elections. For these reasons, we will partly leave aside the cases of Peru and Honduras.

A truly iconic election was that of Petro in Colombia. Even more so than Mexico, the country had never sent a person of the left to the *Casa de Nariño*. Several figures, including Petro himself in 2018, had come close, ranging from Jorge Eliecer Gaitán in 1946, to other former mayors of Bo-

Different kinds of "Lefts"

DICTATORSHIPS
Cuba, Nicaragua, Venezuela

SOCIAL DEMOCRACIES
Bolivia, Brazil, Chile, Colombia

POPULIST COUNTRIES
Argentina, Mexico, Peru

LEFT-WING GOVERNMENTS: 1998 – 2009

LEFT-WING GOVERNMENTS: 2018 – PRESENT

LEFT-WING GOVERNMENTS: 1998 – 2009 AND 2018 – PRESENT

Lucidity Information Design, LLC

gotá. But this archetypical conservative society had managed to avoid all the Latin American swerves to the left since the 1940s, although it did have to cope with different, powerful guerrilla groups along the way. Petro himself was part of one of them, the M-19.

Thus, this time around, the shift to the left extends further than before, to Mexico and Colombia. Together with Lula´s election in Brazil, this means that well over 80% of the region´s population and a similar share of its GDP are today governed on the left, at least insofar as its self-identification and labeling from outside the left or from abroad is concerned. But if the first regional advent of the left was inaccurately seen as a homogeneous, unified, and collective event, the second coming, so to speak, is even more diverse and uneven. However, before we undertake the analysis

of the common threads and powerful differences within the left in Latin America today, we must briefly address the contrasts between the first wave and the second one.

Differences between the first and second Pink Tide

An initial difference has already been pointed out. Mexico and Colombia, meaning, the second and third largest nations in the hemisphere, are now part of the progressive landscape; similarly, three dictatorships -Cuba, Nicaragua, and Venezuela—instead of one—the island regime in Havana- are also part of it. Secondly, and more importantly, the left today ascends to power under far more adverse international circumstances than 20 years ago. Then, the region and the world were living through

Chinese President Xi Jinping holds a welcome ceremony for former Chilean President Sebastián Piñera before their talks at the Great Hall of the People in Beijing, China, April 24, 2019. Xi and Pinera held talks in Beijing ahead of the Second Belt and Road Forum for International Cooperation. (YIN BOGU/XINHUA/GETTY IMAGES)

prosperous economic times, with spectacular Chinese growth fueling an extraordinary boom of commodity prices. Oil, copper, soybeans, iron, sugar, beef, and many other raw materials or primary goods were in huge demand. High prices allowed governments imbued with a social mission to fund anti-poverty programs, like *Bolsa Familia* in Brazil, as well as spending on health, education, and housing. Money was available for huge infrastructure projects, often linked to the export of high-priced commodities.

Today the situation is far less favorable to these policies. The pandemic itself, then the recession that followed, and the subsequent Chinese and American economic downturns, have all put a lid on raw material prices, on foreign investment, on international lending, and on social expenditures domestically. While clearly some Latin American economies (Colombia, Uruguay, Bolivia) fared better than others (Mexico, Peru), all of them face potent headwinds today. The possibilities of budgetary largesse for social programs are far less promising than two decades ago. In addition, many of these governments are confronted with constraints that were weaker or

were simply non-existent the last time around. Beyond anti-free trade *rhetoric*, countries like Chile, Honduras, Peru, Colombia, and Mexico have all signed free trade *agreements* with the United States. No one has so far shown any willingness to withdraw from them. Thus, despite the best intentions of leaders and the enthusiasm of their supporters, electoral victories do not guarantee radical social change. All Latin American economies have been battered by the 2020 recession; poverty and inequality have risen as a result; tax revenues have fallen as economic recovery takes longer than expected. Meeting the demands of the street and the polls will not be easy.

Thirdly, as we shall explore in further detail below, the new lefts of today are, in some cases, far more environmentally minded, and more anti-extractivist than their predecessors. In Chile, Peru, and Colombia, in particular, governments seek to reduce their countries' reliance on commodity exports and to impose more severe controls on mining industries and depredatory agri-business. They may not succeed entirely, given their economies' dependence on the hard currency earned by these exports, but they will try. Commodity

sales do not only face lower prices and demand; many environmental groups and activists within the left´s constituency in these countries oppose more mining, farming, and drilling.

A fourth important change is that while the first group of leaders 20 years ago all had popular followings, they were largely electoral coalitions. On this occasion, the presidents elected were so thanks to powerful popular movements stemming from previous, impressive protests—as in Chile and Colombia—or that developed once they came to power. Environmentalists, original peoples, women, LGBTQ activists, unions and students all emerged as active players in most of these countries, in one way or another. They sometimes swept the new left contingent into power—in Chile, for example— or became a thorn in their side once elected: women in Mexico, Mapuche Indian leaders in Chile, Afro-Colombian activists in their country. In Brazil, where Lula´s popularity remains enormous among the poor and with popular movements, there was a degree of skepticism and discontent among some groups about his lack of enthusiasm for their causes during the campaign. He will soon be obliged to define his polices on these matters, as well as how to repair the enormous damage done to the country during the Bolsonaro years.

A last difference, in this unexhaustive list, is the emergence of China as a player in Latin America. Back in 2001, when the People's Republic joined the WTO, few countries had strong economic ties with Beijing. Former President Jiang Zemin was still concentrating on economic growth at home, and deflecting or blunting American attempts to limit China´s emergence as a world power. Today, President Xi Jinping governs a nation that is the first trading partner for Argentina, Brazil, Chile, Peru, and Bolivia, a major creditor of Venezuela, and a significant investor in mining, infrastructure, and land in other regional economies. Its tensions with the United States are far more acute than two decades ago. China has built the scaffolding of a blue water navy, has begun to establish bases or fueling ports far from its coasts, and initiated a "soft power" drive through the 36 Confucius Institutes in Latin America. For some countries and Latin leaders, this evolution entails great opportunities to create a so-called "active non-alignment;" for others, it is a temptation that must be resisted, as Mexico has, so far at least. But the international configuration today is far removed from what it was in 2000, for example, when Ricardo Lagos was elected as the first socialist president of Chile since Salvador Allende.

Despite these differences with the past, it is tempting to detect a new pink tide today: a broader, deeper, more ambitious wave than before. This continues to be a superficially attractive construct, especially useful for the media and for advocates of this type of change in Latin America. It would seem that from the Rio Grande to Patagonia, from Buenaventura to Recife, the left has finally arrived, having learnt lessons from the past and with a novel vision for the future. And indeed, it is not difficult to distinguish an apparently uniform political trend in this current wave, as many scholars concluded with regard to the former one. For some, this reflects a necessary and desirable shift to the left in countries where inequality has become unbearable, especially after the Covid-19 pandemic and the economic recession that accompanied it. Others detect in this ideological tsunami a significant threat to the region and to the United States, especially in view of the extremism of some of the new rulers and recent Russian and Chinese inroads in Latin America.

In fact, things are more complicated. If there were two lefts in the early 2000s, characterized by a broad degree of diversity among them and within each group, the same is true today, at least regarding the heterogeneity of the different lefts in power. To simplify matters, similarly to the way we broke down the lefts 15 years ago into two ample categories, today we can clearly identify three "lefts" in Latin America, that have little in common

among them. One caveat: in the same fashion that the two lefts of years past were not rigid groupings, or perfect fits, with some actors moving from one category to the other over the years, and some members of one group featuring characteristics more representative

of the other group, today´s three lefts constitute a broad classification. Few, if any, of these parties, movements, leaders, or presidents are archetypal. They belong to one group or another with nuances, shifts, and imperfect inclusions, that may also evolve over time.

The current three 'Lefts'

Before describing these "lefts," it is worthwhile repeating that all the leaders of this second wave define themselves as progressive and actually do have much in common. There are obvious and perceptible nationalist, statist, and populist tendencies in governments such as those of Mexico, Argentina, Colombia, Honduras, Bolivia, and Peru, not to mention the longstanding characteristics of the Cuban, Nicaraguan, and Venezuelan dictatorships. There are reasons for doubting whether Lula´s new presidency will repeat the prudent and moderate economic policies of his first term (2003-2006), or the reckless approach of his successors´ second one (2015-2016). With the exception of Chile and occasionally Peru, practically none of the other left-wing governments are willing to criticize human rights violations and the lack of democracy in

the dictatorships' group. Many of these countries share an ambiguous stance regarding the Russian invasion of Ukraine: Bolivia and Honduras have voted with Cuba, Nicaragua, and Venezuela in defense of Putin´s aggression, while Mexico—sometimes together with Bolsonaro´s right-wing regime in Brazil—Argentina, Peru, and Chile approved resolutions in the UN and the OAS condemning the Russian invasion but publicly expressed their neutrality or refusal to take sides.

It is also undeniable that all of these movements and leaders are largely a response to the poor management of the Covid-19 pandemic by center or right-wing governments in Latin America. Their programs or government action all have a strong social and populist content. They revive age-old grievances against Latin American and foreign elites, insisting on the need to priori-

Colombian President, Gustavo Petro (R), presents his running mate Francia Marquez (L) in Bogota on March 23, 2022 while campaigning for office. (JUAN BARRETO/AFP VIA GETTY IMAGESS)

(L to R) Nicaragua's President Daniel Ortega, former Cuban President Raúl Castro and Venezuelan President Nicolas Maduro talk as they prepare to pose for the family photo of the Bolivarian Alliance for the Peoples of Our America (ALBA) summit at the Miraflores presidential palace in Caracas on March 5, 2018. (FEDERICO PARRA/AFP VIA GETTY IMAGES)

tize the poor, expand social programs, strengthen the state´s control over natural resources and key industries, and have a prickly relationship with the media. Similarly, and perhaps unavoidably, in the minds of the newly elected leaders, or at least in those of their supporters, a clear anti-American stance is nearly always discernable. Given that many of the demands made by these new governments relate to mining, energy, land, and foreign investment, there may be frictions with U.S. interests and policies in the months and years ahead.

Dictatorships

More important, however, are the significant differences between these governments and movements, and they define our three categories. A first group includes the tryptic of dictatorships: Cuba, Nicaragua, and Venezuela. While these regimes systematically seek to associate themselves with the rest of the pink wave, and the latter nearly never criticizes them, there is an abysmal gap between them. All of the new leaders, from 2018 onward, have been democratically elected; none of the dictatorships were. All of their countries enjoy basic freedoms, market economies, engage in globalization,

and maintain cordial relations with Washington. None of the dictatorships do. The military is clearly subordinate to civilian rule; in the dictatorships the line between the two is thin and fuzzy. The three authoritarian regimes are often criticized by members of the international community, human rights NGO´s, and the world media, for the absence of any type of democratic expression or governance. No matter how much the three dictatorships attempt to link themselves with the rest of the left through groups like the Sao Paulo Forum—dating back to the 1990s—or the *Grupo de Puebla*—founded in 2019—and regardless of the fear of criticizing them that they inspire in any party, movement of government of the left in Latin America, they belong to a different species.

Social Democracies

A second category includes the regimes or parties that have, or have had, an unmistakable social-democratic inclination, at some point or another. They do not necessarily belong to the Socialist International, though some of the parties they include do. Some do not consider themselves social-democratic in the European sense, or even identify with the German, Spanish, or Scandi-

navian socialist movements. But their origins, evolution, and current stances place them near that *mouvance*. They are democrats; they believe and participate in globalization and market economies; they favor pro-active, vigorous social policies and programs; they are committed to tax reforms or the consolidation of high tax takes; they get along with Washington, whoever is in office, and tend to tone down the anti-American rhetoric, not to mention anti-imperialist policies. Once again, the taxonomy is not a perfect one. The new governments that can be classified in this category may retain or reacquire some remnants of traditional populist, statist, nationalist, and authoritarian themes. They are mostly coalitions, where not all of the components think or act alike. With these additional caveats, we can begin the classification in Category 2: the new "new" left.

The recently inaugurated Chilean president and his governing alliance should clearly be included. He belongs to this group because of his own statements and programmatic ambitions, his team of aides, his links with his predecessors, like former presidents Ricardo Lagos and Michele Bachelet, and his performance during the first months of his term. Gabriel Boric's coalition does include an anachronistic and uncompromising left-wing, made up of the Communist Party, the Mapuche original peoples' movement, and several members of the former Constituent Assembly, elected before he was. This Assembly was tasked with drafting a new Constitution, which it did, and to submit it to the country for approval by referendum. Boric identified himself closely with the new draft, labeled by many as extreme. It went down to defeat by an overwhelming margin. Despite this tilt to the left, Boric's preference seems to be to follow in the steps of the above-mentioned predecessors, taking into account a series of new factors in the Chilean social and political equation. This amounts to what former Chilean economy minister and senator Carlos Ominami called the "new Chilean way."

It involves several differences with the previous Concertación or Nueva

Mayoría administrations that governed the country for more than 25 years. First, the present coalition considers itself closer to—and attempts to be more representative of—popular movements. President Boric made a point of designating a cabinet with a large female composition, including in some of the main jobs such as Interior, Foreign Affairs, spokesperson, and Defense. He has also staked out a number of stances that are heavily oriented toward climate change and protecting Chile´s highly-endowed but fragile environment, in response to activists and constitutional framers in this field. He may even have gone too far, insofar as one of the reasons the Constitution was roundly rejected by the September 4th plebiscite was an excessive attachment to environmental protection, including strong anti-extractivist articles, in the world´s largest copper producer. Copper still accounts for more than two thirds of total exports. Lastly, Boric made a point during his campaign and for the first months of his term, of addressing original peoples´—mainly Mapuche—demands concerning their lands, legal systems, traditions, language, and representation. Again, he may have exceeded himself. There is little doubt that the Constitution´s defeat was due to the welcome but strident inclusion of indigenous people´s rights, particularly a parallel legal system, this in a country with a tradition of an independent, respected, and honest judiciary.

In its potent message on women´s rights and its strong green inclination, the new Chilean administration resembles a "new" social democratic left, not unlike Germany or part of Scandinavia. Its approach to fiscal and social policy is also similar to traditional social democratic programs. Boric's first reform sent to Congress was a major tax initiative, seeking to raise the country's tax take by 5 points of GDP during his four-year term. The proceeds would be used to finance educational, health, and social security expenditures that were the main demands of the vast protest movement that exploded in Chile in late 2019. While the fate of this major overhaul of an undertaxed economy remains in doubt, this is a clear difference with the traditional Latin American left, which either spends money it does not have, nationalizes health and education institutions instead of expanding them with tax revenues, or simply does not spend at all.

Lastly, the "new Chilean way" has a much deeper respect for human rights and democracy that many other segments of the Latin American left don't have. The government has openly distanced itself from the Nicaraguan and Venezuelan dictatorships, though not from Havana. It has stubbornly refused to resort to repression in dealing with radical, semi-armed Mapuche groups, and has promised a major reform of the national police—known as Carabineros—especially in light of their dismal performance during the 2019 protests. It has sided with most western nations in condemning Putin´s invasion of Ukraine, and has shied away from the Mexican and Argentine attempts to weaken the Organization of American States and its human rights branch. Nor has it endorsed the quixotic search for an OAS without the United States and Canada, but with Cuba, Venezuela, and Nicaragua.

The other movements or governments that belong to this second category are, in order of the adequacy of their "fit," Gustavo Petro in Colombia, Luiz Inácio da Silva in Brazil, and Luis Arce in Bolivia. The latter has managed to extend his predecessor's orthodox economic policies, financing his ambitious and partly successful social programs with high natural gas and lithium prices, and to continue the expansion of indigenous peoples' majority rights in Bolivia. Not much more has happened, but that is a great deal. Growth for 2022 is forecast at nearly 4%, more than the regional average, and inflation, deficits, and the currency's value have remained under control. While Arce has not deviated from Evo Morales' constant confrontations with Washington on practically every issue under the sun, the conflicts have centered on foreign affairs, drug policy, and rhetoric. His democratic convictions, like those of Morales, are suspect, however, especially with the jailing and show trail of Jeanine Añez, the interim president who occupied the post from 2019 through 2021, between Morales' resignation and Arce's inauguration. She was sentenced to 10 years of prison for having violated the Constitution on becoming president in 2019. Many criticized the sentence and

Mapuche indigenous people hold flags of approval of the new Constitution in Temuco, Chile, on August 9, 2022. Chile's constitutional convention, made up of 154 members who are mostly political independents, spent a year creating the new document to replace the constitution adopted during the Augusto Pinochet dictatorship (1973–90). (MARIO QUILODRAN/AFP VIA GETTY IMAGES)

Brazilian former president (2003–10) and newly elected president Luiz Inacio Lula da Silva greets supporters during a campaign rally at the Praça da Liberdade in Belo Horizonte, Minas Gerais, Brazil, on October 9, 2022. (IVAN ABREU/NURPHOTO VIA GETTY IMAGES)

trial, and Arce's behavior in the whole affair leaves much to be desired regarding the rule of law. Still, his regime belongs in the category, if only barely.

This is also the case of Lula in Brazil. Although it is more difficult to determine exactly what policies he intends to follow in his third term, which begins on January 1, 2023, the constant reminders of his own achievements and policies during his first term allow one to expect a somewhat similar performance. If anything, he was criticized during his presidential campaign against Jair Bolsonaro for declining to introduce a forward-looking vision for the country. He limited himself to recalling "how well things went" the last time around. For his first four years as president, Lula espoused orthodox economic policies, showed practically no authoritarian bent, and pursued social policies that were both effective and sensibly financed. This was all less true during his second term, and not at all under his successor, but rhetoric and a few foreign policy excesses aside, his administration was difficult to distinguish from a typically social-democratic one.

The expectations for his third term are mixed, partly as a result of his discreteness during the campaign. This is particularly true regarding Lula´s

stances on what makes Boric, and partly Petro, such attractive examples. Once installed in the Planalto, the PT was never too enthusiastic about popular movements, social issues, and contributing to a different international legal order. Even today, matters such as women's rights, abortion, gay rights, the environment, and human rights in the region and the world, are questions the PT -and Lula- are not entirely comfortable with. Brazil is perhaps the epitome of an extractivist country: oil, iron, soybeans, coffee, sugar, beef, and orange juice are all decisive exports, and Lula has not entirely come to terms with the conundrum of administering that type of economy, while following an anti-extractivist course. The size of the evangelical churches and vote in Brazil, Lula's nostalgia for the Cuban dictatorship, the incredibly complex issue of the Amazon for Brazilian politics and traditions of sovereignty, all make a transformation of the PT's agenda on all of these matters a highly delicate affair.

Gustavo Petro addressed this same extractivist issue during his campaign, and in this domain at least, he is closer to the newer Latin American left than Lula is. The problem lies in the fact that Colombia depends more on commodity exports than Brazil does, and the

commodities it sells abroad are environmentally at least as confounding. Oil and coal are a major source of hard currency, but agricultural exports (coffee, cut flowers) and mining are also. How to limit or reduce commodity exports under these circumstances is not simple. The new president also follows the social democratic model by having submitted an ambitious tax reform to Congress on his first day in office, that includes higher taxes on mining and oil. And like Boric, he has made a point of linking his election and mandate to popular movements, ranging from students who participated in protests in 2020, to women and Afro-Colombians, represented, among others, by his Vice-President, Francia Márquez.

He has also stood by his democratic credentials and his outreach to the center by forging alliances with centrist parties like the old Liberal Party, and appointing moderate, veteran officials to his cabinet, while also including representatives of popular movements or of the left. In this sense, Petro seems to be treading a Chilean-like social-democratic path, despite his reputation for authoritarian behavior, especially as mayor of Bogotá earlier in the century. His quip after the Chilean referendum ended in a dramatic defeat for the new Constitution—"Pinochet is back"—was symptomatic of that shoot-from-the-hip approach.

Where Petro may have difficulties in wearing the same stripes as Boric is in connection with the dictatorships in Nicaragua, Cuba, and neighboring Venezuela. Like his predecessor Juan Manuel Santos, Petro seeks to negotiate a peace agreement with the last remaining, formal guerrilla group, the ELN. Most of their leaders are either in Cuba or in Venezuelan safe havens. It is practically impossible for a negotiation to take place without being on the best of terms with Havana and Caracas. Moreover, after nearly four years of no diplomatic relations with his neighbor, and nearly two million Venezuelans living in Colombia, and the official land border between the two countries practically shut, it makes sense for Petro to reestablish ties with Nicolás

Maduro. But doing so inevitably entails being friendly to him, distancing his government from the opposition—many of whose leaders live in Colombia—and in general acquiescing to the dictator's perpetuation in power. A bad sign regarding the dictatorships was the Colombian representative's absence during an August vote at the OAS condemning Daniel Ortega´s persecution of the church in Nicaragua. The three dictatorships go together, and it is difficult to be friends with one, without befriending all of them. Still, unless proved otherwise, for the reasons outlined above, and many others, such as Colombia's conservative soul which will ultimately constrain him, Petro fits in the social-democratic mold, and belongs to our second category.

Populist Countries

This is not true of Alberto Fernández in Argentina, mainly because of Peronism and the foreign debt—Argentina´s double whammy since the 1940s—and partly because of the division of power with one of his predecessors, now vice-president Cristina Fernández de Kirchner. A massive foreign debt inherited from the previous government has not facilitated matters, but high inflation, price and exchange controls, strident rhetoric, and flirting with Russia and China are all features that question his social-democratic credentials. The massive subsidies on public-owned services such as power, public transport, and gasoline are part of the old Peronist legacy, and Argentine heads of state only cut back on them at their own peril. When President Fernández finally reached an agreement with the International Monetary Fund on his country's 44-billion-dollar debt to the financial agency, Vice-President Fernández opposed it, and her son, Máximo, head of the Peronist caucus in Congress, resigned from the movement. While Alberto Fernández has not gone on a nationalization spree, on oil, power, lithium, and export taxes he belongs to the traditional Argentine mode. His democratic credentials remain largely intact, and on some social issues such as abortion, he has actually

adopted liberal stances. Conversely, he continuously declines to criticize the Latin dictatorships, and his stance on the invasion of Ukraine has been ambiguous at best. His term will be over in 2023; if Cristina is not condemned for a corruption scandal that threatens to ban her from holding public office in perpetuity, she will probably seek to succeed him. Her attacks on the judiciary and the media, during her two previous terms as president, place her clearly outside the social-democratic column. The two Fernándezes, as well as the Peronist movement itself since 1946, either belong in their own category (Borges famously quipped: "Peronism is neither good nor bad; it is incorrigible"), or fit in the populist column where they can be lumped in with López Obrador in Mexico.

Boric, Petro, Lula, and in their own way, the Fernández dupla, remain close to the center of the political spectrum, because their electoral systems include run-offs that cannot be won without alliances beyond their core electoral base. On the other hand, López Obrador governs only for his base, in a country with no second electoral round. One can win—Felipe Calderón did, in 2006—with barely more than a third of the vote. Because of his past PRI history and his own temperament, López

Obrador in Mexico is clearly prey to an authoritarian temptation. He constantly attacks the country's autonomous agencies, from the electoral authority to the transparency institute, and multiple civil society organizations, the media, and the intellectual community. The entire judicial branch of power, including the Supreme Court, have been victims of his daily, morning press conferences. He has militarized public security, and delegated myriad tasks to the Army and Navy, from building trains and bank branches to running the country's customs offices and ports and distributing medicines as well as arresting foreign migrants. Little has actually occurred in consequence, but as his administration winds down, the risks of a crackdown are growing. His energy policies are not only environmentally regressive, but seem highly statist and nationalist, harking back to the era of powerful, corrupt, and inefficient state oil and power monopolies. He has created a lithium state monopoly, discouraged or banned private generation of renewable energy sources, and sought food self-sufficiency, a strange goal for a country with scarce arable land.

He is thus no friend of environmentalists -hacking a 1500 km railway through the southeastern jungle and rainforest- nor of popular movements,

Andres Manuel Lopez Obrador salutes attendants after his virtual victory in the elections for the presidency of Mexico in the Media Center at the Hilton Hotel on July 1, 2018, in Mexico City, Mexico. (MANUEL VELASQUEZ/GETTY IMAGES)

5

be they women, the LGBTQ community or original peoples' groups. His government has made no progress on abortion nor on gay marriage—both legalized by the Supreme Court, not by Congress—nor on decriminalizing marijuana, all goals many of his supporters were expecting. He is said to have remarked once to Felipe González, the former Spanish, social-democratic prime minister, that the Spaniard was nothing better than a "shitty reformist," meaning not a revolutionary. He also confessed to novelist Gabriel García Márquez that the writer was the second most admirable figure of the Latin American 20th century, the first one being Fidel Castro.

While he wrapped up the negotiations with the United States and Canada on a new free-trade agreement (USMCA) in 2019, and has helped both Presidents Trump and Biden by keeping Central American migrants at bay, López Obrador seems unable to refrain from the type of anti-foreign and particularly anti-*Yanquí* rhetoric and gestures that classical Latin American populists have always espoused. He cannot leave USMCA, but he has placed the country in the middle of endless trade and investment conflicts with American, Canadian, and Spanish companies. He cannot be assimilated to the three dictatorships—Mexico is nowhere near that distress—but nor can he be grouped together with the social democratic Latin American left we have attempted to describe. He is closer personally, ideologically, and in terms of public policies, to Fernández in Argentina, to Castillo in Peru, and perhaps even to Xiomara Castro in Honduras. As I wrote back in 2006, history is destiny in these matters. Countries with strong populist traditions like Mexico with Lázaro Cárdenas, Argentina with Perón, and Peru with Haya de la Torre and APRA, tend to revive them.

Conclusion

There is no new pink tide in Latin America. There are different, contradictory, on occasion antagonistic governments in power or movements contending for it. What separates them

is more significant than what they have in common, apart from rhetoric and nostalgia. Their success or failure, however, depends on the lessons they learned—if at all—from the previous experience. There are many conclusions to be drawn from the first wave of left-wing governments at the turn of the century. Here are three.

First, the new boys on the block need to find a way to drag the Latin American elites toward more progressive, compassionate, and redistributive social policies. The point is not only to ensure that Congressional majorities—when they exist—approve these reforms, but also to persuade the rich and famous to support and even applaud them. In the first phase of the left in power, either many of the reforms were not carried out, or resistance to them watered down their effect. Health care systems, a major overhaul of public education, radical change in housing policy, and the consolidation of women´s rights -in a nutshell, the construction of a proper welfare state in Latin America, with the support of the powers that be, is the main challenge facing the social-democratic regimes today, and even the populist ones. The business community in Mexico refuses to clash with López Obrador, but simply disinvests and rejects any notion of tax reform. Consequently, it doesn´t happen. Boric and Petro began their administrations with attempts at tax reforms and in full consultation with the local elites, but the jury is still out on these efforts' success.

This goal will be difficult to achieve, because of the apparent absence of the "worst of evils," which always implies the existence of a "lesser evil." The social democratic welfare states in Europe were built on these premises. A social compact was the "lesser of two evils," the other being Bolshevism and a socialist revolution. There is no such danger today in Latin America—Cuba is a back-water—except for the type of social uprisings that took place in Chile, Colombia, and Ecuador. They may not suffice.

The second lesson the second season of the left must assimilate regards cor-

ruption. Justly or not, the left in power in El Salvador, Ecuador, Argentina, Bolivia, and Brazil during the century's initial decades was swamped by scandals of pay-offs, bribes, sweet-heart contracts and deals, and outright larceny. Presidents were jailed, impeached, exiled, or dethroned in disgrace. Some fought back, others fled, but the notion that the Latin American left, unlike the right, was honest, simply vanished. It wasn't more honest than anyone else. That is not to say that all of the members of the first pink tide were corrupt—certainly not the Chileans and Uruguayans—but rather that too many of them ended up being so. This surprised many people. The charges of corruption disappointed or dismayed the left's own followers, who could not believe that their beloved leaders of and from the people engaged in the same shenanigans the conservative elites had made Latin America famous for.

The logic of the left not believing that it could fall prey to the same temptations was simple. Its icons did not steal, because they represented the people. They had made courageous sacrifices, endured jail and torture, survived coups and repression, and it was obviously impossible for such heroes to succumb to traditional temptations. What the left refused to acknowledge was that the roots and deep causes of corruption in Latin America lay not in the elites' undeniable selfishness and greed—and thus was endemic only to them—but rather in a series of historical, cultural, social, and economic factors that affected the right, the left, the center, and practically everybody everywhere in the region. The fact that as early as the end of the 19th century, the only exceptions to widespread corruption were Chile, Uruguay, and Costa Rica, and that they remain so today, illustrates the pervasiveness and perpetuation of the scourge, more than the virtues of the exceptions. Without a pro-active, institutional and frontal attack on corruption, the new wave of the left will not be spared the sins of the older generation. There is no such thing as an ideological anti-corruption vaccine or gene.

The third conclusion the new left may draw from its predecessors' experience regards the region's role in the world. Latin America counts less today in the world concert than at any time in recent history. There are many reasons for this, but one in particular stands out. The continent has been unable to speak with one voice on virtually any issue at least since the late 1990s. Perhaps the last time the entire region, together with the United States and Canada, came together for a significant undertaking was the signing ceremony in Lima of the Inter-American Democratic Charter on 9-11. The condemnation of the military coup that overthrew Honduran president Mel Zelaya in 2010 perhaps marks another singular episode.

A likely explanation for this solitude may lie in the way foreign policy and international relations became heavily ideological from the early 2000s onward, largely as a result of Hugo Chávez's activism. Partly because of his opposition to FTAA and his founding of ALBA, partly because of his spats with Colombian neighbor and adversary Álvaro Uribe, partly in response to Cuban urging, the Venezuelan leader soon pit one part of Latin America against the other, mainly for ideological reasons, but often with consequences that went far beyond that. On climate change, on human rights, on the collective defense of democracy, and the fight against corruption and pandemics, on drug enforcement, the nations of Latin America split up into two or more camps. All camps were soon silenced in the international arena.

The new tide of the left must not repeat the same mistakes this time around. The international context is different, and more adverse. The rivalry or conflict between the United States and China, the Russian invasion of Ukraine, the possibility of a new pandemic and the proliferation of human rights violations across the globe all make a "de-ideologization" of these countries' foreign policies more necessary than ever. These factors also demand a sustained effort to unite behind the few global causes on which the region can make a difference.

Former Venezuelan President Hugo Chavez speaks during the inauguration of the Bolivarian Alternative for the Americas (ALBA) Summit on April 19, 2010, in Caracas. The summit was held coinciding with celebrations of the Bicentenary of the Venezuelan independence.
(MIGUEL GUTIERREZ/AFP VIA GETTY IMAGES)

One innovative idea in the regard has been put forth recently by a group of Chilean foreign policy specialists. Its title is perhaps not the most fortunate one, but the substance behind it is clearly imaginative. "Active nonalignment" brings back, of course, dismal memories of the 1950s and 1960s. But given the growing presence of China in South America, and the intensifying American insistence on limiting that presence, the notion of not taking sides on the main issues that confront the two super-powers seems attractive. If such an approach allowed the region as a whole to converge on certain causes—climate change, pandemics, reform of the United Nations, an international legal system—and to differentiate itself from Beijing and Washington, it would be doubly useful, enabling Latin America to reacquire a certain voice on the world stage on important issues. The foreign policy fiascoes we witnessed during the first wave would then perhaps be avoided by the second one. There is one exception to this approach. Unfortunately, given the reluctance of the left in Latin America to "name and shame" human rights violators in the region and elsewhere, this is a cause

on which that single voice will remain silent. A pity, since the vast majority of the sub-continent's inhabitants live in democracies, and denouncing human rights violations in Cuba, Venezuela, and Nicaragua, or China and Saudi Arabia, should be a priority, not a problem.

The shift to the left in Latin America since 2018, and chiefly this year, is a more complex process than the "second pink tide" slogan suggests. Nonetheless, there is a shift, one that was probably necessary and even inevitable. Much of what the first wave achieved withstood the passage of time, of rotation in power, the pandemic, and the ensuing recession. Some of its accomplishments evaporated, and many of its errors were costly, and durable. This new wave may last longer, achieve more, and eventually leave power in better shape than the previous one. Or, because of its diversity, its radicalism in some cases, and the social pressure for change, it may disappear from the scene soon, thanks to an undesirable backlash against incompetence, extremism, and an adverse international environment. All in all, an exciting dichotomy, and a fascinating time for the region.

discussion questions

1. Why do you think left-wing governments have been largely popular over the past 25 years in Latin America?

2. Was the first "pink tide" successful at governing Latin America? Do you think the second one will leave a similar legacy? Explain why or why not.

3. Why is the second "pink tide" even more diversified that the first, being split into three categories rather than two?

4. How should the United States interact with the three different types of left-wing governments? Explain for each category: dictatorships, social democracies, and populist countries.

5. Why do you think we only see "pink tides" in Latin America? Why are left-wing politics so popular in Latin America as compared to Europe?

suggested readings

Cameron, M. A, **Latin America's left turns: Politics, policies, and trajectories of change.** Lynne Rienner Publishers, July 31, 2010. 289 pp. This accessible look at Latin American politics explores how—and to what effect—diverse forces on the left have not only captured the imagination of vast swathes of the continent's population, but also taken hold of the reins of government.

Castañeda, Jorge, and Marco A. Morales, **Leftovers: Tales of the Latin American Left.** Routledge, New York, July 7, 2008. 268 pp. Castañeda explores the differences between the left-wing governments in Latin America during the early 2000s.

Crandall, Russell, **The United States and Latin America after the Cold War.** New York: Cambridge University Press, September 2008. 278 pp. The United States and Latin America after the Cold War looks at the almost quarter-century of relations between the United States and Latin America since the Berlin Wall fell in 1989. An academic and recent high-level U.S. policymaker, Crandall

argues that any lasting analysis must be viewed through a fresh framework that allows for the often-unexpected episodes and outcomes in U.S.–Latin American relations.

Levitsky, Steven, and Kenneth M. Roberts, **The Resurgence of the Latin American Left.** Johns Hopkins University Press, September 1, 2011. 496 pp. Latin America experienced an unprecedented wave of left-leaning governments between 1998 and 2010. This volume examines the causes of this leftward turn and the consequences it carries for the region in the twenty-first century.

Reid, Michael, **Forgotten Continent: A History of the New Latin America.** Yale University Press, November 14, 2017. 441 pp. An in-depth exploration of the current challenges countries across Latin America face and their priorities for the future.

Webber, J. R., & Carr, B, **The New Latin American left: Cracks in the Empire.** Rowman & Littlefield Publishers, October 4, 2012. 402 pp. This provocative, multidisciplinary work explores the dramatic resurgence of the Left in Latin America since the late 1990s.

Don't forget to vote!

Download a copy of the ballot questions from the Resources page at www.fpa.org/great_decisions

To access web links to these readings, as well as links to additional, shorter readings and suggested web sites,

GO TO www.fpa.org/great_decisions

and click on the topic under Resources, on the right-hand side of the page.

Famine: a renewed threat in the 21st century?

by Daniel Maxwell

A camp on the outskirts of Dollow, Jubaland, Somalia, in April 2022, where people displaced by the ongoing drought have gathered in search of aid. Somalia has suffered five failed rainy seasons in a row, making this the worst drought in decades, and 6 million people are in crisis levels of food insecurity. The problems are being compounded by the rising costs of food prices because of the Ukraine war. (SALLY HAYDEN/GETTY IMAGES)

In July 2011, the United Nations declared a famine in Somalia, which eventually killed an estimated 258,000 people. Eleven years later, in mid-2022, Somalia faces a nearly identical set of circumstances—in terms of both causes and consequences—regarding famine. And in 2022, Somalia isn't the only country to face these circumstances.

Famine has long been a scourge to humanity. According to South African economist Stephen Devereux, one of the foremost global experts on the topic, famine killed more than 70 million people during the 20th century—nearly as many as died in World War II. But after the 1960s, both the frequency and the magnitude of famine began to decline. Ethiopia (as well as other parts of northeastern Africa) suffered a major

famine in the mid-1980s, shaping the understanding and image of famine for a whole generation. But since then, only relatively limited—and increasingly rare—instances of famine occurred, until Somalia in 2011. Many observers thought that famine had been overcome: technological advances in food production and distribution, economic growth, and a much-expanded global humanitarian response capacity had combined to finally make the inevitability of famine a thing

DANIEL MAXWELL *is Henry J. Leir Professor in Food Security, Friedman School of Nutrition Science and Policy, and Research Director, Feinstein International Center, Tufts University, Boston, MA.*

South Sudanese refugees try to repair their hut in flooded waters from the White Nile at a refugee camp that was inundated after heavy rain near al-Qanaa in southern Sudan, on September 14, 2021. (ASHRAF SHAZLY/AFP VIA GETTY IMAGES)

of the past. Somalia 2011 was a harsh awakening. It was not clear at the time if it was a one-off occurrence resulting from a freak combination of factors or if it was the harbinger of changes to come in the context of massive shifts in the global food system and climate.

By 2017, the answer was clear, with two more famines declared (in northeastern Nigeria and South Sudan) and several "near misses" including a subsequent crisis in Somalia and, perhaps even more worryingly, a severe state of acute food insecurity in Yemen. Even if it did not quite reach the level of famine, a huge proportion of the population was affected—mostly from the effects of a brutal civil war being fought there.

With the onset of the global Covid-19 pandemic in 2020 and its knock-on effects on economies, employment, supply chains, and mobility, many observers feared the worst in terms of acute food insecurity, and indeed the World Food Program warned of "biblical famine." In actual fact, while the number of hungry people globally increased substantially, no instance of actual famine was found, but one

suspected case did emerge late in the year—again in South Sudan—but it was only peripherally related to the Covid pandemic, being driven instead by more localized factors including violent conflict and flooding associated with extreme weather events. But the effects of the Covid pandemic have proven to be long-lasting, and the global numbers of acutely food insecure people increased throughout 2021.

By 2022, the list of famine-risk countries had grown to six including Somalia once again, neighboring Ethiopia and South Sudan, as well as Yemen, Afghanistan, Nigeria. Other parts of the Sahel also faced the risk of famine in 2022, and the number of acutely food-insecure people reached its highest level in recorded post-World War history, and perhaps its highest level ever. By September, 2022, famine had been projected for parts of Somalia unless levels of humanitarian assistance were ramped up significantly, but no famine had been definitively declared yet.

Recognizing the increasing risk of these crises, the world faces a great decision: how can famines be prevented in the future? But several questions need to be addressed first: What is famine? What causes it, and why is it, once again, seemingly a major threat? Are the current drivers or causes of fam-

ine idiosyncratic and coincidental or long-term trends that signal the return of famine as a cause of global concern? These are all highly relevant questions in 2022.

Definition

"Famine" is a powerful word that elicits an emotive response in ways that "hunger," "food insecurity," or "humanitarian emergency" do not. More definitions of famine exist than can be accounted for in one paragraph, but very broadly, "famines" can be defined as extreme events in which a large number of people in a given population or geographic area suffer inadequate access to food, usually because their livelihoods have been damaged or destroyed. This leads to widespread malnutrition, ill health, and death. In most famines, deaths (politely referred to in contemporary discourse as "excess mortality") are frequently caused by infectious disease rather than outright starvation, in large part because severe malnutrition compromises human immune systems, making people—and especially young children who frequently comprise the majority of famine deaths—much more susceptible to diseases like measles or even common diarrhea. Over half the deaths in Somalia in 2011 were children under the age of five years.

Thus, famine is the confluence of a complex set of interactions that include an extreme lack of access to adequate food but manifested in acute malnutrition, ill health, and ultimately, excess mortality. While most contemporary definitions of famine include death or excess mortality, not all do—especially among populations actually at risk of famine. Affected populations may worry about destitution and the destructions of their livelihoods as much as they worry about hunger or death.

Researchers and humanitarians have long tried to precisely define famine—and the definition has long revolved around malnutrition and mortality, even though the proximate driver was recognized to be hunger. In the early 2000s, attempts to classify acute food insecurity as something specific and measurable (as opposed to

Before you read, download the companion **Glossary** that includes definitions, a guide to acronyms and abbreviations used in the article, and other material. Go to **www. fpa.org/great_decisions** and select a topic in the Resources section. (Top right)

"hunger," which had a political meaning but otherwise referred to a physical sensation that was impossible to quantify) resulted in an index or scale known at the Integrated Food Security Phase Classification or IPC. IPC was invented in Somalia to demonstrate graphically (to the warlords who ruled their own areas in the country at the time) why certain areas were receiving more food assistance than others. IPC ingeniously linked several measurable human welfare outcomes—including but not limited to food insecurity, malnutrition, and mortality—into an index of severity classifications (or "phases") which could then be mapped by geographic area, with each "phase" given an increasingly alarming color on the map. IPC analysis is now regularly conducted in over 50 countries in Africa, Asia, the Middle East, and the Latin America/Caribbean region.

Although the original intent of IPC was to analyze and map acute food insecurity more generally, it's definition of "Phase 5"—the most extreme end of the scale—has become the default technical definition of famine. Famine is defined by IPC as a combination of very poor human welfare outcomes in a given population: at least 20% of a given population with effectively no access to food (and all coping mechanisms exhausted); at least 30% of children under five suffering acute malnutrition (meaning a very low weight for the height of the child—the most common manifestation of malnutrition in a crisis); and a crude death rate of at least 2 persons dying per day for every 10,000 people in that population. Two deaths per day per ten thousand population might not sound like a lot of mortality, but it is eight to ten times the "baseline mortality" of the death rate under "normal" circumstances in most countries, and five to six time the "normal" death rate even in countries with extremely challenging public health limitations.

Recent experience has shown that frequently, not all these thresholds are likely to be breached at once, and it is actually extremely difficult to get data on all these indicators in famine

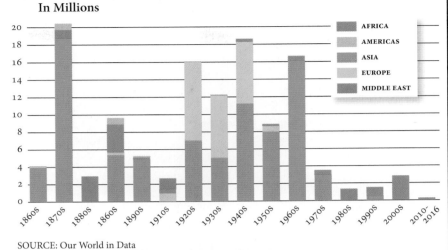

Fig. 1: Famine Mortality by Region and Decade: 1870–2010
In Millions

SOURCE: Our World in Data

Lucidity Information Design, LLC

conditions, in part because almost all contemporary famine or near-famine circumstances take place in wars or violent conflict, making it difficult to access affected populations, much less to carry out a statistically representative assessment of their conditions. Nevertheless, this is the standard definition of famine that is accepted today. It is worth pointing out that these indicators are all about current status and consist of rates (mortality) or prevalence (food insecurity and malnutrition). Historically, famines were often judged by total mortality, not by current status rates or prevalence.

This current technical definition of famine raises several concerns. First, many aspects of famine are not included in the technical definition: destitution, distress migration, breakdown of social institutions, and many others—the IPC definition reflects only current-status indicators focused on things that can be objectively measured and which have clear thresholds. But that may oversimplify famine.

Second, although the current definition includes a minimum population size (at least 10,000 people), it is based almost exclusively on the current severity of the crisis. But crises at a slightly lower level of severity than famine, but which affect a greater number of people or which last longer (or both) can result in much greater loss

of human life and livelihoods: loss of life can be heavy in IPC Phase 4, even if no "famine" is ever declared. This is precisely what happened in South Sudan with the limited famine that occurred there in 2017. While some 380,000 people died as a result of the crisis in in South Sudan between 2014 and 2018, only about one percent of the excess mortality in that crisis actually occurred during the "famine" as currently defined. In Somalia in 2011, the deaths of 258,000 human beings were attributed to the famine, but an estimated 43% of those deaths occurred before famine criteria were met and the actual famine was declared—and much of the remaining mortality occurred outside the areas declared to be in famine.

History

Famines have happened throughout human history, and indeed have often shaped history. The great potato famine in Ireland in the mid 1840s was so named because a potato blight caused the destruction of the subsistence crop on which Irish peasants relied, even though the more fundamental causes had to do with the nature of land tenure under British colonial rule. This led to massive displacement and flight from the country. Famine death and displacement not only depopulated Ireland—the country only recently regained its pre-famine population level,

6

China: A team of workers labouring in a stone quarry in heavy rain during the "Great Leap Forward" (1959–61). (PICTURES FROM HISTORY/GETTY IMAGES)

more than 150 years later—it also significantly reshaped the population of cities in the eastern United States, most notably Boston and New York.

Given the prominence of the Ethiopian famine in the mid 1980s in shaping the views of the current generation

An elderly woman holds flowers and candles to commemorate those who perished as a result of the Holodomor, the plague of hunger, during a memorial ceremony in Ukrainian city of Donetsk on November 26, 2010. (ALEXANDER KHUDOTEPLY/AFP VIA GETTY IMAGES)

regarding famine, many people believe famine has primarily occurred in Africa, but this is untrue. By far the biggest loss of life in famines in the past 150 years has been in Asia and Europe as depicted in Figure 1 (which does not include the Irish famine). Although often considered to be the result of crop failure and climatic hazards, famine has long been associated with either wars and violent conflict or totalitarian rule (or both). The Asian famines in the 1870s were triggered by droughts that we now understand to be a function of the El Niño Southern Oscillation or ENSO effect. The impacts of these droughts were significantly worsened by colonial policies and mismanagement of the consequences of the droughts, resulting in widespread loss of life. The aftermath of World War I and the Russian revolution saw widespread starvation in Europe, and again in the lead up to and during World War II. Stalinist policies of collectivization and attempts to erase a Ukrainian identity led to one of the worst famines of the 20th century—known as the Holodomor, which literally means "death by hunger" or "killing by starvation" in the Ukrainian language.

In terms of loss of human life however, the most serious famine of the 20th century was the "Great Leap For-

ward" famine in China, which started in the late 1950s and lasted, most experts agree, until about 1962 (thus it is depicted in Figure 1 across two different decades—had it all occurred in the same decade, the figure per decade as Figure 1 depicts them would have been twice as large!). Widespread drought in the 1970s in the Sahel region of West Africa led to famine deaths there, as did the Biafran war or the Nigerian civil war in the late 1960s up to 1970, though famine death totals in the 1960s were still predominantly in Asia.

With the decline in totalitarian government in the latter decades of the 20th century, the incidence of famine also declined as did the number of people dying from famine—but one final major famine did occur in North Korea in the mid 1990s. Given the impossibility of accessing affected populations in North Korea, the death toll is disputed—some estimates put it much higher than the estimate depicted in Figure 1. The early part of the 21st century saw almost no famine (though high mortality in places like the Democratic Republic of the Congo, which was at least partially related to hunger and malnutrition, and Darfur).

Causes

A number of explanations have been put forward for what causes famines.

Population growth. The cause of famine was long thought to be food shortages—interpreted as production failures or shortfalls—and population growth. The thinking of Thomas Malthus in 1809 long dominated most thinking and policy about famine. He postulated that population growth will always outpace technological advances in food production, meaning that in the medium to long term, some people were bound to starve to death—hence famines. Even as recently as the 1974 world food crisis, that kind of thinking tended to dominate both famine analysis and public policy. A lot of emphasis was put on the "population explosion" as the cause of the crisis. "There are too many mouths to feed!" screamed a September 1974 headline at the height of that global crisis.

Fig. 2a: Famine Deaths, 1870–2010

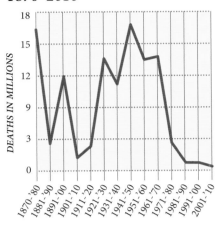

SOURCE: World Peace Foundation

Fig. 2b: Population Growth, 1870–2010

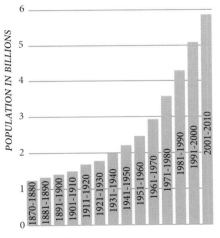

SOURCE: World Peace Foundation

Lucidity Information Design, LLC

The work of Alex de Waal (2018) demonstrates that the lack of relationship between population growth and famine in recent history. Figure 2 takes the same global data as Figure 1 but superimposes it over global population growth. While there might have been some correlation between population growth and famine deaths at one point in time, that relationship clearly falls apart over the past 60 years, and there is no linear relationship at all over the past 150 years.

Entitlement failures. It wasn't until the publication of Amartya Sen's famous book, *Poverty and Famine*, that famine came to be seen primarily as an issue of inadequate access to food, rather than an outright food shortage. Analysts had noted at least as far back as the great Irish famine that grain and livestock were being exported from Ireland even while its citizens were starving, which should have been enough to convince people that an outright food shortage wasn't causing the famine: the issue was that Irish peasants were too poor to purchase the food they needed, and the subsistence crop on which they relied had failed because of the potato blight. Sen argued that it was the entitlement to food (the ability to buy, grow, or in some other way access adequate food—through transfers or gifts for example) that was the problem, not necessarily an overall food availability problem.

Behavioral responses. Studying entitlements led observers to look at the behavioral responses of famine-affected people—a field a studies that came to be labeled "coping strategies." This perspective suggested that famines should be viewed as a process rather than simply an event. This revolutionized the understanding of famine dynamics and helped to birth the notion of famine early warning. But it didn't necessarily explain what caused the decline in entitlements.

Multi-hazard causation. Famine had long been associated with some kind of natural hazard—often drought, sometimes flood, sometimes a crop or animal disease (a bacterial blight in the case of the Irish famine)—and therefore with a production shock or a sharp decline in production. But it is also clear that famine is frequently associated with war and violent conflict. Most famines are triggered by a combination of factors, some of which might be natural hazards while others might be human made. And while some populations may be largely dependent on their own production for their consumption, most people in today's world are dependent on markets—both labor markets and food markets—for their access to adequate food and nutrition. And frequently, shocks such as droughts or conflict can rapidly change market conditions (the war in Ukraine in 2022 is an example). Shocks can drive the price of food up, and in many cases reduce the income that people depend on—dramatically reducing the purchasing power of vulnerable people.

That was precisely what happened in Somalia in 2011 (Figure 3). The amount of food that a could be purchased with one day's wages varied by regional labor market prior to the crisis but dropped between 50% and 80% by the height of the crisis and the declaration of famine in July 2011. Similar declines were noted for pastoralists who depended on selling their livestock to purchase food. In an emergency partially triggered by drought of course,

Fig. 3: Terms of Trade (Labor to Food) in Somalia: 2010–2012

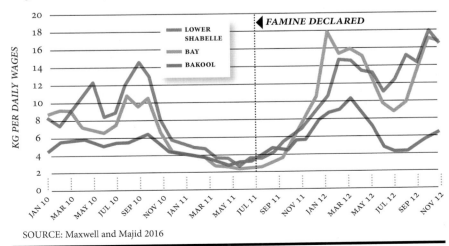

SOURCE: Maxwell and Majid 2016

Lucidity Information Design, LLC

View of a group of starving and emaciated children from the Biafra region standing together at a mission hospital during the Nigerian-Biafran civil war in Nigeria in August 1968. Members of the Igbo tribe rebelled in 1967 to demand a separate Republic of Biafra. The war and famine lasted until 1970, when the Biafran Republic forces surrendered to the nationalist government. (ROLLS PRESS/POPPERFOTO VIA GETTY IMAGESS)

food isn't the only life-giving necessity that becomes extremely expensive—the cost of water also doubled or tripled depending on location. The steep decline in purchasing power depicted in Figure 3 that happened in late 2010 was one indication of the severity of the crisis; the fact that purchasing power didn't improve for months was certainly one of the factors that tipped a "bad year" over into being an outright famine. But with the return of the rains in late 2011, rural labor markets recovered somewhat, and the price of imported grain dropped rapidly. These factors combined to improve purchasing power and bring the famine to an end.

Conflict. However, the common causal factor in almost all contemporary famines or "near famine" emergencies is war or conflict. Indeed, of the countries currently facing famine risk, almost all are in some kind of violent conflict (South Sudan, Somalia, Ethiopia, Nigeria, Yemen, parts of the Sahel) or in an immediate post-conflict transition (Afghanistan). Some of the effects of violent conflict are clear: people are displaced from their usual forms of livelihood, grain stores are looted, livestock are killed or stolen. Violent conflict frequently means that

not only are people displaced, but also have difficulty accessing assistance or alternative employment.

While sometimes starvation or famine may seem like simply the unfortunate outcome of violent conflict, it is also sometimes the intent. The use of hunger or starvation as a weapon of war is nearly as old as war itself—early references to this practice go back to Roman times. Starvation was used as a weapon by the Nazi "hunger plan" during World War II to starve an estimated 4 million Soviet citizens, including during the famous siege of Leningrad in 1941–42. Widespread famine, estimated to have resulted in more than a million deaths, was the result of the blockade of Biafran forces during the Nigerian civil war between 1967 and 1970, with much of the mortality in the final months of the siege. More recently, siege warfare was used to devastating effect during the Syrian civil war, with place names like Aleppo, Homs, and Eastern Ghouta becoming household words in the global press. There are accusations currently that Russia is weaponizing food in the invasion of Ukraine by blocking Ukrainian exports of wheat, maize, and sunflower oil, preventing Ukraine from getting

the income from its exports. This also makes the contemporary global food crisis significantly worse by pushing up the prices of these products, which has roiled global food markets well beyond these specific commodities.

Response failures. In his review of recent famine research, Stephen Devereux noted that contemporary famine could be classified into "old" and "new" famines. "Old" famines were those fundamentally triggered by climatic, environmental, or pest- and disease-related drivers and resulted primarily in production failures. "New" famines are those triggered by political crises and might include production shocks and likely the market failures noted in Sen's famous book, but also might fail to mitigate or prevent such crises or response failures.

The notion of response failure was new to the understanding of famine causation, but it wasn't a new concept. One of the key changes in public policy regarding famine and famine prevention (or at least preventing mass mortality) that grew out of the experience of the Sahelian and East African famines of the 1970s and 80s, together with the observation that famines are the result of a process and not simply unexplained events, was the birth of famine early warning.

Early warning was the notion that, if famines were the result of identifiable processes, then causal factors could be systematically tracked and used to predict when and where famine were likely to occur. And they could trigger public policy interventions to mitigate the causal factors, or at least provide timely assistance to affected populations. The most famous of these efforts was the U.S.-funded Famine Early Warning System Network or FEWS NET, which began in 1985. FEWS NET combines IPC-style analysis with the tracking of market trends, seasonal climatic forecasting, and other causal factors predict food security status and trends, and it has been shown over time to be quite accurate in its forecasts.

In its early days, the rationale for FEWS NET was that the United States was the major humanitarian donor in the world, and the main tool at its disposal at that time was food aid—an in-kind transfer of food to famine-affected, or in many cases, chronically food-insecure populations. Food aid in that era came primarily from the United States and other industrialized, agriculture-exporting countries, and was used for a variety of purposes besides famine prevention. For the chronic cases, projecting requirements was not difficult, but for a rapidly developing emergency (whether or not it deteriorated into famine by today's definition), food aid was the primary—and in many cases practically the only—means that governments or humanitarian agencies had at their disposal. But food aid was a very unwieldly mechanism to respond to an urgent crisis: it had to be purchased, shipped thousands of miles both internationally across oceans and domestically within affected countries before it could be distributed to affected populations. This process required as much as five months, meaning that such crises had to be predicted five or six months ahead of time, so that assistance could be mobilized and, even if a crisis couldn't be prevented, at least human life could be protected. At least, that was the idea behind famine early warning, and as noted, the predictive component has worked fairly well. And of course, recent advances in machine learning and artificial intelligence are adding substantial analytical capacity to early warning as well.

But the policy response component has not worked as well. As early as 1995, it was clear that while early warning was providing reasonably accurate information about the likelihood of famine or acute food security and nutrition crises, policymakers (governments, donors, humanitarian agencies) were repeatedly failing to act on this information to prevent these crises or at least mitigate the human suffering caused—a phenomenon that came to be known as the "early warning/response gap" or as "response failure". This phenomenon of clearly predicting a food security crisis without a corresponding response has been noted repeatedly in food security crises since then, including during the current set of crises.

In some cases, these response failures have legitimately been the result of poor information, albeit rarely. More likely they resulted from institutional mistrust of figures generated, or because of political and security constraints. In Somalia in 2011, it was well known that food aid in particular was being diverted by conflict actors, and one of the main conflict actors was Al Shabaab, an Islamist group affiliated with Al Qaeda. Any aid agency that was responsible for aid leakage to Al Shabaab faced both the risk of prosecution under laws such as the U.S. Patriot Act, and also massive reputational risk (for "abetting terrorism"). This led to widespread aversion by humanitarian agencies to respond robustly to the crisis until a legal work-around was established (which only happened after the famine was declared).

Limited understanding of famine dynamics. Even if understood as a process, the actual dynamics of famine were not well understood. The understanding of these dynamics has improved over recent years as well. In an influential paper, Paul Howe added a component to our understanding of famine that up to that point had simply been noted as a kind of idiosyncratic factor. He identified five steps in the process leading into and out of famine. These include an initial "pressure" (or causal factors combined with underlying vulnerabilities), which tips a particular population into food insecurity and/or malnutrition. But some other

factor, labeled the "hold," keeps that pressure in place long enough to begin to force negative feedback loops between food consumption, livelihoods, malnutrition, and disease ("self-reinforcing dynamics") that lead to the actual "famine system" itself— before some "rebalancing" leads to a reduction in mortality (Figure 4). While early warning has long focused on what Howe labeled the "pressure" and the "self-reinforcing dynamics" leading to a famine, it was the notion of the "hold" that helped to crystalize some of the dynamics that were recurrent but not always noted in famine analysis, or were only noted in an idiosyncratic way (for example, in Somalia in 2011, it was the access and movement constraints imposed by Al Shabaab, along with the constraints of the counter-terrorism regulations by Western donors that constituted the "hold" that led to that famine).

An earlier paper by Howe (2006) had noted that the policy priority of states, armed groups, and humanitarian actors also significantly shaped the nature of famine prevention or response.

Current Situation

Even though all this is known and established, 2022 has once again seen the rise in numbers of acutely food insecure people—to nearly 200 million.

Figure 5 depicts the global food crisis map from mid-2022 from FEWS NET.

Table 1 shows how the total number

Fig. 4: **Howe's "Famine System" Model**

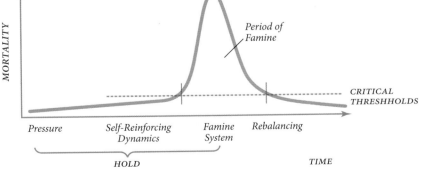

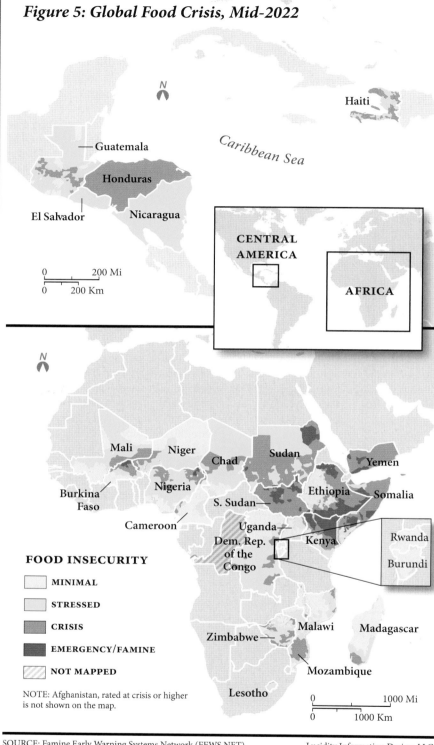

Figure 5: Global Food Crisis, Mid-2022

FOOD INSECURITY

- MINIMAL
- STRESSED
- CRISIS
- EMERGENCY/FAMINE
- NOT MAPPED

NOTE: Afghanistan, rated at crisis or higher is not shown on the map.

SOURCE: Famine Early Warning Systems Network (FEWS NET)

Lucidity Information Design, LLC

Table 1: Number of Acutely Food Insecure (IPC P3+) People: 2016–2022

	2016	2017	2018	2019	2020	2021	2022
Total IPC P3+ (Millions)	108	124	113	135	155	161	193
IPC Phase 5 (Thousands)	ND	ND	ND	ND	401	510	584

* Two actual famines declared (one retrospectively)
** One "famine likely" declared
SOURCE: FAO and WFP 2022

Lucidity Information Design, LLC

and, once again, pushed the number of acutely food-insecure people higher by nearly 20 million—mostly caused by the lockdowns and the economic knock-on effects. One of the major sources of income in food-insecure countries such as Yemen or Somalia is remittances from a global diaspora sent back to the home communities that migrants have left behind. But the kinds of employment opportunities available to these migrants (mostly in the Gulf states in the case of Yemenis, practically everywhere in the case of Somalis) were among those hardest hit by the pandemic and the lockdowns—resulting in an immediate cessation of remittance incomes.

While this led to a good deal of worry, in fact, only one "famine likely" was identified in 2020, quite late in the year, in southeastern South Sudan, and it was mostly driven by violent conflict combined with excessive flooding in back-to-back years. The year 2021 was mostly dominated by the fear of a famine in the warn-torn Tigray Region in Ethiopia, compounded by a near total blockade of the region for much of the year. Given the extreme constraints on access, little humanitarian response was possible, adding to the fears of a famine, but because of the same constraints, little current-status information about the population was available.

The year 2022 began with some of the highest numbers of food-insecure people ever recorded. Global food

of people needing food aid (IPC P3+) has increased over recent years, including the number of people in IPC Phase 5 where numbers are available.

In mid-2022, an estimated 26 million children under 5 years old in these same, crisis-affected populations were acutely malnourished. Five million of these were severely wasted and at immediate risk of dying.

In 2020, of course, the Covid-19 pandemic added a novel causal factor prices had been ticking upwards since the beginning of the pandemic and by early 2022 had reached levels equivalent to the prices in 2011 (which saw not only the famine in Somalia, but also the "Arab Spring," which was driven by many factors, a key trigger being the extremely inflated price of wheat—and therefore bread, the staple food of urban populations across the Middle East and North Africa). Then Russia invaded Ukraine, roiling markets and causing the prices of wheat and maize to skyrocket.

Nearly all countries facing a severe food security crisis are dependent on imports, so any price increases on global markets are quickly transmitted to local populations in food crisis. The price and availability (of both wheat and maize) was the most obvious, but this shortly led to spill-over effects as consuming nations began to switch to other, less expensive staple grains, boosting price levels across nearly all food commodities.

Second and less obvious was that many of the food insecure, wheat-dependent countries are in the Middle East and North Africa, which has a relatively short supply route from Black Sea ports in Ukraine and Russia. But alternative markets were much more distant—in North America, Argentina, or Australia. Third, as a major exporter of petroleum, Russia immediately drove the price of shipping higher in response to sanctions against it. And finally, in an effort to secure domestic consumption, several countries introduced export bans on wheat (India) and vegetable oil (Indonesia).

All of this sent the number of acutely food-insecure people spiraling upwards once again, to nearly 200 million (but note that these latest numbers are estimates, not based on new assessments). The World Food Program estimated in May that the cost of its operations had increased by 44% since the war started in February and large funding deficits for humanitarian response are now almost universal. The global Humanitarian Response Plan (which of course includes more than just food and nutrition support) was only 30% funded as of mid-July, and that was after some

major donors had increased their allocation following an assessment of the impact of the invasion.

These challenges combined with drought conditions in the Sahel, and a fourth straight failed rainy season in the Greater Horn of Africa led to a massive drought emergency, primarily affecting Ethiopia, Somalia, and even Kenya—a country that is not usually a source of worry about famine. The Horn of Africa is now suffering it fifth poor rainy season in a row, which is unprecedented in recent, recorded history." These countries were still recovering from the Covid-19 pandemic and the desert locust upsurge. In addition, Ethiopia, South Sudan, and Somalia remained mired in conflict. Other countries in Central and Southern Africa were affected as well. But people everywhere were affected by the rapid increase in the price of food.

Although no new famines (by IPC criteria) have been declared, 2022 looks set to be perhaps the worst year on record for acute food security crises. Already, the number of people in need is greater than in any year on record. Recent reports suggest that the October-to-November rains in the Greater Horn of Africa may also be below average, implying that for several countries this crisis could be quite prolonged—in sharp contrast to the relatively rapid end to the 2011 famine.

There remains some fear that 2022 may well see a series of protracted crises like those mentioned above in which the IPC thresholds for famine are not quite reached (or for which data doesn't even exist) but in which a much larger population is in an emergency for a much longer period of time than has been the case in the recent past. Total mortality from a series of such food security and nutrition crises could well exceed that of recent famines, without "famine" ever having been found or declared … and of course, without the emotive power of that word to provoke a more robust response.

Policy options for famine prevention and response

Adequate knowledge and experience exist to prevent famine and certainly to prevent mass mortality in food and nutrition crises. The question is about the political will to utilize several tools in a timely way. Four of those tools are discussed below: famine early warning, humanitarian response, anticipating and mitigating causal factors, and accountability and preventing the use of hunger as a weapon.

Famine early warning. Improved information and early warning have clearly been one of the success stories in the fight against famine. Very few if any contemporary food and nutrition crises—let alone actual famines—have come as a complete surprise. Forecasts might differ (predicting some seasonal weather outcomes always has a degree of uncertainty and predicting other shocks—particularly conflict—is never straightforward). There are instances (North Korea in the 1990s, Tigray in 2021) where governmental authorities

do not allow assessments of famine conditions, so the details are sometimes vague. But by and large, information is not the constraint to preventing famine—the problem is whether early warning information is acted on..

Humanitarian response. For most of human history, if there has been any response to famine, the attempt has been limited to containing the crisis and trying to prevent human suffering and death (of course, in some cases, causing death was the intent!). Traditionally, this has been in the form of providing food assistance—and between the end of World War II and the turn of the 21st century, this was almost entirely in the form of in-kind food aid: maize or wheat grown in the American Midwest or other exporting nation and shipped to the affected location. Following the Indian Ocean tsunami in 2004, the use of cash transfers—rather than food transfers—became more common. The prevalence

Mothers wait for high nutrition foods and health services at Tawkal 2 Dinsoor camp for internally displaced persons (IDPs) in Baidoa, Somalia, on February 14, 2022. Desperate, hungry and thirsty, more and more people are flocking to Baidoa from rural areas of southern Somalia, one of the regions hardest hit by the drought that is engulfing the Horn of Africa. (YASUYOSHI CHIBA/AFP VIA GETTY IMAGES)

of in-kind food aid was driven more by supply side considerations than careful consideration of whether it was the best resource: it was a resource that the United States and other food exporting countries could make available cheaply and it helped to prop up domestic producer prices—a big political concern in the United States and other food exporting countries between the 1950s and the 1990s. But cash, particularly with the globalization of the banking industry, could be transmitted more or less instantaneously (in contrast to the months it takes to ship food), supported local markets (rather than addressing surplus-supply issues in exporting countries), and enabled people to address their own needs (rather than simply assume they needed food).

The World Food Program was mostly absent from affected parts of Somalia in 2011, so the infrastructure for delivering in-kind food aid didn't exist, and cash was used instead—and had a very successful impact. Cash is now a much more dominant form of humanitarian assistance—both to protect food security and for other objectives such as shelter, water, health care, etcetera. Sometimes this kind of support is provided in the form of a voucher that can be exchanged for goods or services, providing donors some assurance that it will be spent on the intended form

of support (for instance, food vouchers must be spent on food).

Along with the switch to cash, support to malnourished children has also been revolutionized through the use of ready-to-use therapeutic foods (RUTFs). A more community-based approach to managing acute malnutrition has been developed in which mothers or care givers are taught to use the RUTFs and other basic measures of nutritional care. Unless the child is also gravely ill, s/he does not need to be admitted to a residential care facility (which required the mother or care giver to stay with the malnourished child—at the expense of caring for her other children). Together with improvements in coordination and other technical responses, humanitarian assistance has improved dramatically in the 21st century, but it has also become more expensive to provide, and in nearly all cases involving famine, faces severe constraints on access.

Anticipating and mitigating causal factors. While humanitarian assistance has primarily been reactive, new initiatives, based on improved early warning, are attempting to be much more anticipatory in nature, with "early" or "anticipatory" action becoming major initiatives in recent years. This means acting on early warning to prevent or mitigate a crisis, not simply preparing to respond to it. Early or anticipatory

action might provide cash assistance to mitigate the effects of a shock (before it becomes a humanitarian emergency) or help people protect their livelihoods and assets, enabling them to weather the shock themselves. Frequently it takes the form of "crisis modifiers" or other flexible funding that can be utilized to quickly respond to worsening circumstances before they get out of hand, without having to conduct new assessments, propose new projects, etcetera. With the growth of social safety net programs to deal with chronic poverty and hunger, an increasingly effective measure is to enable those programs to be "shock responsive" or to expand in capacity and coverage in times of crisis to include people acutely affected by drought or other shocks—even if they can manage on their own in "normal times." Strong evidence suggests that intervening earlier is not only more effective in preventing famine and the human damage that famine causes, it is also less expensive to prevent the deterioration into famine than to wait and deal with widespread malnutrition and illness.

The World Bank and the UN Office for the Coordination of Humanitarian Affairs (OCHA) launched major initiatives in 2018 to link improved early warning to both rapidly implementable contingency plans and non-traditional sources of finance including private sector insurance and disaster bonds. This kind of preparedness has been shown to be highly effective in some kinds of crises though the magnitude of crises faced in 2022 likely require anticipatory action at a much larger scale than has been available to date. This also is linked to longer term programs aimed at building resilience at the household and community levels—including risk management capacity to enable local communities to better withstand shocks without external assistance.

Accountability and preventing the use of hunger as a weapon. Much of the debate about how to prevent famine from recurring revolves around accountability: famines don't just happen; someone either causes them or, at a minimum, allows them to occur despite knowing they are happening or likely to happen. So, mechanisms to hold conflict actors, policymakers and humanitarian actors accountable have become increasingly important. At the same time, attempts have been made to deal with conflict drivers of famine in a way similar to how anticipatory action deals with natural hazards. The longest standing of these tools is International Humanitarian Law (IHL) under which the use of food or hunger as a weapon is considered a war crime. But it is incredibly difficult to demonstrate, to the degree of certainty necessary for a court to accept, that food is intentionally being used as a weapon.

A different approach was the unanimous passage of UN Security Council Resolution 2417 in May of 2018, which noted the links between violent conflict and hunger—and famine. Its passage was a victory for advocates seeking accountability for starvation, but its impact to date beyond its reporting function has been unclear. International advocates as well as humanitarians on the ground are seeking ways of leveraging the power of a UN Security Council resolution to prevent famine and food security crises, but the actual effects are still uncertain. Global Rights Compliance, a group of international lawyers concerned with the issue, notes that "while the normative framework has been strengthened, compliance has deteriorated." In brief, while efforts are being made, much remains to be done to prevent famine—whether resulting from acts of commission or omission—in conflict and warfare.

Averting famine in the future

So, what do we need to do to avert famine in the future? Given the status of budgets in 2022, careful prioritization and devotion of scarce resources to the most affected is going to be necessary. In the medium- to longer-term, we must focus on several things:

First, we must acknowledge famine as a political crisis as well as a humanitarian crisis. If conflict is the common causal factor, improved means of working in conflict must be developed.

Workers fill bags with rice inside a World Food Program warehouse, in Gonaives, Haiti, Aug. 5, 2022. (ODELYN JOSEPH/AP IMAGES)

These include better conflict analysis, stopping the politicization of humanitarian analysis and assistance, and building stronger support for IHL—not only among states but, critically, among non-state armed groups. It is equally important to address and reduce conflict and, ultimately, to peacefully resolve conflict, leveraging tools like UNSCR 2417. All this requires high-level leadership.

Second, we have to make some hard decisions about who leads in famine prevention—especially in conflict emergencies where governments are at war with their own people or are parties to conflict that drive the food security crisis. Most traditional efforts to counter famine have been led largely by international humanitarian agencies—the UN and international NGOs. But experience has repeatedly shown these organizations face severe access constraints in famine, often introducing inappropriate assistance or relying on inappropriate methods. Major efforts at the localization of humanitarian action are now a policy imperative, and nowhere needed more urgently than in addressing famine.

Third, other drivers of famine remain, and we must do a better job of preparedness and be more adept at anticipating crises, intervening early, and building resilience. This means paying attention not only to early warning, but

also to what information is telling us more broadly: the fact that we haven't had a declared famine (yet!) in 2022 is good, but we need to pay attention to the hundreds of thousands of people who could be killed by hunger, malnutrition, and resulting diseases this year even if "famine" (by contemporary criteria) is not declared.

Finally, we must prioritize accountability. The foremost famine analysts of this generation (de Waal and Devereux) both note that famine will never be stopped until those who cause it (or who allow it to happen) are held accountable. UNSCR 2417 was a unique statement about accountability in this regard, as was the 2019 amendment to the Rome Statute extending prohibitions on the use of starvation as a weapon to non-international armed conflict or civil wars. Even the 2020 Nobel Peace Prize awarded to the World Food Program implicitly recognizes the importance of multilateral action and accountability. So, there is a strong international ethical consensus on accountability for famine and starvation. These tools need to be leveraged more, and while there is a strong need to be in dialogue with affected communities and local organizations, leadership here has to come from the top.

If we're able to do these things, perhaps we can once again turn the tide against famine.

discussion questions

1. The Famine Early Warning System Network has been successful at predicting coming famines; however, policymakers have often failed to act on this information to prevent these famines. How can policymakers be convinced to act?

2. Should the West step in and aid countries in the Middle East and Africa that are no longer receiving food shipments from Ukraine and Russia? Why or why not?

3. Is the sending of cash as a humanitarian response a step forward from the use of food aid? Why or why not?

4. Should the use of hunger as a weapon be considered a war crime? Why or why not?

suggested readings

Applebaum, Anne, **Red Famine: Stalin's War on Ukraine**. First United States edition, New York: Doubleday, October 10, 2017. 496 pp. An exploration of the history of the Holodomor.

Buchanan Smith, M., and S. Davies, **Famine Early Warning and Response –the Missing Link.** London: IT Publications, 1995. 228 pp. Drawing on case studies from Ethiopia, Sudan, Chad, Mali, and Kenya (focusing on Turkana district) during the drought years of 1990–91, this book investigates why early warning signals were not translated into timely intervention. It examines, for the first time, the role of early warning information in decision-making processes, particularly within key donor agencies. The book concludes with practical policy recommendations, on who "owns"early warning information, how it is used, and looks at how to speed up the logistics of emergency relief.

Devereux, Stephen, **Famine in The Twentieth Century**. Working Paper 105. Institute of Development Studies, January 1, 2000. Devereux argues that if famine is to be eradicated during the 21st century, it requires not only technical capacity in terms of food production and distribution, but also substantially more political will, at national and international levels, than has been seen to date.

Hedlund, Kerren, Nisar Majid, Daniel Maxwell, and Nigel Nicholson, **Final Evaluation of the Unconditional Cash and Voucher Response to the 2011–12 Crisis in Southern and Central Somalia**. London: Humanitarian Outcomes, 2014. This report sets out to determine the effectiveness of the unconditional cash and voucher interventions in southern and central Somalia. This evaluation considers the broader context that led to the failure of the humanitarian community to respond in a timely and adequate manner to the suffering of the Somali people. And the ever-present dilemma of delivering humanitarian assistance and fueling an aid economy where aid, and the vulnerable populations for whom it was intended, are exploited by those with power.

Maxwell, Daniel, and Kirsten Gelsdorf, **Understanding the Humanitarian World**. London: Routledge, May 8, 2019. 222 pp. Maxwell and Gelsdorf highlight the origins, growth, and specific challenges to, humanitarian action and examine why the contemporary system functions as it does. They outline the main actors; explore how they are organized and look at the ways they plan and carry out their operations. Interrogating major contemporary debates and controversies in the humanitarian system, and the reasons why actions undertaken in its name remain the subject of so much controversy, they provide an important overview of the contemporary humanitarian system and the ways it may develop in the future.

Waal, Alex de., **Famine That Kills: Darfur, Sudan. 2nd ed**. New York: Oxford University Press, January 13, 2005. 288 pp. In 2004, Darfur, Sudan, was described as the "world's greatest humanitarian crisis." Twenty years previously, Darfur was also the site of a disastrous famine. *Famine that Kills* is a seminal account of that famine, and a social history of the region. In a new preface prepared for this revised edition, Alex de Waal analyzes the roots of the current conflict in land disputes, social disruption and impoverishment.

Don't forget to vote!

Download a copy of the ballot questions from the Resources page at www.fpa.org/great_decisions

To access web links to these readings, as well as links to additional, shorter readings and suggested web sites,

GO TO www.fpa.org/great_decisions

and click on the topic under Resources, on the right-hand side of the page.

Iran at a crossroads
by Lawrence G. Potter

A protest to mark 40 days since the death in custody of 22-year-old Mahsa Amini, whose tragedy sparked Iran's biggest antigovernment movement in over a decade in Saqez, Kurdistan Province, Iran, on Oct. 26, 2022. (ZUMA PRESS, INC. / ALAMY)

In the fall of 2022, Iran was at a crossroads. The most serious and widespread anti-government demonstrations since the revolution were set off by the arrest and death in police custody of a young woman, 22 year old Mahsa Amini, last September 16. She was charged with "bad hijab," i.e. improper veiling. Although the government shut down the internet, dramatic video of the protests, many led by women, and the lethal response by security forces, aroused worldwide anger and concern.

Two months on, the protests had spread to some 100 cities throughout Iran and over 300 people had been killed. By early November over 14,000 people had been arrested, and over 1,000 demonstrators were on trial. This level of defiance and anger was something not seen before, and the govern-

ment's brutal crackdown so far has not deterred the men and women protesting. The slogan of the revolt, "Woman, Life, Freedom" [*Zan, Zendegi, Azadi*], reverberated throughout Iran. Suddenly, the hijab, or head covering, which has been mandatory for all women to wear since April 1983, became the most important issue in the country.

The protest focused on cultural reform and an end to

LAWRENCE G. POTTER *teaches in the School of International and Public Affairs at Columbia University and was deputy director of Gulf/2000, a major research and documentation project on the Persian Gulf states based there, from 1994 to 2016. He is a longtime contributor to* GREAT DECISIONS *and published "The Persian Gulf: Tradition and Transformation" in FPA's* Headline Series *Nos. 333–334 (Fall 2011).*

A protester holds a portrait of Mahsa Amini during a demonstration in Istanbul on September 20, 2022. (OZAN KOSE/AFP VIA GETTY IMAGES)

key pillars of the state, such as the "Islamic" nature of its rule and suppression of women. Everywhere women were ripping off their headscarves and burning them, and even publicly cutting their hair in protest. Schoolgirls removed their veils and chanted anti-government slogans. Original demands of justice for Mahsa and making hijab optional morphed into demands calling for the downfall of the Islamic Republic. This has quickly led to a crisis of legitimacy for the regime.

There has been widespread support for the protesters in Iran, and rallies have been held in cities around the world to show solidarity. Although leaderless, by mid-November major groups such as students, teachers, and factory workers, and those in the oil industry, had gone on strike, as shops and bazaars closed, recalling tactics that helped to bring down the shah. The uprising spread to the most prestigious school in the country, Sharif University of Technology in Tehran, where many students were beaten or shot. Demonstrators chanted, "Death to the Dictator" (a reference to the Supreme Leader, Ayatollah Ali Khamenei) and "We don't want an Islamic Republic." The question is, would this lead to the downfall of the revolutionary regime, and if so, what would replace it? What should, or could, the U.S. do about it?

Iran, which had appeared more stable than many other Middle Eastern states, is riven by serious domestic problems. They include mismanagement of the economy, widespread corruption and a continuing brain drain due to lack of opportunity. The government blundered a response to the covid crisis (with 7.5 million cases and 145,000 deaths), partly due to a refusal to import western-made vaccines. A critical environmental crisis and water shortage, with over 70% of the country currently suffering from an extreme drought, has had dire effects throughout the country. Today more than a third of people live in poverty, and there is a feeling of hopelessness about the future – in a survey last July, half of respondents aged 18 to 29 said they would leave if they could.

Domestic tension increased after the inauguration of Ebrahim Raisi as president of Iran in August 2021. The election was widely regarded as being rigged, with only half of eligible voters going to the polls. Hardliners are now in charge of all branches of government, and reformers who played a prominent role in earlier years have been sidelined. Ayatollah Khamenei accused the United States and Israel of supporting the demonstrators and so far has not offered any concessions.

Historians note that, even under the monarchy, Iranians have a history of rebelling against the government and demanding their rights. Coalitions uniting secular and religious forces have repeatedly demanded change and sometimes gotten it. The best example is the Iranian revolution of 1978-79, but there is ample precedent, including the Tobacco Revolt in 1890-91, the period of national awakening when the first constitution was granted, 1906-11, the tumultuous events of 1952-53 when Prime Minister Mohammad Mosaddeq almost overthrew the shah, and an anti-shah uprising inspired by Ayatollah Khomeini in June 1963. Since the Islamic revolution, the most serious threat to the regime came in 2009 with the rise of the Green Movement to challenge the outcome of the re-election of President Mahmoud Ahmadinejad. This is when chants of "Death to the Dictator" were first heard in Iran.

Unlike the middle-class composition of the Green Movement, which was focused on the capital, Tehran, widespread revolts in 2017 and 2019 were drawn from more lower-class elements in the provinces. They were motivated by a variety of economic issues, such as teacher's salaries, water shortages, delays in paying wages, high gas prices and inflation.

The current revolt is led by a new generation that feels it has nothing left to lose. As opposed to the time of the revolution and the Green Movement, today there is no organized opposition, a program for change or even identifiable leaders, making it hard for the government to stop the uprising. The protesters lack the armed support that was available to the opposition during the revolution. There is new resistance by artists, as shown by the protest anthem by Shervin Hajipour called "Baraye" [meaning "for" or "because of"]. This highlights what people are fighting for and is made up of many contributions from a Twitter hashtag.

Before you read, download the companion **Glossary** that includes definitions, a guide to acronyms and abbreviations used in the article, and other material. Go to **www. fpa.org/great_decisions** and select a topic in the Resources section. (Top right)

The turmoil in Iran comes at a dangerous time in the Middle East, with a rise in sectarian tensions and increased Iranian intervention in nearby states with weak governments, such as Iraq and Syria. Arab monarchies in the Persian Gulf, as well as Israel, regard Tehran as their primary threat. An Iranian attack on Saudi Arabian oil tanks and pipelines in September 2019 shocked the Gulf monarchs and called into question the value of U.S. protection. Iran recently sold a large number of attack drones to Russia for use in Ukraine, angering the U.S. and European states.

Since the revolution Israel has been an ideological enemy and favorite rhetorical target. It is believed to have carried out a number of spectacular attacks on Iranian security targets. They include the assassination of Iran's top nuclear scientist, Mohsen Fakhrizadeh, in November 2020, two explosions at a key nuclear facility in Natanz in July 2020 and April 2021, and the assassination of Al Qaeda's second in command in Tehran in August 2020. Clearly, Israel has inside information and collaborators inside the country. "The attacks have also cast a cloud of paranoia over a country that now sees foreign plots in every mishap," according to the *New York Times*.

So far regional states have not made any significant efforts to engage Iran, although last spring there were quiet talks in Baghdad between Iran, the UAE and Saudi Arabia. But neither side is ready to engage in confidence-building measures, let alone adopt Iran's solution, a region-wide security organization including all littoral states that it would dominate.

When President Barack Obama met with Saudi King Salman in Riyadh in April 2016, he pressed the king to "share" the neighborhood with Iran—an appeal the king did not appreciate. Despite talk of "pivoting to Asia," U.S. forces remain in the Gulf and engage in a dangerous cat-and-mouse game with Iran.

Progress has now stalled on the issue of greatest interest to outsiders, resuming the nuclear deal reached between Iran, the U.S. and other states. The deal

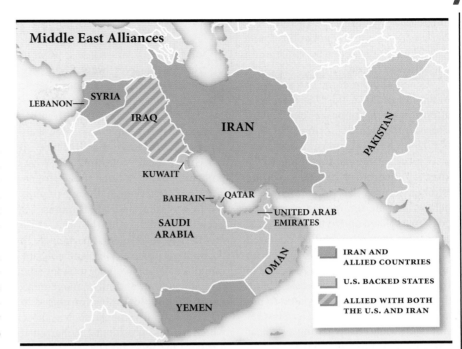

Lucidity Information Design, LLC

was a foreign policy triumph for President Obama that was intended to defuse a serious threat and set out a framework for improved relations. President Donald Trump, however, who disparaged the accord as "the worst deal ever," unilaterally withdrew the U.S. in May 2018, and extensive negotiations for its revival under the Biden administration have proven fruitless.

As negotiations came to a standstill in the fall of 2022, the U.S. shifted its attention to the popular revolt, with President Biden declaring on October 15 he had an "enormous amount of respect for people marching in the streets." Secretary of State Antony Blinken assured that "we are going to help make sure the Iranian people are not kept isolated and in the dark." U.S. envoy for Iran Rob Malley declared that the U.S. would focus on sanctions and other pressure tools in response to Iran's crackdown on protesters, and that President Biden is prepared to use military means against Iran as a last resort to prevent it from getting a nuclear weapon. On November 3, President Biden assured supporters that "we're going to free Iran."

Iran in crisis

Forty-three years since a popular revolution overthrew Shah Mohammad Reza Pahlavi and an Islamic Republic replaced the dynasty that had ruled the country since 1925, Iran has changed in many ways. Under the shah, rapid modernization, the alliance with the United States and imposed Westernization led to serious social strains. The revolution brought the age of mass politics to Iran, and left Iranians–especially women–with the conviction that they were entitled to participate in the political process. Unfortunately, the initial idealism gave way to autocratic rule, corruption and mismanagement, which the revolution had promised to end. Reform movements, such as those which elected presidents Mohammad Khatami in 1997 and Hassan Rouhani in 2013, have been repeatedly stymied.

Prof. Ervand Abrahamian, a lead-ing historian of Iran, believes that the Islamic government has survived for four decades because of its emphasis on populism and commitment to improving the lot of the poor by creating a welfare state and giving priority to social over military expenditure. There has been a strong commitment to provide infrastructure, and facilitate mobility.

Since the revolution, there have been many changes. The population surged from 36 million in 1978 to 88.6 million by mid-2022. The rate of infant mortality has dropped since the 1970s, and adult literacy rates have skyrocketed from 37% to 87% now. Mainly agricultural until World War II, Iran is now three-quarters urbanized. The sharp division historically between city and countryside has now been erased, with electricity, water and internet services now provided throughout the country.

Iran: Land of the Lion and the Sun

Iran, which means "the land of the Aryans," claims a tradition of kingship reaching back 2,500 years. Like Iraq, Iran was conquered by Arab Muslim invaders in the 7th century A.D. It was later an important part of the Abbasid Empire, centered in Baghdad. Iran was subject to a series of invasions by Turkic (non-Persian) peoples from Central Asia from the 11th to the 15th centuries, and was ruled almost continuously by leaders of Turkic origin until 1925. Iran was never colonized by a European power, and the constant goal of Iranian foreign policy has been to maintain the country's independence.

The Pahlavi Dynasty of Reza Shah (1925–41) and his son, Mohammad Reza (1941–79), tried to create a modern, secular state and promoted a strong Iranian nationalism. Both were authoritarian rulers, identified with the military, and were strongly anti-Communist. They did not tolerate internal dissent. Mohammad Reza Pahlavi was known for his friendship

with the U.S., which helped return him to the throne in 1953 after he briefly fled the country during the oil nationalization crisis. The shah's close ties to the United States became one of his main liabilities at the time of the revolution.

Pahlavi rule was brought down in January 1979 by a coalition of religious groups, middle class merchants (*bazaaris*), and liberal reformist and leftist groups. Leadership of the country was then assumed by the ulama or Muslim clergy, under the direction of Ayatollah Ruhollah Khomeini (1902-89). The monarchy was abolished and the country became an Islamic Republic in April 1979. The country's spiritual guide and successor to Khomeini is Ali Khamenei (b. 1939) who served as president from 1981–89 and is regarded more as a political figure than a religious scholar. He long ruled in collaboration, and sometimes rivalry, with Ali-Akbar Hashemi-Rafsanjani (1934–2017), who served as president from 1989 to 1997.

Iran today is an ethnically diverse nation of some 88.6 million people. The principal groups are Persians, Turks and Kurds and Arabs. There are no reliable figures on the religious breakdown, but Shiites constitute the majority of the population, with Sunnis (especially tribal peoples who live in border areas) the largest minority. There are a small number of non-Muslims, primarily Bahais, Christians, Jews and Zoroastrians.

According to the 2016 Census, more than half of Iran's villages have been deserted as people have sought work in cities. The population of major urban areas has mushroomed: that of the capital, Tehran, was 4.8 million in 1978 and 9.4 million now. The lack of jobs, housing and entertainment in cities has led to serious discontent.

Many issues about how to define Islamic government have continued to divide the country. These include the legal status of women and whether veiling should be required, debates over the role of the state in the economy, and whether the ulama (Islamic clergy) should rule directly in Iran (which never happened in the past). The government's obsession with controlling the personal lives of citizens, especially women, has led to the lack of freedoms. At a time of austerity in Iran, many question Iran's policy of intervening in and providing aid to allied states like Iraq, Syria, Lebanon and Yemen.

An important theme of the revolution was the emphasis on Islam's role in resisting the western cultural onslaught and restoring moral order. This led to laws requiring that women cover their hair and bodies, and be segregated from men. It has resulted in a never-ending struggle between men, women and state enforcers (sometimes referred to as the "morality police") who seek to monitor public morality, particularly in large urban areas. There was an increase in harrassment under President Raisi compared to Rouhani, which has led to consternation and defiance, especially by the younger generation.

Although not equal under the law, since the revolution women have aspired to play a more prominent role. More than 60% of university students at present are women. Religiously observant families, who avoided sending their daughters to school under the shah, began to send their veiled daughters to school and on to jobs afterward. For the lower classes, women were empowered. Others pushed back hard against new restrictions unknown under the shah, such as mandatory hi-

Iranian Supreme Leader Ayatollah Ali Khamenei (C) and Islamic Revolutionary Guard Corps commander Hossein Salami (L2) participate in the Khatam al-Anbia Air Defense University graduation ceremony in Tehran, Iran on October 30, 2019. (IRANIAN SUPREME LEADER PRESS OFFICE /ANADOLU AGENCY VIA GETTY IMAGES)

jab and segregation by sex, such as on busses. Women are disadvantaged by unequal laws regarding marriage, divorce, child custody and inheritance, as well as workplace sexual harrassment. In 2021, a law was passed severely curtailing access to abortion and contraception.

The downside of the revolution is apparent everywhere. Only one in ten gain admission to public universities, although many more enter private ones. There is a strong link between unemployment and drug addiction, which is taking a serious toll on society. Iran has the highest proportion of opium users of any country in the world, according to the World Health Organization. The human rights situation is dismal, and Sunni Muslims, as well as minority religious groups such as Christians, Jews and Bahais, are subject to restrictions.

The middle and lower classes, and those without connections to the government, are under extreme economic pressure. The gross national income per capita in purchasing power parity (PPP) in 2021 is estimated by the Population Reference Bureau to be $15,760 . Since the government ended subsidies on food and medicine imports last May there has been a rise in inflation, which

last August was running at a rate of 52%. In October 2022, the World Bank forecast economic growth for Iran this year at 2.9%.

Iran is subject to stringent U.S. economic sanctions that seek to halt most imports and ban international transactions. The mainstay of the Iranian economy is petroleum exports, which due to sanctions are depressed. In September 2022 Iran was exporting about 800,000 barrels of oil a day, mostly purchased by China, but if sanctions are lifted within months might ramp up production from 2.5 million barrels at present to 3.8 million barrels. With fluctuating exchange rates, rampant corruption and lack of protection under the law, many foreign companies are not about to invest there regardless of sanctions. Iranian banks are cut off from the world financial system and suffer from mismanagement, capital shortfall, and a lack of transparency. Still, Iran brags about its "resistance economy."

The rise of youth culture

A majority of Iranians today have grown up with no memory of the shah or life under a secular government. The population is young; around sixty percent are below the age of 30. The average age of marriage for males is 27.8

years, while for females it is 23.1 years, and late marriage is reportedly fostering a sexual revolution. A demographic transition has begun, with much lower fertility rates (about 1.6 children per woman in 2021, in contrast to 6.5 children per woman in 1986) – the lowest rate in the region and below replacement level.

In an information age young Iranians are much better informed than their parents' generation about the outside world, and 84% of the population uses the Internet. In July 2022 Iran had an estimated 40 million Facebook accounts. Because of the internet and social media, people are well aware of what they are missing. During the current protests the government has often shut down the internet, and many people resort to Virtual Private Networks (VPNs) to get through. In recent years the government has collaborated with China to censor the internet and introduce facial recognition so it can spy on its citizens. During recent protests people were attacking cameras and masking to conceal their identities.

State and society are now at a crossroads, with widespread anger over the government's inability to make real reforms, improve living conditions and expand personal freedoms. The contrast between the narrow group of old men and ideologues who currently run Iran and its youthful population could not be greater. The youth of Iran are thoroughly disillusioned after decades of Islamic government and want to replace it, not reform it. Islam per se is not the issue; the protesters are against the clerical system of government imposed after the revolution.

"The whole country's collective consciousness is to be focused on the existential fight for the future of the country," according to Hadi Ghaemi, with the Center for Human Rights in Iran (located in New York). "Young people will not have a future if the Islamic Republic continues on its current course, if the status quo persists...It is an unprecedented situation. I cannot compare it to any other time."

As noted by Professor Narges Ba-

joghli, an Iranian anthropologist who made a long-term study of the Islamic Revolutionary Guard Corps (IRGC or Revolutionary Guards), "in the Islamic Republic, a revolutionary system has become the status quo, and now the Republic faces the question of how to keep its system 'alive.' This question entails two main challenges: how to safeguard the socioeconomic and class status of its leaders and how to appeal to younger generations and their demands for political participation." She found that the Guards, like other Iranians, were deeply divided, often on generational grounds.

The war within

The project of the revolution to Islamize society has backfired to the extent that many young Iranians want nothing to do with religion, and some even speak of Iran as a post-Islamic state. Reportedly, many Iranians are disenchanted with Shiism and are turning to Sufism (a mystical version of Islam) or to other faiths such as Christianity, Zoroastrianism and Bahaiism. In an online poll of 50,000 Iranians conducted by Gamaan, a Dutch research group, in 2020, half of the respondents said they had lost or changed their religion, and less than a third identified as Shia.

Since its inception, the Islamic Republic has been saddled with a unique form of dual government. While the president is elected and runs the state bureaucracy, there is a "parallel state" or "deep state" that the Supreme Leader presides over that aims to protect him and the legacy of the revolution. Over the years Khamenei has expanded a network of security, intelligence and economic forces that is totally loyal to him. His office accords him great power: he appoints the head of the judiciary, as well as commanders of the Revolutionary Guard and Basij, a volunteer militia, in addition to members of the Guardian Council (who vet election candidates) and ministers of foreign affairs, intelligence, defense and the interior. He has the final say in most matters.

The original "reign of the ayatollahs" has now morphed into control

by the security services, above all the Revolutionary Guards, who are expected to fight hard to preserve their power. The Guard has been in the forefront of exerting Iran's influence abroad, for example through Shia militias it recruits and sponsors. It seeks to preserve Iran's revolutionary legacy and has strong economic interests in a state that has rewarded them well. They will make it very difficult to select a moderate successor to the leader, however much the majority of Iranians may wish it.

The succession

Since the establishment of Iran as an Islamic state in 1979, only two people have held the top position of *rahbar,* or leader: Ayatollah Ruhollah Khomeini (1902-89), the leader of the revolution; and after his death in July 1989, Ayatollah Ali Khamenei (b. 1939). Opposition to and suspicion of the U.S. has been a cornerstone of Khamenei's worldview, and he believes that any warming of relations might doom the regime.

According to the constitution, the successor will be chosen by the Assembly of Experts, made up of 88 Islamic jurists. The Revolutionary Guards, however, will also play a key role. "When Khamenei dies, the deep state will ensure that whoever replaces him shares its hard-line views and is committed to protecting its interests," according to experts Sanam Vakil and Hossein Rassam. An obvious candidate is Ebrahim Raisi, and another possibility is the current leader's son Mojtaba, 53. He has close ties to the Revolutionary Guards, but is not very popular and many would resist a family succession. Others caution that the ability of Khamenei to drive events may be overestimated, especially in light of the hostility towards him by large segments of the population.

It seems unlikely that the Revolutionary Guards will try to take over Iran, as they prefer to exercise power in the shadows and remain unaccountable. They need the ulama to legitimate their power and do not have the skills to run the government and manage the economy. But the IRGC, widely feared for its brutal crackdowns on civilian demonstrations, today has a serious generation gap and is not unified. "At the moment, the IRGC's greatest political strength may be the weakness of its opponents," according to U.S.-based experts Ali Reza Eshraghi and Amir Hossein Mahdavi.

Prospects

By late fall 2022, it was unclear where the uprising is going. Media reports do not always reflect what is happening outside Tehran, where everyday life goes on, and the slogan "Women, Life, Freedom" may not express people's most pressing concerns, such as keeping their jobs and not getting arrested.

"One of the things that is striking about the government system in Iran is its robust consolidation over the last 43 years," Prof. Kian Tajbakhsh of Columbia University observed to the BBC. "This is a regime that has relatively successfully combined an ability to provide basic goods and services to much of the population, and combined that with a kind of coercive authoritarian power and a relatively closed political system. So I would say past experience suggests that they will ride this out."

The opposition's lack of leadership and a clear program does not bode well for their success. While there have been many strikes, they have been sporadic and not like the major, sustained general strikes during the revolution. Some sectors, such as the bazaar, bus drivers and other workers have not yet participated in earnest. The government shows no sign of giving in, perhaps because the protesters are not seeking only a modification of some policies, but its wholesale removal. With the closure of the political parties of the reformers there is no outlet for the opposition.

Longtime analyst Shireen Hunter reminds us that "the outcome of the turmoil that would follow a sudden collapse of political power in Iran could well be worse than the current situation, both at home and in Iran's relations with other countries."

As of this writing, there is no clarity on the future trajectory of political change in Iran. A certain number of the population, sometimes cited as 15%, are devoted to the hardline Islamic government, for religious reasons or because their jobs depend on it. (The number may be larger as it does not include the rural population.) There is no opposition in exile, such as monarchists or the Mojahedin, that has a realistic chance of taking power.

Many questions remain. One is whether organized labor forces, such as teachers, university professors, civil servants and oil workers, will commit to a sustained struggle and provide leadership. Another is whether the security forces will remain united in suppressing dissent. This was not the case under the shah, when many police and military refused to fire on protesters. Today the Revolutionary Guards and Basij are expected to be loyal to the government. According to Prof. Azadeh Moaveni, "For the first time in its history, the Iranian state is staring a challenge in the face, knowing many of its forces' sympathies lie with the people."

The way the government sees things, "Iran has prevailed in the face of much international hostility and can be proud to call itself the only truly independent country in the world," according to Alex Vatanka of the Middle East Institute. "But it's an empty slogan and a poor excuse for having turned a proud, ancient nation of Iran into a pariah state."

Iran's foreign policy: neither East nor West

"Like many old civilizations that have experienced great triumphs and great humiliations, Iran is both self-assured and deeply insecure," according to Karim Sadjadpour, a senior fellow at the Carnegie Endowment for International Peace. He notes that many Iranians believe that the great powers conspire to prevent them from being prosperous and independent. In the government's view, the greatest threat is American troops in the Persian Gulf, which serve to contain Iran as well as protect the Gulf monarchs. Iran views the GCC states collectively, but not individually, as a threat. The Islamic

Drones in an underground base in Iran. Over the past decades, Iran and militias it supports in Yemen, Lebanon, Syria, and Iraq have increasingly used the weapons to attack its enemies, including Saudi Arabia. (IRANIAN ARMY/AFP)

State, a militant Sunni Islamist group, is considered a mortal enemy that had the audacity to carry out terrorist attacks in Tehran in June 2017 against the Iranian Parliament building and the Mausoleum of Ruhollah Khomeini.

Iran's foreign policy goal since the revolution has been to assert its independence of external powers, as reflected in the slogan, "Neither East nor West." One important difference is that foreign policy is no longer made by one man, the shah, but is the product of contending factions in Tehran. This has resulted, especially in the early years, in confusion about Iranian intentions. The battle between the "idealists" and "realists" led initially to the ascendancy of the former, who placed an emphasis on Islam over Iranian nationalism and sought to export the revolution. As the idealism of the early years waned and attempts to export the revolution failed, a less confrontational style developed. By the mid-1980s, Iranian rhetoric had cooled and Iran sought better relations with other states.

A study by the International Crisis Group concludes that "Iranian leaders' first priority...is to ensure the Islamic Republic's perpetuation...Iran has long sought to compensate for its sense of encirclement and relative conventional military weakness by achieving self-sufficiency in asymmetric military capabilities and increasing its strategic depth. Iran has heavily invested in its ballistic missile program [and] built a network of partners and proxies to protect against external threats."

Many outsiders believe that its foreign policy is ideologically driven, as at the time of the Iran-Iraq War (1980–88). However, according to Vali Nasr, a professor at Johns Hopkins School of Advanced International Studies in Washington, "its foreign policy is far more pragmatic than many in the West comprehend. As Iran's willingness to engage with the United States over its nuclear program showed, it is driven by hardheaded calculations of national interest, not a desire to spread its Islamic Revolution abroad."

The two military campaigns waged by the second Bush Administration, the first in 2001 to liberate Afghanistan and the second in 2003 to liberate Iraq, have significantly enhanced Iran's standing in the region by neutralizing longtime foes. However, Iran now feels extremely vulnerable since it is surrounded by U.S.-backed states, including Iraq, Pakistan and the GCC. The reality is that Iran can do little to counter U.S. military domination of the Persian Gulf.

Tehran frequently has asserted its view that the littoral states themselves should assume prime responsibility for Gulf security. Iran's major objective, most recently presented by President Rouhani at the UN in January 2021 as the "Hormuz Peace Plan," is a nonaggression treaty of the Gulf states. However, the GCC states are not ready to sign on. With no strong Iraq as a counterweight to Iran, they are driven closer into the western embrace. As long as an Islamic government is in power in Tehran, there is little likelihood the security proposal could be accepted by the other side.

Iran's regional policy

Iranians' view of the Arabs is colored by fourteen hundred years of historical encounters, and most recently, the bitter eight-year war it fought to a stalemate with Iraq. During that time many Arab states contributed to the Iraqi war effort while few helped Iran. As pointed out by Prof. Mehran Kamrava of Georgetown University, "Iran and its Arab neighbors have never tried to view the region's strategic landscape from a win-win perspective in which both sides would benefit. Instead, all too often they have approached strategic competition with each other as a zero-sum game." Kamrava notes that "the Persian Gulf's security dilemma [is] intractable and self-sustaining," due to the lack of trust in the region among the Arab states as well as between Arabs and Persians.

Regional tensions increased after the United States removed Saddam Hussein from leadership of Iraq and, for the first time, installed a Shia-led government in Baghdad. This helped fuel a perception on the part of the six Gulf Cooperation Council states led by Sunni Arabs–Saudi Arabia, Kuwait, Qatar, Bahrain, the United Arab Emirates and Oman– that the Shia, previously regarded as a misguided religious sect, were now a serious security threat to the region. There was fear that large Shiite populations in places like Iraq, Bahrain, Saudi Arabia and Kuwait might be mobilized to support Iranian goals.

Iran's regional strategy is guided by a policy of "forward defense," the aim of which is to avoid fighting on its own territory. This is carried out by the Quds Force, the overseas arm of the Revolutionary Guards, which recruits and trains Shi'i militias in Yemen, Iraq and Syria, in addition to aiding insurgent groups such as Hezbollah in Lebanon and the Houthis in Yemen. There have been many incidents closer to home, such as confrontations between Iranian forces in speedboats harassing American warships and the increasing use of drones in the Persian Gulf. The devastating attack by Iranian drones on Saudi oil processing facilities at Abqaiq in September 2019 was an important reminder that, should it wish to do so, Iran could act with impunity to destroy cities on the Arab side of the Gulf.

Iran wants to preserve Iraq's territorial integrity, prevent the emergence of an independent Kurdistan (lest it serve as an inspiration to Iranian Kurds), and ensure the continuation of a Shi'i-dominated government in Baghdad – all goals of the U.S. There are also religious interests. Two of the holiest cities for Shiite Muslims, Najaf and Karbala, are located there, and Iranian pilgrims have always visited them. The Shiite seminaries in Najaf were the main center for the faith until the rise of rival Qom in Iran in the twentieth century, and since the fall of Saddam there has been an increased flow of Iranian pilgrims. The most senior Shiite religious leader in Iraq, Ayatollah Ali Sistani, is of Iranian origin and has good ties with Iran, as do many government figures.

Iran aims to counteract political and economic sanctions of the U.S. and Europe by cultivating better ties with countries such as India, Russia and China, which benefit from cheap oil. It has also been supportive of political groups that oppose Israel, such as Hamas in Gaza and Hezballah in Lebanon. Although Russia is a historic enemy of Iran, in the fall of 2022 it bought large numbers of Iranian drones for use in Ukraine.

The U.S. and the Islamic Republic have worked together in the past to achieve some common political goals, such as the overthrow of the Taliban and installation of the government of Hamid Karzai in Afghanistan in 2001. Notably, the two cooperated militarily to defeat the Islamic "Caliphate" (Daesh) in Iraq and Syria in 2019.

U.S. policy toward Iran

Dealing with Iran has bedeviled every U.S. administration since the revolution, starting with Jimmy Carter. Many in Washington have long memories, and cannot forget the humiliation of the hostage crisis (1979–81). Antipathy to Iran and Iranians has remained ingrained and made it hard to reconcile.

There is no constituency for Iran in Congress. Because of this, the Obama administration did not submit the Iran nuclear deal for its approval and it remained only an executive action that could be canceled by the next president. Israel was adamantly opposed to the deal when it was first negotiated, and has put strong pressure on President Biden not to renew it.

There are now lobby groups formed and supported by Americans of Iranian heritage, such as the National Iranian American Council in Washington. NIAC calls attention to human rights abuses and has pushed for more humane policies regarding visas. They have advocated renewal of the JCPOA, leading to accusations that they are supporters of the regime, and have urged that ways be found to negotiate with the Iranian government to mitigate the damages done by sanctions. NIAC agrees with the Biden administration that the priority right now is to respond to the protests and let the Iranian people determine their own future.

"Multiple U.S. administrations have attempted to coerce or persuade Iran to reconsider its revolutionary ethos, but have failed," according to Mr. Sadjadpour. "The reason is simple: U.S.-Iran normalization could prove deeply destabilizing to a theocratic government whose organizing principle has been premised on fighting American imperialism....By and large, the U.S. has sought to engage a regime that clearly doesn't want to be engaged, and isolate a ruling regime that thrives in isolation."

Policies for the future

The prerequisite to formulating effective policies is accurate information, which in the case of Iran has been seriously lacking or else simply disregarded. The governments of the U.S. and Iran have become the prisoners of their own rhetoric, often abetted by the news media. Even at the height of the Cold War, the U.S. had an embassy in Moscow and carried out a dialogue on many subjects. If the U.S. can enjoy normal relations with former adversaries such as the Soviet Union or Vietnam, it should be possible to do so for Iran in spite of memories of the hostage crisis. As Henry Kissinger once said, "revenge is sweet, but it's not foreign policy."

John Limbert, former hostage, ambassador and professor, has reflected on the "ghosts of history" that have prevented Iranians and Americans from talking to each other. He notes, "One of the perverse effects of the long Iranian-American estrangement has been the two sides' inability to talk about issues that concern both, even when such talks could benefit both parties. In a reasonable world, American and Iranian officials would have begun talking decades ago about such issues–not as friends but as states with interests." American and Iranian negotiators did get to know each other very well during the nuclear talks, but the landscape has changed in the wake of the cancelation of the deal and the installation of a hardline government in Iran. At present there is strong congressional opposition in Washington to improving bilateral relations.

There is now a serious lack of U.S. expertise on Iran which has hindered relations. Few Americans have been to

Official visit of U.S. President Jimmy Carter to Tehran, Iran, December 31, 1977. President Carter toasts the new year with Shah Mohammad Reza Pahlavi. (JEAN-CLAUDE DEUTSCH/PARIS MATCH VIA GETTY IMAGES)

Americans and Iranians: strained encounters

Since the Iranian revolution, relations between Washington and Tehran have been characterized by mutual hostility and aborted attempts at reconciliation. This has arisen out of policy differences and, behind that, mutual misperceptions that have left each nation with sharply differing historical memories of the other.

Americans had little contact with Iran before World War II, when 30,000 U.S. troops were sent there to help secure a supply line to Russia. After the war, Washington backed Iran's demand that Soviet troops be withdrawn from its northwest province of Azerbaijan. When the Soviets retreated, Iran looked on the United States as a protector. The young shah, Mohammad Reza Pahlavi, sought U.S. military and economic assistance, and the C.I.A. helped restore him to power after he was briefly forced out of the country in 1953. Over the next quarter century (1953–79), Washington developed a close relationship with the Pahlavis, who turned Iran into an anti-communist bulwark and became good customers for U.S. arms.

After Britain's withdrawal from the Persian Gulf in 1971, the Nixon administration depended upon Iran, along with Saudi Arabia, as one of the "twin pillars" to provide security there. The shah was regarded by most Americans as a modernizer who continued the work of his father, Reza Shah (1925–41) of centralizing power, strengthening the military and building a secular state. In 1978, on the eve of the revolution, some 50,000 Americans were living and working in Iran, and between 1962 and 1976 almost 2,000 Peace Corps volunteers served there. Iran, as President Carter declared in a New Year's eve toast in Tehran on December 31, 1977, appeared to be "an island of stability in one of the more troubled areas of the world." How could he, and America, have gotten it so wrong?

The Iranian version

The Iranian encounter with the United States is a story of disillusionment and betrayal. For the first half of the 20th century Iranian impressions of America, limited though they were, had been positive. Unlike European imperial powers such as Britain and Russia that had long interfered in Iranian affairs, the United States was regarded as a disinterested observer with no designs on Iranian territory. Iranians assumed that because of its democratic ideals the United States would support Iran's nationalization of its major financial resource, oil, during the early 1950s. Many were bitterly disappointed when the U.S. instead backed its ally, Britain, in the dispute, and intervened in Iranian affairs, first by helping to depose the popular nationalist leader Mohammad Mossadegh in 1953 and then helping maintain an autocratic shah in power for the next 25 years.

When President Carter was asked about the Mosaddeq incident in 1980 he referred to it as "ancient history." Yet many Iranians have not forgotten, for they believe that these actions cut short Iran's last chance for democracy. In a CNN interview in 1988, former President Khatami denounced Washington's "flawed policy of domination" of Iran, specifically mentioning the 1953 coup. Many regarded the shah as a creature of the Americans, who shared blame for his increasingly autocratic ways, the human rights abuses of his secret police, SAVAK, and his coddling of the military. His willingness to deal with Israel and supply it with oil was also at issue. For a large segment of the popular classes who were bypassed on the road to prosperity, the shah's westernization efforts and his contempt for the ulama, or Islamic clerics, prompted resentment. They regarded the ulama as the preservers of Iranian cultural identity, and accepted Ayatollah Khomeini as their leader. Eventually, they joined with others, some secular, to make the revolution.

On the eve of revolution in the late 1970s, the U.S. government was unaware of the strength of domestic opposition in Iran, had virtually no contacts with the ulama, and continued to back the shah until almost the bitter end. Many Iranians were surprised by American's hostility to their revolution, and relations were strained to the breaking point during the hostage crisis (November 1979–January 1981). Since then, the U.S. image of Iran has been one of demonstrators shouting "death to America" and turbaned ayatollahs denouncing the United States as the "Great Satan." But Americans' image of Iran is now seriously out of date.

It used to be said that Iranians are the most pro-American people in the Middle East, although their government is the most anti-American—just the opposite of the situation prevailing in Arab countries. The U.S. image was seriously dented following the mistaken downing of an Iranian civilian airliner by a U.S. warship, the Vincennes, in the Persian Gulf, in July 1988, leading to a loss of 290 Iranian lives.

After the tragedy of 9/11, candlelight vigils were held in sympathy in Tehran. Because many young Iranians are heavy internet users they are familiar with American films and pop culture. Many thousands of Iranians took refuge in the United States after the revolution and maintain close connections with families back home. Official U.S. statements emphasize that policymakers have a problem only with Tehran's policies. It may be that after the U.S. withdrawal from the nuclear accord, and the many privations brought on by U.S. economic sanctions, the younger generation is changing its opinion of Americans.

Iran in the past forty years, and diplomats and professors with expertise in Iran have mostly retired. In the 1980s and 1990s the State Department did not even train Persian-speakers. "The point is that the United States should be talking to the Islamic Republic not because doing so is easy or even likely to produce immediate and positive results, but because both sides might find significant common interests in doing so," according to Ambassador Limbert.

A whole generation in Iran is familiar with American culture through social media and films, but lacks any personal knowledge of the country its government likes to refer to as "the Great Satan." In 1978 there were some 100,000 Iranians studying abroad, half in the U.S., and 50,000 Americans were working in Iran. Before Covid-19, 11,450 Iranian students were enrolled in American colleges, according to the Institute of International Education. The risk is increasing that new generations of Americans and Iranians will forget the past legacy of cooperation and become permanently estranged.

The evolution of U.S. policy

Since the triumph of the revolution the U.S. and Iran have been estranged. President Clinton's policy of "Dual Containment" sought to exclude both Iran and Iraq from playing a role in the Persian Gulf. During the Iran-Iraq War (1980-88), although the U.S. was ostensibly neutral President Reagan tilted to Iraq. At the time of the Gulf War and the expulsion of Iraqi forces from Kuwait (1990–91), Iran earned U.S. gratitude by not intervening. When Secretary of State James Baker outlined his postwar goals to Congress in February 1991, he said that Iran could play a role in future security arrangements in the Gulf. But such a role did not materialize.

The U.S. responded positively, if cautiously, to the election of President Khatami in Iran in 1997. In an important policy statement, Secretary of State Madeleine Albright on June 17, 1998 urged Iran to join the U.S. in drawing up "a road map leading to normal relations." In March 2000, she

U.S. Secretary of State John Kerry leaves after addressing a press conference on Iran nuclear talks at Austria International Centre in Vienna, Austria on July 14, 2015. Major powers clinched a historic deal aimed at ensuring Iran does not obtain the nuclear bomb, opening up Tehran's stricken economy and potentially ending decades of bad blood with the West. (CARLOS BARRIA/AFP via Getty Images)

went as far as any American official has gone in making a qualified apology for the U.S. role in overthrowing the Mossadegh government in 1953. The U.S. attempt to engage Iran, unfortunately, did not succeed.

Administration policy on Iran, Iraq and indeed the entire Middle East, was influenced above all by the attacks of September 11, 2001, which highlighted the dangers of terrorism and weapons of mass destruction. In the aftermath of 9/11, the United States worked with Iran to evict the Taliban and install the Karzai government in Afghanistan. Any goodwill and cooperation, however, was cut short by President Bush's designation of Iran as part of an "axis of evil" in his January 2002 State of the Union address. Iran was accused of seeking to acquire nuclear weapons, obstructing the Arab-Israeli peace process, supporting terrorism and violating human rights. From then on the United States let the Europeans, especially Britain, France and Germany, play a lead role in conducting negotiations over the nuclear issue.

Whereas U.S. policy for a decade after the Gulf War was to maintain the status quo, the younger Bush opted for major change by waging a preventive war to oust Saddam in 2003. In the wake of the U.S. invasion of Iraq

and removal of Saddam Hussein, the United States lost a golden opportunity to reach a "grand bargain" proposed by Iran to normalize relations.

The Obama administration

When President Obama took office in January 2009, he held out hope of discussing issues with Iran "without preconditions and on the basis of mutual respect." He said, "We will extend a hand if you are willing to unclench your fist."

By the fall of 2009, things had changed following revelations of a secret enrichment plant under construction south of Tehran at Qom. In the most spectacular and successful project, the U.S. secretly worked with Israel to develop the Stuxnet computer worm, which infected and disabled computers in Iranian nuclear plants between June 2009 and May 2010. By seriously harming these computers, the U.S. achieved by cyberwarfare what would have been the aim of a military strike.

In its second term the Obama administration, led by Secretary of State John F. Kerry, focused on Iran and achieved their signal foreign policy victory. With its partners—Britain, France, Germany, Russia, and China— in July 2015 the United States negotiated the Joint Comprehensive Plan of

U.S. Republican presidential candidate Donald Trump speaks at a rally organized by the Tea Party Patriots against the Iran nuclear deal in front of the Capitol in Washington, DC, on September 9, 2015. (NICHOLAS KAMM/AFP VIA GETTY IMAGES)

Action, or JCPOA, which achieved the paramount goal of preventing Iran from acquiring a nuclear weapon in return for an easing of sanctions.

The age of Trump: maximum pressure

The Trump administration repeatedly said it wanted to negotiate a "better deal" with Iran, but failed to do so. It re-imposed UN sanctions on September 19, 2020 under "snapback" provisions of the deal. Following Trump's re-election loss, in the remainder of its term the administration imposed a "flood of sanctions" not related to the nuclear deal, such as on its ballistic missile program, assistance to terror organizations and human rights abuses. Additional sanctions were placed on Iranian banks which seek to sever Iranian ties to the outside world.

Ambassador Wendy Sherman, who led the team negotiating the agreement, acknowledged that it was not perfect, but pointed out it achieved the top U.S. goal, which was to preclude Iran from getting a bomb. She wrote, "Trump has turned Iran into a nearly impossible problem for future administrations. His behavior has given U.S. allies less reason to trust Washington on future deals or to take U.S. interests into account. He

has thrown away a hard-nosed nuclear deal that set a new standard for verification, and he punched a hole in a highly effective web of sanctions and international consensus that made the Iran deal–and future deals like it–possible."

A nuclear-armed Iran would be a nightmare scenario, and many experts see the non-renewal of the nuclear accord as a huge mistake. According to reporter Barbara Slavin, "eventually... talks will resume because there is no other viable option." She notes that "a revised nuclear agreement with Iran would not just roll back its nuclear program – which hovers dangerously at the point of breakout – but lessen the sanctions that impoverish ordinary Iranians while filling the pockets of corrupt smuggling rings. It would allow Iranians to re-engage with Western businesspeople, particularly Europeans who desperately need new sources of energy after Russia's invasion of Ukraine."

In a major escalation of tension with Iran, President Trump, charging that Iranian Major General Qasem Soleimani, commander of the Qods Force, "was plotting imminent and sinister attacks on American diplomats and military personnel," ordered his assassination by drone strike in Baghdad on January 3, 2020. Suleimani was con-

sidered the mastermind of Iranian security operations in the region, close to President Khamenei and regarded as a hero in Iran.

Biden's policy dilemma

President Joseph R. Biden was elected in the fall of 2020 on a platform of returning to the nuclear deal with Iran, and favored removing sanctions if Iran resumed compliance with the JCPOA. However, once in office he hesitated to do so, and extensive negotiations to renew the deal so far have not been successful. In the run-up to the fall 2022 congressional elections it seemed clear that the deal would not be renewed due to objections from both sides. With Iran no longer under supervision by the International Atomic Energy Agency (IAEA), it has the ability to build a nuclear weapon quickly. It has already enriched uranium to 60% purity, slightly under the 90% needed for a weapon. Experts believed that "breakout" could occur within weeks and Iran would become a threshold nuclear state.

Biden did take a strong stand against the Iranian government's attacks against demonstrators. He stated last October 3, "I remain gravely concerned about reports of the intensifying violent crackdown on peaceful protesters in Iran, including students and women, who are demanding their equal rights and basic human dignity...For decades, Iran's regime has denied fundamental freedoms to its people and suppressed the aspirations of successive generations through intimidation, coercion, and violence. The United States stands with Iranian women and all the citizens of Iran who are inspiring the world with their bravery."

Biden has sought to do what he could, but it is minimal–nothing like the resources sent to shore up the Ukrainian government. The Treasury Department changed the rules to facilitate internet access with Iran, and issued exemptions for social media and cloud technology. Entrepreneur Elon Musk offered to provide Starlink, a satellite internet system, to Iran to help increase the flow of information. Senator Bob Menendez, Chairman of the Senate Foreign Relations Committee, said the United States "should lead the international community" in condemnation, and "we should be using our surrogate broadcasting in the region to let the Iranian people know what is going on in their country."

Policy options

How should the United States respond to the current uprising? Should it intervene? Experts are divided as to whether this is a prelude to revolution, or a disaster in which the state will inevitably crush the protests. The Green Movement, which had widespread support and success in standing up to the state, fizzled out after seven months. Gary Sick, a senior expert on Iran at Columbia University advises, "Above all, we should be modest in our expectations...patience should be the name of the game. At a minimum, we should exercise utmost care that our policies toward Iran provide the necessary breathing space for a movement that Iranians themselves must create under the most difficult circumstances possible."

Other Iran-watchers also advocate caution. Professor William O. Beeman, a professor of anthropology at the University of Minnesota, has been a close observer of Iran for decades. He remarks, "above all, the United States must not try to control events in Iran. This is different from supporting the Iranians fighting for their human rights and right to personal freedom. Any direct American intervention will taint any group that emerges as a challenge to the current regime, and doom it to failure. Iranians must determine their own destiny, something they feel they have not been able to do for many centuries."

Iranians remember how the last revolution turned out and have been afraid to make another one. Although many in Iran itself and the Iranian diaspora yearn for the Islamic regime to be replaced, Prof. Mohsen Milani has cautioned that U.S. policymakers "should not confuse discontent with a willingness to launch a revolution."

***

After decades of estrangement, there is little trust between Americans and

A protest in Los Angeles against the Iranian regime on Oct. 22, 2022. Chanting crowds have rallied in Berlin, Washington D.C, and Los Angeles in solidarity with protesters facing a violent government crackdown in Iran. (RICHARD VOGEL/AP IMAGES)

Iranians. In the future, hopefully both countries can break the historic pattern of never being able to reciprocate the other's advances. Treating Iran as a permanent enemy has not achieved U.S. aims, and if the nuclear accord is not renewed in some form the world must face the prospect of a nuclear-armed Iran. When talks eventually resume, other issues besides the nuclear one should be on the table, such as security in the Persian Gulf, preventing drug smuggling via Afghanistan, and opposing terrorist groups like Al Qaeda and the Islamic State. Insisting on negotiating other issues important to the U.S., such as putting limits on Iran's ballistic missile and drone program, could doom any talks.

As highlighted by the unprecedented fall protests, the Iranian government has lost all legitimacy and young people, in particular, feel there is no hope for their future. Where this leads we do not know, and it seems Iranians will have to carry out their resistance with little prospect of material support from abroad. But whether there is political change in the near future or not, a sharp line has been drawn between state and society, with widespread acknowledgement that a hybrid system of government devised four decades ago no longer works and the majority of the people does not want an Islamic government.

The U.S. does not have the ability to "fix" Iran, and has forfeited much of the goodwill of Iranians it built up over decades. In the postwar era, generations of Iranians and Americans visited each other's country and many Iranians settled permanently in the United States in enclaves like "Tehrangeles". In acknowledgement, all U.S. presidents since George W. Bush have celebrated the major national Iranian spring holiday, Nowruz, at the White House.

In the memorable phrase of President George H. W. Bush in his inaugural address, "goodwill begets goodwill," referring to Iran. The question is how to start the cycle again. Continuing to exclude Iran as a legitimate player in the region is not a sustainable position.

In the long run—however long this is—ties will improve, because it is in Iran's interest and is what most Iranians want. Iranians are very proud of their heritage, and are pained that their country is regarded as a pariah state. They have been waiting for decades to rejoin the world and regain its respect. When this happens and Iran becomes a "normal" state, tensions in the Persian Gulf will lessen and the Iranian dream of a regional security agreement may be realized. And U.S. troops can finally come home.

Discussion Questions

1. The U.S. has been able to reconcile with former enemies, such as Vietnam and, until now, the Soviet Union. What is it about Iran that makes it so hard to do so?

2. What are the "ghosts of history" that both Iran and the U.S. have to face in dealing with each other?

3. The Iranian revolution was 43 years ago. How has the country changed since then?

4. How important is ideology in Iran today? Is it still a revolutionary state? Has the revolution ended? What are its foreign policy goals?

5. According to Vali Nasr, "Iran is an indispensable component of any sustainable order in the Middle East." What are the implications of this?

6. Is Iran or Saudi Arabia a greater source of insecurity in the Persian Gulf? Is Iran only strong in the region since the Arabs are weak? How does instability in the Arab world help Iran?

7. So far attempts by the U.S. to isolate and punish Iran have hurt the Iranian people but not led to policy changes by the government. Do you think it is time for Washington to alter its policy?

8. What should the U.S. do about Iran's nuclear program? Iran now has a peaceful nuclear energy program – do you think it will transition into a nuclear weapons program? If so, what are the consequences for the Persian Gulf countries?

9. Should the U.S. not push for a renewal of the nuclear deal at this time, as it would lead to more money and less pressure on the government at a time people are revolting?

Suggested Readings

Abrahamian, Ervand. **A History of Modern Iran,** 2nd ed., 2018. New York: Cambridge University Press, 2018. Excellent overview by leading historian.

Ansari, Ali M., **Modern Iran Since 1797: Reform and Revolution,** 3rd ed. New York: Routledge, 2019. An important and up to date interpretative history of modern Iran.

Cooper, Andrew Scott. **The Fall of Heaven: The Pahlavis and the Final Days of Imperial Iran.** New York: Picador, 2018. The rise and fall of the dynasty, with sources from all sides.

Farman Farmaian, Sattareh, with Dona Munkar. **Daughter of Persia: A Woman's Journey from Her Father's Harem Through the Islamic Revolution.** New York: Three Rivers Press, 2006. An amazing memoir of Iran in the 20th century by eyewitness.

Ghazvinian, John. **America and Iran: A History, 1720 to the Present.** New York: Vintage Books, 2021. A major new assessment, widely praised.

Kamrava, Mehran, **Triumph and Despair: In Search of Iran's Islamic Republic.** London: Hurst, 2022. Account of Iran from the revolution until today, by leading scholar. "After forty years, the Islamic Republic remains a country in search of itself."

Mottahedeh, Roy P. **The Mantle of the Prophet: Religion and Politics in Iran,** 2nd ed. Oxford: Oneworld Publlications, 2008. A remarkable book explaining why Iran had a revolution in 1978-79.

Nasr, Vali. "Iran Among the Ruins: Tehran's Advantage in a Turbulent Middle East." **Foreign Affairs,** vol. 97 no. 2 (March/April 2018): 108-18. Iran is an indispensable component of any sustainable order in the Middle East, and the U.S. cannot roll back its influence.

Sadjadpour, Karim. "What the U.S. Gets Wrong About Iran," Guest Essay, **The New York Times,** August 12, 2022. "The U.S. has sought to engage a regime that clearly doesn't want to be engaged, and isolate a ruling regime that thrives in isolation."

https://www.nytimes.com/2022/08/12/opinion/iran-america-nuclear-policy.html

Sherman, Wendy R. "How We Got the Iran Deal and Why We'll Miss It." **Foreign Affairs,** September/October 2018. The lead negotiator of the deal explains why it was a mistake to cancel it.

Vakil, Sanam. "Iran's Crisis of Legitimacy: An Embattled Regime Faces Mass Protests–and an Ailing Supreme Leader." **Foreign Affairs,** September 28, 2022. Public anger in Iran is focused on the legitimacy of Khamenei and the system he represents. https://www.foreignaffairs.com/middle-east/iran-crisis-legitimacy-mass-protests-ailing-leader

Don't forget to vote!

Download a copy of the ballot questions from the Resources page at www.fpa.org/great_decisions

To access web links to these readings, as well as links to additional, shorter readings and suggested web sites,

GO TO www.fpa.org/great_decisions

and click on the topic under Resources, on the right-hand side of the page.

Climate change, environmental degradation, and migration
by Karen Jacobsen

A view of flood-hit areas as families struggle while winter comes in Mehar, Sindh province, Pakistan ,on October 22, 2022. Over 2.2 million houses were damaged, including some 800,000 completely destroyed, across Pakistan. The flood also washed away 435 bridges and over 8,077 miles of roads while over 1.1 million livestock perished. Also, one in nine children under 5 years of age admitted to health facilities in Pakistan's flood-battered areas are found to be suffering from 'severe acute' malnutrition, according to a UN report. (MUHAMMED SEMIH UGURLU/ANADOLU AGENCY VIA GETTY IMAGES)

By now we are all aware of the ways in which human degradation of the environment, largely caused by greenhouse gas emissions that leads to global warming, are affecting our planet.

When we talk about climate change we mean long-term shifts in temperatures and weather patterns. These shifts may be natural, such as through variations in the solar cycle. But in the last 20 years, a consensus has emerged among climate scientists, embodied in the Intergovernmental Panel on Climate Change (IPCC), that the planet is warming at an unusually high rate, and that this warming has a strong anthropogenic aspect, i.e. it is being caused by the actions of human beings. These actions are mostly through the emission of greenhouse gases (GHG) that occur as a result of burning fossil fuels (coal, oil and gas) and other factors like clearing land and forests (that release carbon dioxide), landfills for garbage (that are a major source of methane emissions). Almost all sectors of our global economy—energy, manufacturing, transport, construction, and agriculture are significant emitters of GHG.

Global warming leads to increased heat and drought in

KAREN JACOBSEN *is the Henry J. Leir Professor in Global Migration at The Fletcher School of Law and Diplomacy at Tufts University, and directs the Refugees in Towns Project at the Leir Institute for Migration and Human Security. Her current research explores urban displacement and global migration, with a focus on the livelihoods and financial resilience of migrants and refugees, and on climate mobility.*

8

some places, and increased intensity of storms, wind and rainfall in other places. Sometimes the same region experiences all of these affects. For example, see the BOX about the Khyber Pakhtunkhwa region of Pakistan. Global warming is also linked to sea level rise: between 2006 and 2016, the rate of sea level rise was 2.5 times faster than during the 20th century. The impact of sea level rise potentially affect billions of people living in coastal areas, particularly the many small island developing states (SIDS). See Box about SLR in Cuba. All these consequences are thought of as *climate change impacts*, and it is these impacts that can contribute to the mobility—both emergency displacement and longer—erm migration of people.

Many studies make projections about what is likely to happen as a result of climate impacts in the future. These studies make projections about heat: extremely hot zones could cover 20% of the earth's surface by 2070, compared to less than 1% now, affecting one third of the global population; about wildfires: by 2100, wildfires could increase by 50%; and particularly about flooding: coastal flooding events that currently happen once every 100 years could happen annually by 2100.

Human beings are degrading the planet in multiple other ways that both contribute to global warming and create environmental problems that impact people's ability to survive and thrive. The deliberate destruction of rain forests for timber, plantations (like oil palm) and grazing land for cattle, have consequences for indigenous people and their traditional ways of life. Urban growth and uncontrolled urban sprawl in the form of new housing, shopping malls and parking lots lead to deforestation, increased pavement and plastic pollution all of which can contribute to flooding (by blocking drainage); the

! Before you read, download the companion **Glossary** that includes definitions, a guide to acronyms and abbreviations used in the article, and other material. Go to **www. fpa.org/great_decisions** and select a topic in the Resources section. (Top right)

destruction of farmland and increased urban heat island (UHI) effects. Urban growth also pushes houses out into what's called the Urban-Wildlife Interface, where the forest meets suburbia. This means houses and towns are often directly in the path of wildfires. Ocean plastic pollution, the eradication of the world's forests, the loss of species diversity—all have consequences for the livelihoods of millions of people whose livelihoods depend on oceans, forests and wild lands. People living in cities, especially, but not only on coasts, are increasingly affected by flooding and urban heat intensification. Whether in cities or small towns or rural areas, in developed or developing countries, we are all caught up in the changes that are coming. People's homes and assets, livelihoods, health, food security, plans for their children, and hopes and dreams are all affected when they are hit by hurricanes or floods, caught up in multi-year droughts, or see their traditional livelihoods disappear with the flora and fauna of their landscapes. Some will move away, others—possibly most—will stay where they are to deal with what comes, and some will return after they move away. This article explores some of these issues; like climate change itself, climate-related migration is a burgeoning area of research and scholarship, and there are several handbooks and overview articles, as well as many case studies.

Many different terms are used to describe people moving for climate-related and environmental reasons: ecomigrants, environmental or climate refugees, and climate displacees. The terms and language we use are part of the broader discourse about climate migration, which we discuss further below. I will use the term "climate mobility" and "climate migrants" here, to avoid acronyms and lengthy terms, and because the terms are widely used. Both terms include the idea of mobility and displacement that results from environmental degradation together with climate impacts.

This article examines some of the issues around climate mobility that I find particularly interesting and wor-

thy of further research and discussion. Part 1 begins by examining who leaves in the face of environmental hazards, and why some people move and others don't. Although there is much scholarly and media focus on climate migrants, as with all migration, not everyone leaves. Many, even most, stay behind for various reasons, as we explore. Part 1 continues with how we talk about climate-related migration, what language and metaphors are used in the media and in research reports, and what the implications of such language are for how we respond. We then look at where people who move go, and how many climate migrants there are – and how confident we can be in the data and models

Box: Floods and drought in Khyber Pakhtunkhwa region of Pakistan

In Pakistan's Khyber Pakhtunkhwa region (what used to be known as the North West Frontier Province), droughts threaten farmers in the southern zone, while the northern and Central zones experiences Glacial Lake Outburst Floods (GLOFs) caused by melting from rising temperatures on the Hindu Kush and Himalayas mountain ranges. Some 3,044 lakes have developed in the Gilgit-Baltistan and Khyber Pakhtunkhwa regions, putting seven million people at risk. One district, Chitral, has experienced more than 13 GLOFs over the last 17 years. Displaced households live in temporary shelters for years. Some households have left their native valleys permanently.

Most of this internal migration within Khyber Pakhtunkhwa is towards the region's cities, including especially the regional capital of Peshawar. These cities have also been hosting large numbers of Afghan refugees for the past thirty years. Today there are more than 670,000 Afghan refugees registered with UNHCR, and probably many more who are unregistered. The growing numbers of both internal climate-displaced migrants together with Afghan refugees are creating serious difficulties for the city of Peshawar.

BOX: How climate change and environmental degradation combine to create climate mobility

Sea-level rise (SLR) is one of the most well-known forms of climate change and is often cited as a cause of migration. But sea level rise often results from a combination of climate change and environmental degradation. In Isle de Jean Charles, on the Gulf Coast region of Louisiana, for example, SLR has resulted from the destruction of wetlands (as a result of activities by the U.S. Army Corps of Engineers and the Gulf of Mexico's petrochemical industry), as well as a lack of investment in mitigation. Some of the residents of the Isle de Jean Charles tribal community have already left, and formal resettlement efforts are ongoing. The media have described this community as the first climate migrants in the United States, but the sea level rise in Isle de Jean Charles is a result of environmental degradation and climate change.

Destroyed houses on the Island of Jean Charles, an indigenous community located on the coast of Louisiana, which was severely impacted by the passage of Hurricane Ida in 2021. In recent years, the area has suffered from an emptying population as a result of rising sea levels and the intensity of climatic events. The residents of the island were considered by the government as the first climate refugees in the United States. (LALO DE ALMEIDA/FOLHA-PRESS/PANOS /REDUX)

2020 Oregon wildfires. Climate change is increasing the intensity and frequency of many climate-related hazards, and populations that migrate after these hazards occur could be classified as climate migrants. For example, in 2020 in Oregon, 40,000 people temporarily evacuated in response to wildfires. The fires also destroyed five towns, prompting longer-term migration. Although climate change can increase the intensity of wildfires and other climate hazards, such events are also a product of natural resource management and other social structures that influence the way that the built environment is managed.

that project estimates. Part 2 turns to policy and other responses to climate-related migration. First we look at how international organizations, such as UN agencies, and other global initiatives are trying to help countries deal with climate-related migration. Then we explore the responses of city and national governments and finally we look at how civil society – particularly the private sector (businesses, corporations), and local initiatives by affected indigenous communities are responding to climate-related migration. What is being done now? What is not being done? What could be done? What should be done? Finally, we end with a look ahead to see what the future holds by way of initiatives in the pipeline and new technologies that might mitigate climate-related migration.

Part I. The problem – how we think about, talk about and measure climate-related migration

How climate change, environmental degradation and migration are related

Across the world, global warming, geophysical hazards (like earthquakes, which are also potentially caused by global warming) and other forms of environmental degradation undermine people's ability to survive and thrive in their home settings. Some of these people will move away; others will stay, either because they don't have the resources to migrate, or because they choose to stay in their homes and try to make the best of it. In this regard, climate migration is like all migration: when people are faced with threats or difficulties, many more stay, compared to the number who migrate. This is because migration requires resources – money, knowledge, networks, physical health, and other nontangible characteristics like willingness to take risks. There are also social and cultural factors that mitigate against out-migration – family obligations, place attachment. Not everybody – households or individuals - has the tangible and non-tangible assets needed for migration, and many have strong positive reasons to stay. This means that although millions of people are now, and in the future will be threatened by the impact of climate change, only some of them will be able to move, or will choose to move. Thus, although we are barraged with media predictions that hundreds of millions of people will become climate migrants, many scholars believe these numbers to be vastly exaggerated.

When scholars and researchers study climate mobiity we bring together two fields of study: the study of migration of people, and the study of climate change and environmental degradation. Both fields make two broad distinctions that map quite well (but not perfectly) onto each other. Migration scholars distinguish between **displacement and migration**; climate scientists distinguish between **sudden onset and slow onset** impacts.

Displacement occurs when people are forced to leave their homes suddenly, with little choice in the matter. For example, if a family's home village or town is being shelled or attacked by armed groups, most people (but not all) will flee. Similarly, if one's town is in the path of a sudden onset disaster, such as a Cat 5 hurricane, or a huge wildfire, many people (but not all) will flee or be evacuated. We refer to such people as having been displaced by **sudden onset events**. Climate change is widely thought to be increasing these kinds of sudden onset events. They include extreme weather events such as tropical cyclones (in the Indian and Pacific Oceans) or hurricanes (in the Atlantic Ocean) and unusually intense precipitation ("rainbombs"), which destroy people's homes and livelihood as a result of wind damage and flooding. Sudden onset events also include massive wildfires (aggravated by drought and heat) and even earthquakes (aggravated by melting ice caps which destabilize tectonic plates).

Migration on the other hand is a more measured process that entails careful decision-making on the part of individuals or more usually, their families, and then planning and preparation for the move. This process can take weeks, months or even years – if preparation includes saving enough money to make a move. A family's decision to move – whether it is the entire family or one family member selected

to be the migrant – is prompted by many factors. People embark on migration to improve their own or their household's financial situation, to join family in other places, for education or health needs, or simply to seek a better or more interesting life. Migration also occurs because households, especially those whose livelihoods depend on the land, like farmers or herders, recognize that their livelihoods are being threatened by the **slow onset** impact of climate change – recurring drought or floods that destroy their crops or livestock, or rising sea levels that wipe out their livelihoods and homes. Farmers and herders have always been faced with drought and flooding, and they have developed strategies to manage such threats. But in recent years, these kinds of threats have become much more frequent, wiping out savings, and reducing people's abilities to endure the loss of a herd or a season's crop. As with displacement, not everyone faced with the same problems migrates. As we shall see, the decision to migrate is influenced by many factors.

How we talk about migrants - Discourse, narratives and language

It is useful to think about how we talk about climate-related migration, what language and metaphors are used in the media and in research reports, and the implications of such language for how we -- and policy makers -- respond. Metaphors are important aspects of all discourses, and the migration discourse (which includes climate migration) is steeped in hydraulic metaphors – floods, tsunamis, waves, inundation, 'drowning in refugees,' the list goes on. When it comes to climate-related migration, the hydraulic metaphors are couched in alarmist, apocalyptic language, with an emphasis on so-called "climate refugees." As Giovanni Bettini points out, climate-related migration

"is frequently depicted as a future crisis, narrated with images of massive, unrestrainable and threatening floods of 'climate refugees' from the global south in a post-climate change apocalypse. Words like catastrophe, threat and urgency are extensively em-

ployed: titles such as "Here comes the flood", "The Human Tide" or "The Human Tsunami" are symptomatic of such tendencies."

As Bettini argues, such strong tones might be justified given recent predictions of the humanitarian impacts we can expect, assuming current global warming trends continue. "Climate change threatens a large share of the world's population and gilding the bitter pill would be an act of irresponsibility, denial or intentional deceit." Yet, the discourse is highly problematic, first because it is based on thin evidence, and second because it has serious consequences for how we respond to climate-related migration. Let's consider both of these problems.

First, the discourse assumes very large numbers – hundreds of millions – of climate migrants are on the move, but in fact the evidence for this claim

BOX: SLR and small island states: the case of Cuba

Like many Small Island States, Caribbean island economies depend on tourism, agriculture, and fishing, all of which are threatened by hurricanes and rising sea levels. In Cuba, storms and hurricanes have driven the sea further inland, contaminating crops and aquifers (seawater intrusion causes the salinization of agriculture land), threatening mangrove forests and grasslands, and wiping out beaches. To date, sea levels have risen less than three inches (seven centimeters), but by 2100, SLR is projected to increase to 33 inches (85 climate migration) which could affect 24,000 square kilometers of land, submerging about 20% of it – nearly 5.8% of Cuba's territory. The Cuban shoreline contains 250 towns and villages with over 3.5 million inhabitants. Migration from Cuba has been increasing over the past five years; as their homes and livelihoods are impacted by rising seas, with little help from their government, more people are likely to move to Cuba's towns, and from there, perhaps further afield.

is weak. In recent years, the IPCC has backed off its earlier forecasts that hundreds of millions of "climate refugees" would be on the move. They and other experts now recognize that the estimates are contested, the numbers lack solid evidence, and there is no consensus on them. Second, 'apocalyptic narratives' can have a counterproductive effect on communicating the urgency of climate-related migration. There is the problem of compassion fatigue, i.e. media consumers become numb to the constant drumbeat of doom and gloom, and stop reading about it. The narratives also tend to focus on so-called "climate refugees." a misnomer that also places the emphasis on the migrants themselves, rather than on the broader picture that includes the situation in their sending areas. Third, such narratives and evidence-lacking predictions of millions of "climate refugees" serves to entrench climate migration as a looming security crisis, again with little evidence, but which is reflected in the response by policy makers to harden borders and try to prevent migration, as we discuss below. The critique of apocalyptic and false narratives about climate-related migration is not about denying or trivializing climate change and its impacts on human societies or on mobility. Rather the intention is show how climate migration is used by policy makers to drive other agendas, including those that support finding ways to keep migrants out.

Who leaves and who stays?

Different kinds of climate and environmental impacts determine whether people can – or choose to - remain on their land and in their homes, or whether they are forced to move, either immediately or over a period of time. People can be temporarily displaced, moving back to their homes when the flood dissipates, or they can lose their homes permanently. People might decide to stay where they are and ride out the flood or wildfires or drought, only to decide months or years later that they can't face another one. They might decide that everyone in their household

Leaders of the UN climate conference, from left, Dr. Hoesung Lee, chair of the IPCC (Intergovernmental Panel on Climate Change), Simon Stiell, U.N. climate chief, and Alok Sharma, president of the COP26 climate summit, attend the opening session at the COP27 UN Climate Summit, Nov. 6, 2022, in Sharm el-Sheikh, Egypt. (PETER DEJONG/AP IMAGES)

should move—which might entail selling their house and land and livestock —or that one person should stay behind to look after their assets, or that one person should go first to set up a base for the others to follow later.

The decision to leave, to stay, to stay but leave later—is complicated by many household-specific factors, and in most cases – unless people have been forcibly displaced by a sudden onset event like a flood or wildfire that has completely devastated their home—is taken over a period of time. Households living in the same affected area can make very different decisions, depending on their social, economic and demographic situation. As noted, the ability to migrate requires that a household has the financial means to do so. A move within the country will cost less than travel to another country – which costs considerably more, and depending on the source country, can require paying a smuggler's hefty fees. Financial constraints are one of the most important determinants of who leaves or stays, and climate impact can exacerbate poverty by reducing a household's livelihoods and assets. For example, successive drought years could mean a family has had to dig into their savings or sell their as-

sets, rendering them less able to gather the funds to needed to migrate. Climate impacts could thus mean the very poor are less able to migrate and more likely to stay. But wealthier people might also be more likely to stay – because they have more ability to diversify or adapt their livelihoods, or put in place mitigation infrastructure that reduces climate hazards.

Financial constraints are not the only reason people do or do not move. There is a vast scholarship on the many reasons why people migrate, and when faced with climate or environmental hazards, whether sudden or slow onset, these reasons also influence people's decision to move. Similarly, there are multiple reasons for why people do not migrate, and there is interesting research on the reasons for immobility in the face of climate or environmental hazards. Migration researchers recognize that in any place experiencing out-migration, there are just as many people, if not more, that do not migrate, because they cannot or because they do not wish to, or some combination thereof. In regions experiencing war and violence, people can be trapped or 'stuck' – their mobility constrained by besieging forces or armed conflict or roving militias. In these circumstanc-

A view of fiords as they melt due to climate change near Svalbard Islands, in the Arctic Ocean in Norway on July 19, 2022. Approximately 1.5 million square kilometers of sea ice has melted in the arctic region, which is the most heated by the effects of global climate change and the studies with satellite data since 1970 indicate that ice is decreasing every year. (OZGE ELIF KIZIL/ANADOLU AGENCY VIA GETTY IMAGES)

es, a sudden onset climate event like a flood or hurricane can mean no-one is able to move, as much as they need to.

Even where it is possible to migrate, and people do have the means, there are many reasons why people elect to stay. They might lack adequate social networks outside their community of origin, and thus not have sufficient support in destination areas. (The presence of social capital is one of the main determinants of migrants' destinations.) People also choose to stay because of 'place attachment', a phrase that includes family obligations, and other socio-cultural reasons that keep people home. For example, people might be reluctant to leave their ancestors' burial grounds. They might simply stay because they feel "this is my home." They might have religious faith that their gods will protect them and their villages.

Another factor that influences whether people leave or stay is how governments or other actors support or undermine the ability of people to mitigate climate impacts. The policy responses of both national governments or cities to migrants and displaced people can influence people's decisions about their destinations, how successfully they adapt to their new homes, and whether they return home or not. To sum up, when

we think about the impact of climate change and environmental degradation on people, we tend to think about migration, but it is just as important that we consider those who do not migrate, and what happens to them.

Where do climate migrants go?

One of most important considerations facing all migrants is where to head for. Destinations can differ depending on whether a family has been displaced or is planning to migrate. Displaced people might initially rush to the nearest safe place, but even during the emergency they might try to move to places where they know people who can help them. Later, when they are safe, many will consider more carefully whether to move elsewhere or to return to their homes. One of the most important factors determining onward destination is whether a family has connections there. Such connections could be a relative who will help them, or there might be a historical relationship through family, trade, or other connections between the place of origin and the destination.

People who are displaced by a sudden onset event move relatively short distances to nearby safety, perhaps elsewhere in their city, or if they are

rural dwellers, to nearby villages or cities. This means most climate displacement from sudden onset events occurs within countries, i.e. it is internal rather than international. Over time, or with slow onset climate events as rural livelihoods become untenable, the trend is for people to move to cities. So the overall pattern of climate migration tends to be internal and rural to urban. But there are many exceptions to this pattern. Some international migration occurs, especially if people live near borders, or if they have family networks in other countries. There is also plenty of rural-rural migration. In general, there is very little tracking over the long term of what happens to people displaced by disasters or where they end up, and even less tracking of people who migrate for climate related reasons. See BOX Hurricane Katrina

How many climate migrants?

Climate-related migration results from different causes and complex decision making, and manifests in different scales across time and space. This complexity makes it difficult to decide who exactly the climate migrants are amongst the wider population of migrants, and it means that we really don't have a very good idea of how many people have migrated or been displaced, and how many are planning to migrate soon or sometime in the future. Nor do we know exactly where people go – there are few registries tracking such movements – or how many people return to their homes after being displaced, or after having migrated.

It is easier to track the numbers of people who've been displaced by disasters, especially because most disaster displacement occurs within the same country. One organization that tracks climate-related migration, is the Internal Displacement Monitoring Center (IDMC). According to IDMC, in 2020 there were 30.7 million new disaster displacements, mostly resulting from weather-related disasters like floods and storms. Some of these people returned. IDMC's global map of those remaining at the end of 2020 can be found below.

Part 2 Policy responses

There is now a widespread response to global climate-related migration on the part of global organizations, national and city governments, global corporations and businesses, and civil society. There is also an extensive literature on these responses, some good examples are listed in the Recommended Readings section.

International responses

In the past five years, multilateral organizations, such as the United Nations Framework Convention on Climate Change (UNFCC), the International Organization for Migration (IOM), and the United Nations High Commissioner for Refugees (UNHCR), have begun to promote climate migration as an emerging global priority. These and other global organizations, such as the International Committee of the Red Cross (ICRC) have committed resources and personnel; convened donor governments and other actors; and developed frameworks, guidance, and recommendations. Climate migration is mentioned in the United Nations' Global Compact for Safe, Orderly and Regular Migration (United Nations General Assembly, 2018) and in other UN decisions. However, unlike the 1951 Refugee Convention and its 1967 Protocol, the international treaty governing the treatment of refugees, to date there is no treaty governing the treatment of climate migrants – and as noted above, no state or international organization recognizes the concept of 'climate refugees.'

National Responses

Most climate mobility occurs within states rather than across borders, and so how national states (and politicians) react, the kinds of laws and resulting policies they enact, and whether these policies get implemented – are all crucial to understanding the outcomes of climate-related migration.

A recent review of national policy approaches by the RAND Corporation provides some useful insights. They define *climate mobility policy* as "the official government laws, regulations, and directives designed to shape the mobility actions and outcomes of people affected by climate change." The authors point out that the definition includes "some policies that do not explicitly adopt the terminology of climate migration, such as international development support provided to low- and middle-income states with the effect of boosting resilience, but excludes policies that are not to a reasonable degree aimed at climate mobility, such as automobile emission standards designed to reduce greenhouse gas emissions associated with climate change."

The RAND authors call climate migration "a policy arena in formation" with states following different paths, and they provide a useful framework for understanding how nation-states are developing policies to respond to climate migration. National governments pursue climate mobility policies for five main reasons: security and rule of law, rights, development, preservation of customs and cultures, and "resilience." These reasons can reinforce each other but can also lead to conflicting policies.

National climate mobility policies are concerned with five main categories: mobility control, social protection, built environment and physical adaptation, government reform, and planned relocation. These five types reflect the needs of both climate migrants and their host communities. Governments making climate mobility policy could use these as a checklist of issues.

Back in 2011, the highly regarded Foresight report put out by the British government found that environmental change can lead to six distinct 'human mobility outcomes' which represent challenges to policy makers. Two of these outcomes involved non-movement - where people are either trapped or choose not to leave, and two outcomes are associated with mobility – migration or displacement. Associated with each of these two mobility out-

In this aerial view, heavily damaged mobile homes are seen in Fort Myers Beach, Florida a month after Hurricane Ian made landfall on September 28 as a Category 4 hurricane, causing an estimated $67 billion in insured losses and at least 127 storm-related deaths in Florida. (PAUL HENNESSY/SOPA IMAGES /LIGHTROCKET VIA GETTY IMAGES)

Box: Food security in the face of climate change: A community-based response

Climate change impacts on wildlife habitat are intersecting with a growing demand for country food and rising market food prices to impact food security in the Inuvialuit Settlement Region. In response, Inuvialuit are taking an integrated, community-based approach. As changing temperatures have meant that traditional, below-ground freezer storage has become unreliable and unsafe, the Inuvialuit Regional Corporation (IRC) is installing industrial community freezers in each of the Inuvialuit communities. Using a rebate from the Arctic Energy Alliance's Community Renewable Energy Program, a 2.5 kW grid-tied solar photovoltaic system was installed at the Inuvialuit Community Freezer in Inuvik. Solar panels are being installed on community freezers in other Inuvialuit communities as well— creating renewable energy generation capacity as well as solar installation training opportunities. Promoting food sharing through community freezers is being complemented by the development of country food processing facilities in many communities, as well as an initiative to commercialize country food distribution.

Climate Change Strategy in 2019. It is the only comprehensive Arctic-focused climate change strategy in Canada, with coordinated policies and actions.

The future

In 2011, the *Foresight* report said:"Preventing or constraining migration is not a 'no risk' option. Doing so will lead to increased impoverishment, displacement and irregular migration in many settings, particularly in low elevation coastal zones, drylands and mountain regions. Conversely, some degree of planned and proactive migration of individuals or groups may ultimately allow households and populations to remain in situ for longer."

Eleven years later, we have come a long way to recognizing the difficulties and even futility of trying to prevent climate-related migration, and we have developed ways to mitigate displacement from disasters. What does the future hold by way of these efforts? This concluding section looks to the future and identifies two developments that are already and might in the future inform new approaches to climate-related displacement and migration. One concerns new technologies, including those that provide new information and those that mitigate climate impact. The second development relates to how business and corporations are affected by climate-related migration, and what we might expect from them by way of innovation.

New technologies

Early warning systems have long been a way to prevent harm to people from disasters, and potentially prevent disaster-related displacement. In recent years, these systems have become more sophisticated and accurate at forecasting weather, giving communities time to be warned of impending disaster. In some countries, efforts are made to include people with disabilities. In the Philippines, for example, early warning

comes are operational and geopolitical policy related challenges.

The RAND authors point out that "A climate mobility strategy can have valuable forcing functions" - i.e. be a catalyst for change, when it comes to issues such as the rights of migrants, national security, and reinforcing the resilience of communities or pillars of cultural heritage. The authors emphasize that the impact of climate change on a population is influenced by broader national policies. Thus, they recommend that, rather than having a

Soldiers lower a boat into the water to help evacuate people in the municipality of La Lima, Nicaragua, an area flooded due to the overflowing of the Chamelecon river after the passage of Hurricane Iota, on November 18, 2020. Storm Iota, which made landfall in Nicaragua as a "catastrophic" Category 5 hurricane, killed at least ten people as it smashed homes, uprooted trees and swamped roads during its destructive advance across Central America. (PHOTO BY WENDELL ESCOTO / AFP) (PHOTO BY WENDELL ESCOTO/AFP VIA GETTY IMAGES)

single comprehensive climate mobility strategy, countries should integrate climate mobility considerations into other policies and only adopt climate-specific policies where necessary.

How communities take things into their own hands—Indigenous people as agents of change

For indigenous groups, climate change threatens place-based attachments and culturally specific practices in their traditional homes. At the same time, they have cultivated adaptive capacities based on their recognition of the interdependence of all life forms and the importance of preserving sustainable resources and ecosystems. Thus indigenous groups have always been involved in their own environmental conservation, adaptation and mitigation and have developed effective practices for biodiversity conservation and climate adaptation and mitigation. Such traditional strategies, combined with innovative ideas and new technologies, can mitigate the effects of climate change, and prevent the need for people to migrate. A good example is how the Inuit people of Canada have mobilized around climate change. Inuit Tapiriit Kanatami, the national organisation for Inuit in Canada, released their four-year National Inuit evacuation systems incorporate both sound and visual signals to improve accessibility. In Nepal, humanitarian and government officials receive training on disability-inclusive shelter arrangements, such as ramp access and sanitation facilities located on the ground floor. Another modeling approach is '**hazard risk mapping**' which uses demographic information and vulnerability assessments to identify exposed areas and households at risk. By anticipating climate impacts such as erosion and sea level rise, these kinds of maps and models can help plan for ensuing displacement at the local and national levels.

Innovative farming techniques, such as new crop and breed varieties, are being developed to reduce the impact on farming livelihoods of both sudden impact disasters and long-term problems like drought and heat. Mitigation of such impacts can reduce the need for rural people to migrate when their livelihoods fail. As IDMC points out, however, new technologies are not always necessary (or effective). "Long-known and sometimes forgotten historical practices can often be just as effective." Local food banks can be organized to support people and livestock in diffi- cult years. Sustainable water, land and natural resource management can go a long way towards slowing the effects of climate change or even reverting some of them. Crop diversification can help ensure yields and limit diseases, while the restoration of centuries-old ecosystems can be a turning point in minimizing displacement risk.

Climate-ready businesses – and corporate climate migration

There are at least two ways in which climate change and migration will affect businesses, creating both opportunities and threats to their infrastructure locations, business models and supply chains. First, many companies large and small, will need to relocate their infrastructure and offices to areas that are less prone to weather and climate extremes. This '**c**orporate migration' is

Members of the Red Cross help to evacuate people after the overflow of Bambito river due to the heavy rains caused by Hurricane Eta, in Bambito, Panama, November 5, 2020. (LUIS ACOSTA/AFP VIA GETTY IMAGES)

already underway, and some business writers predict that many towns could see an exodus of large employers in the future as oceans encroach on coastal areas and inland areas prone to flooding or wildfires see increased challenges. Some examples of relocations to higher ground in the past three years include tech giant Hewlett Packard Enterprise, which is in the process of moving its former Houston-area campus to its new global headquarters in Spring, Texas, after experiencing extensive flooding in 2016 and then in 2017 during Hurricane Harvey.

Second, business and corporations increasingly recognize that to forestall climate-related migration that could create labor problems, they will need to create climate-smart productive jobs. The Foresight Africa 2022 report, which identifies priorities for the African continent in the coming year, says that across Africa, 375 million young people will enter the job market in the next 15 years. More than half will be living in rural areas, where livelihoods are highly climate-sensitive and will become increasingly untenable due to crop productivity losses and water stress. Unless there are climate-smart

productive jobs in rural economies, youth will migrate to urban areas, where there is no promise of jobs for them. Policies to address such obstacles and help youth find work in rural areas already exist:

One example is in northern Nigeria, where investment in a solar-powered Kilishi (a highly demanded local meat delicacy) factory enabled a shift from use of firewood to cleaner meat-drier domes and fuel-efficient kilns, conserving forests and bringing prosperity to the local community, while creating employment opportunities for the youth who would have otherwise migrated to cities in other states. The project has successfully attracted youth back from Abuja, the capital city, where they were performing menial jobs with low wages.

Market-driven innovation, along with the push from indigenous people, national governments and international organizations, all hold the promise of solutions to climate-related migration. This promise of solutions offers a stark contrast to the security-driven, apocalyptic narrative that often dominates the media. It behooves us all to understand and work towards these solutions.

discussion questions

1. As you read in the article, many individuals forced to relocate from climate change often cannot afford to. In the case of the United States, what role should the government play in assisting domestic climate refugees? What role, if any, should the U.S. government play in assisting international climate refugees?

2. The author states that the IPCC has toned down most of its forecasts for the future because "apocalyptic narratives" can have a numbing effect and that negative messaging can harm efforts to raise awareness for climate change issues. If this form of messaging is ineffective, what is an effective way to raise awareness and promote change? How can we best convince people to listen?

3. Wealthy individuals are often those that can have the biggest im-pact in helping the climate crisis but are also those that can afford to escape the negative effects of it. How can the world convince them that they should care about climate change and persuade them to use their resources to make a difference?

4. As highlighted in the article, indigenous peoples and their entire lifestyles are often heavily affected by climate change but are rarely given a voice in climate-related decisions. How should we go about promoting dialogue with indigenous peoples and giving them a voice in the climate discussion?

5. The author notes how businesses often have to change their practices and in some cases have to relocate because of the climate crisis. Innovations by the private sector often have a positive impact on the fight against the climate crisis. How can world leadership encourage market-driven innovation related to climate change?

suggested readings

Bettini, G. (2013). Climate Barbarians at the Gate? A critique of apocalyptic narratives on "climate refugees." **Geoforum,** 45, 63–72. Explains and debunks the narratives and language used in discussions of climate migration, and why we should not use the term climate refugees.

Blake, J. S., A. Clark-Ginsberg and J. Balagna (2021). "Addressing Climate Migration: A Review of National Policy Approaches." Santa Monica, CA, RAND Corporation. A good discussion of types of policies related to climate mobility and how policies can influence people's exposure to climate-related hazards, access to mitigation strategies, and ability to move safely and with dignity if necessary.

Up. Bloomberg CityLab. https://www.bloomberg.com/news/articles/2015-08-25/8-maps-of-displacement-and-return-in-new-orleans-after-katrina . Good summary of what happened after Hurricane Katrina.

Foresight (2011). Migration and Global Environmental Change, Final Project Report. The Government Office for Science, London. A "classic" – one of the early and best written report on migration and environmental change, with good explanation of concepts and policies.)

IDMC (2021). **Addressing Internal Displacement in the Context of Climate Change.** Geneva. This organization, the Internal Displacement Monitoring Center, has been gathering information on internal displacement for decades, and provides good insight into the data we have on numbers of displaced and how reliable those data are.)

Fussell, Elizabeth, Lori M. Hunter, Clark L. Gray. 2014. "Measuring the environmental dimensions of human migration—The demographer's toolkit." **Global Environmental Change** 28 (2014)-182–191. Good explanation of how demographers can help provide data on climate-related migration.

Baldwin, A. and G. Bettini (2017). **Life adrift: Climate change, migration, critique,** Rowman & Littlefield. A collection of essays from the interpretive social sciences and humanities that treats climate change and migration as a relation that demands theoretical and historical explanation, rather than a problem requiring technical and expert solutions.

McLeman, Robert and François Gemenne. **Routledge Handbook of Environmental Displacement and Migration.** Routledge, 2018. A review and assessment of existing knowledge and future research priorities related to climate-related migration.

Don't forget to vote!

Download a copy of the ballot questions from the Resources page at www.fpa.org/great_decisions

To access web links to these readings, as well as links to additional, shorter readings and suggested web sites,

GO TO www.fpa.org/great_decisions

and click on the topic under Resources, on the right-hand side of the page.

About the balloting process...

Dear Great Decisions Participants,

As you may already know, my name is Dr. Lauren Prather and I have been working with the Foreign Policy Association (FPA) for the last five years on the National Opinion Ballot (NOB). A version of this letter has appeared in previous briefing books, so I'm only writing a quick hello this year.

My research is primarily focused on international relations. I am a faculty member at the School of Global Policy and Strategy at the University of California, San Diego (UCSD) and have research projects on a range of public opinion topics, from foreign aid to climate change to national security issues. I also teach a class on public opinion and foreign policy for my university.

One of the key difficulties in my research is that the public is often uniformed or misinformed about the topics. This is where you come in! The Great Decisions participants continue to be some of the most informed Americans about foreign policy issues, and the NOB is the perfect opportunity to voice those opinions.

The NOB is also one of the only public opinion surveys in the United States that attempts to gather the opinions of the educated public. Thus, it has great value to researchers and policymakers alike. Some of the questions in which researchers are interested include the following:

- Are the opinions of the educated public significantly different from those of the average American?
- How does public opinion about foreign policy change over time?
- How does public opinion on one foreign policy issue relate to public opinion on other foreign policy issues? For example, are people who support U.S. government policies to mitigate climate change more or less willing to support drilling in the Arctic?
- How do different segments of the population, men or women, liberals or conservatives, view foreign policy choices?

In order to answer the types of questions researchers are interested in, such as how do people's opinions change over time, the NOB needs to have certain attributes. We need to have a way to organize the ballots by participant across all topics. That way, we know, for example, how participant #47 responded to the question about climate change mitigation and how he or she responded to the question about drilling, even if those were in different topics in the NOB. Your random ID number is the **only thing** connected to your responses and **never** your e-mail address. In fact, as a researcher, I must receive the approval of my Institutional Review Board by demonstrating that your data will be protected at all times, and that your responses will be both confidential and anonymous.

If you have any questions or comments, I am always happy to respond via e-mail at LPrather@ucsd.edu. To learn more about my research and teaching, you can visit my website at www.laurenprather.org.

Thank you again to everyone who has participated in the NOB over the years. I have learned a tremendous amount about your foreign policy views and it has greatly informed my own research. In the future, I hope to communicate to the scholarly world and policy communities how the educated American public thinks about foreign policy.

Sincerely,

Lauren Prather

Don't forget to vote!
Download a copy of the ballot questions from the Resources page at www.fpa.org/great_decisions

Global Discussion Questions

No decision in foreign policy is made in a vacuum, and the repercussions of any single decision have far-reaching effects across the range of strategic interests on the U.S. policy agenda. This Great Decisions feature is intended to facilitate the discussion of this year's topics in a global context, to discuss the linkages between the topics and to encourage consideration of the broader impact of decision-making.

1. Consider "Global Famine" in the context of "War Crimes." Can provoking a famine during the midst of war be considered a war crime? If so, should international law be used to prosecute it?

2. Consider "Economic Warfare" in the context of "Global Famine." As shown in both articles, the implementation of western sanctions on Russia has resulted in an increase in the number of food insecure people worldwide, particularly in Africa. Should the west reconsider its sanction policy for this reason?

3. Consider "China and the U.S." in the context of "Politics in Latin America." As China's global reach continues to extend into Latin America, more countries in the western hemisphere continue to fall under China's influence. Should the United States do more to prevent this sway? Why or why not?

4. Consider "Economic warfare," "Iran at a crossroads," and "Energy security." How effective have sanctions against Iran been? Can they work if countries need oil and are willing to ignore sanctions?

Don't forget to vote!
Download a copy of the ballot questions from the Resources page at www.fpa.org/great_decisions

Become a Member

For nearly a century, members of the Association have played key roles in government, think tanks, academia and the private sector.

FOREIGN POLICY ASSOCIATION 1918

Make a Donation

Your support helps the FOREIGN POLICY ASSOCIATION's programs dedicated to global affairs education.

As an active participant in the FPA's Great Decisions program, we encourage you to join the community today's foreign policy thought leaders.

Member—$250

Benefits:
- Free admission to all Associate events (includes member's family)
- Discounted admission for all other guests to Associate events
- Complimentary GREAT DECISIONS briefing book
- Complimentary issue of FPA's annual *National Opinion Ballot Report*

Visit us online at

www.fpa.org/membership

Make a fully tax-deductible contribution to FPA's Annual Fund 2020.

To contribute to the Annual Fund 2020 visit us online at **www.fpa.org** or call the Membership Department at

(800) 628-5754 ext. 333

The generosity of donors who contribute $500 or more is acknowledged in FPA's *Annual Report.*

All financial contributions are tax-deductible to the fullest extent of the law under section 501 (c)(3) of the IRS code.

FPA also offers membership at the SPONSOR MEMBER and PATRON MEMBER levels. To learn more, visit us online at www.fpa.org/membership or call (800) 628-5754 ext. 333.

Return this form by mail to: Foreign Policy Association, 551 Fifth Avenue, 30th Floor, New York, N.Y. 10176

ORDER ONLINE: WWW.FPA.ORG/GREAT_DECISIONS

CALL (800) 477-5836

FAX (212) 481-9275

❏ MR.　　❏ MRS.　　❏ MS.　　❏ DR.　　❏ PROF.

NAME _____

ADDRESS _____

_____ APT/FLOOR _____

CITY _____ STATE _____ ZIP _____

TEL _____

E-MAIL _____

❏ AMEX　　❏ VISA　　❏ MC　　❏ DISCOVER

❏ CHECK (ENCLOSED)

CHECKS SHOULD BE PAYABLE TO FOREIGN POLICY ASSOCIATION.

CARD NO.

SIGNATURE OF CARDHOLDER

EXP. DATE (MM/YY)

PRODUCT	QTY	PRICE	COST
GREAT DECISIONS 2023 Briefing Book (FPA31725)		$35	
SPECIAL OFFER TEN PACK SPECIAL GREAT DECISIONS 2023 (FPA31732) *Includes 10% discount		$315	
GREAT DECISIONS MASTER CLASS GD ON DVD 2023 (FPA31726)		$40	
GREAT DECISIONS 2023 TEACHER'S PACKET (1 Briefing Book, 1 Teacher's Guide and 1 DVD (FPA 31728) E-MAIL: (REQUIRED)		$75	
GREAT DECISIONS CLASSROOM-PACKET (1 Teacher's Packet & 30 Briefing Books (FPA31729) E-MAIL: (REQUIRED)		$775	
MEMBERSHIP		$250	
ANNUAL FUND 2022 (ANY AMOUNT)			

SUBTOTAL $_____

plus S & H* $_____

TOTAL $_____

For details and shipping charges, call FPA's Sales Department at (800) 477-5836.

Orders mailed to FPA without the shipping charge will be held.

This year's edition of the *Great Decisions* DVD features the *Great Decisions* Master Class format. This format will feature 20-30 minute long lectures on the nine topics from this current issue.

Master class lectures are presented by Jeffrey S. Morton, the Pierrepont Comfort Chair in Political Science at Florida Atlantic University and a Fellow at the Foreign Policy Association. He holds a Ph.D. in International Relations from the University of South Carolina and an M.A. from Rutgers University. Dr. Morton has delivered the *Great Decisions* program to live audiences since 1999.

If you have a plan, we want to hear it. Tell your community leaders, your local officials, your governor, and your team in Washington. Believe me, your ideas count. An individual can make a difference.

—George H.W. Bush

$35.00

FOREIGN POLICY ASSOCIATION
551 Fifth Avenue, Suite 3000, New York, NY 10176
Phone (212) 481-8100 Fax (212) 481-9275 Orders: (800) 477-5836
www.fpa.org/great_decisions

$35.00
ISBN 978-0-87124-284-6
53500

9 780871 242846